COSMOPOLIS

COSMOPOLIS

The Hidden Agenda of Modernity

Stephen Toulmin

The University of Chicago Press

This edition is reprinted by arrangement
with the Free Press, a division of
Macmillan, Inc.

The University of Chicago Press, Chicago 60637
Copyright © 1990 by Stephen Toulmin
All rights reserved. Published 1990
University of Chicago Press edition 1992
Printed in the United States of America
99 98 97 96 95 94 93   6 5 4 3

ISBN 0-226-80838-6 (pbk.)
Library of Congress Cataloging-in-Publication Data

Toulmin, Stephen Edelston.
    Cosmopolis : the hidden agenda of modernity / Stephen Toulmin. —
University of Chicago Press ed.
       p.   cm.
    Originally published: New York : Free Press, c1990.
    Includes bibliographical references and index.
    1. Civilization, Modern—History.   2. Philosophy, Renaissance.
3. Philosophy, Modern—History.   4. Europe—Intellectual life.
5. Rationalism.   I. Title.
[CB357.T64   1992]
909.82—dc20   92-18478
                                                                  CIP

⊗ The paper used in this publication meets the minimum requirements
of the American National Standard for
Information Sciences—Permanence of Paper for Printed
Library Materials, ANSI Z39.48-1984

For Donna

'Tis all in peeces, all cohærance gone;
All just supply, and all Relation:
Prince, Subject, Father, Sonne, are things forgot,
For every man alone thinkes he hath got
To be a Phœnix, and that there can bee
None of that kinde, of which he is, but hee.

—JOHN DONNE

Contents

Preface

*T*his book chronicles a change of mind. The discoveries it reports are as much personal as scholarly. After training in mathematics and physics in the late 1930s and early '40s, I was introduced to philosophy at Cambridge after World War II, and learned to see Modern Science—the intellectual movement whose first giant was Isaac Newton—and Modern Philosophy—the method of reflection initiated by Descartes—as twin founding pillars of modern thought, and prime illustrations of the strict "rationality" on which the modern era has prided itself.

The picture our teachers gave us of 17th-century Europe was a sunny one. For the first time, Humanity seemed to have set aside all doubts and ambiguities about its capacity to achieve its goals here on Earth, and in historical time, rather than deferring human fulfillment to an Afterlife in Eternity—that was what had made the project of Modernity "rational"— and this optimism led to major advances not just in natural science but in moral, political, and social thought as well. In retrospect, however, that picture was too uniformly bright, at least if we take seriously the other things that historians of early modern Europe have shown us since Roland Mousnier's pioneer work in the 1950s. A realistic picture of 17th-century life must now include both brilliant lights and dark shadows: both the successes of the new intellectual movements, and also the agonies of the religious wars that were their historical background.

For myself, in the late 1960s I began to be uneasy about the received account of 17th-century ideas. The cultural changes that began around 1965 were (it seemed to me) cutting into our traditions more deeply than was widely appreciated. I tried to capture this point in a draft essay for *Daedalus,* dealing with changes in the philosophy of science from 1945 up to 1970: understandably, the editor urged me to produce a less ambitious text for publication, but the central perceptions remained, to be presented here in Chapter 4. My doubts were reinforced by an essay by Stephen

Shapin, published in 1981, on the correspondence between G. W. Leibniz and Newton's ally, Samuel Clarke; having taught the same text from a narrower point of view at Oxford in the early '50s, I was well placed to see the originality and force of Shapin's reading, which I discuss in Chapter 3. During a year in Santa Monica at the Getty Center for the History of Art and the Humanities, I had a welcome chance to pursue these doubts in the Research Library of the University of California at Los Angeles, and also at the Bibliothèque Nationale in Paris and at other libraries: my debts to colleagues at Santa Monica, and to the Getty Trust, can be seen in Chapter 2.

In the end, the most powerful influence in changing my view of the 17th century was the experience of reading Michel de Montaigne's *Essais* with my students in the Committee on Social Thought at the University of Chicago. Montaigne does not often figure in the curriculum of English and American philosophy departments: still less are his books listed on reading lists in the natural sciences. As we worked through the essays, I was delighted to find how congenial he was to readers in the late 1970s. In arguing a case for the classical skepticism of Sextus Empiricus and Pyrrho, for instance, he came closer than I thought possible to the ideas of my teacher, Ludwig Wittgenstein, and I ended by wondering whether the opening gambit in the chess game of Modern Philosophy had been, not Descartes' method of systematic doubt, but the skeptical arguments of Montaigne himself.

Conversations with Avner Cohen and Phillip Hallie encouraged me to pursue this suspicion, and helped me to see Montaigne's central relevance to the present crisis within philosophy. That move led me in turn into the larger world of 16th-century Renaissance humanism, and showed how far the failures of understanding between Science and the Humanities, about which C. P. Snow was so eloquent, began early in the 17th century, when Descartes persuaded his fellow philosophers to renounce fields of study like ethnography, history, or poetry, which are rich in content and context, and to concentrate exclusively on abstract, decontextualized fields like geometry, dynamics, and epistemology. From then on, the focus of my research was the 17th-century move from a partly practical to a purely theoretical view of philosophy, and that is my central concern here.

In choosing as the goals of Modernity an intellectual and practical agenda that set aside the tolerant, skeptical attitude of the 16th-century humanists, and focussed on the 17th-century pursuit of mathematical exactitude and logical rigor, intellectual certainty and moral purity, Europe set itself on a cultural and political road that has led both to its most striking technical successes and to its deepest human failures. If we have any lesson to learn from the experience of the 1960s and '70s, this (I have come to believe) is our need to reappropriate the wisdom of the 16th-century humanists, and develop a point of view that combines the abstract rigor and exactitude of the 17th-century "new philosophy" with a practical concern for human life in its concrete detail. Only so can we counter the current widespread disillusion with the agenda of Modernity, and salvage what is still humanly important in its projects.

By this stage, my inquiries covered so broad a canvas that I could not hope to present them in fully documented scholarly form in part of a lifetime, or in a book of manageable size. Instead, I have chosen to write an essay that may enable readers to recognize, and even follow, the steps that led me both to a more complex picture of the birth of Modernity, and to more sanguine ideas of how the 17th century's achievements could be humanized, and so redeemed. Rather than encumber my essay with a full scholarly apparatus, I am therefore adding a bibliographical appendix in which I describe my sources and give any indispensable references: for instance, to the 1611 sonnet which (as I argue in Chapter 2) may be the first, unacknowledged printed work of René Descartes. Here, let me add a word about the fine coöperation of M. Peyraud and his fellow workers in the catalogue room at the Bibliothèque Nationale, in helping hunt down and document the "missing volume" in which that sonnet appears.

In all these investigations, I have learned from my discussions with colleagues and friends. Let me here thank those who, at various stages, helped to keep my reinterpretation on the rails: as well as those already mentioned, Geneviève Rodis-Lewis, Richard Watson, David Tracy, Julian Hilton, Thomas McCarthy, and John McCumber. Above all, I am grateful to Klaus Reichert of the Johann Wolfgang Goethe Universität, Frankfurt-am-Main, and to the President of the University, for asking me to inaugurate in May and June of 1987 the visiting professorship generously endowed by Deutsche Bank, with a series of lectures on "Beyond Modernity". The chance to air my ideas in public before the heirs to the scholars who created the sociology of knowledge in the 1930s gave me the confidence to present them here. Parts of my argument have been presented at the University of Michigan, as the Hayward Keniston Lecture; at Washington University, St. Louis; Northeast Illinois University, de Kalb; the University of Illinois, Champaign; the Centre for Working Life in Stockholm; Monmouth College, as the inaugural Sam Thompson Lecture; and Loyola Marymount University, Los Angeles. Lynn Conner has been a great help in the sheer production of a text, while my friend Daniel Herwitz has been a welcome and helpful sounding board at every stage in the work. Only Joyce Seltzer, my editor at the Free Press, knows how much the whole conception of this book owes to her own imaginative commentary, or how far her tactful criticism has shaped its execution. Finally, let me thank Rudi Weingartner and the electors to the Avalon Foundation Chair in the Humanities at Northwestern University, who gave me the chance to complete it around the normal duties of an academic life.

An investigation with the scope I have chosen here cannot hope to be equally convincing at all points; but about one thing I am certain enough. In the reappropriation of the humanist tradition, our political or cultural future is not the only thing at stake. Striking a better balance between the abstract exactitude needed in the physical sciences and the practical wisdom typical of fields like clinical medicine can also be a matter of personal importance. If we reach the Gates of Heaven, and are given the chance to take up our eternal residence on the same cloud as Erasmus and Rabelais, Shakespeare and Montaigne, few of us (I suspect) will demand that we be cloistered permanently, instead, with René Descartes, Isaac Newton, and the exact-thinking but darker-souled geniuses of the 17th century.

Evanston, Illinois
May 1989   Stephen Toulmin

Backing into the Millennium

*T*his is a book about the past, and about the future: about the terms in which we make sense of the past, and the ways in which our view of the past affects our posture in dealing with the future. The beliefs that shape our historical foresight represent (as German philosophers put it) our *Erwartungshorizonten,* or "horizons of expectation." Those horizons mark limits to the field of action in which, at the moment, we see it as possible or feasible to change human affairs, and so to decide which of our most cherished practical goals can be realized in fact.

As we enter the 1990s, the third millennium of our calendar is ten years ahead; and at this, of all times, onlookers might expect us to take stock, reassess our historical situation in history, and shape fresh ideas about directions in which to move—not goals we can pursue individually, but reasonable and realistic ambitions for us to embrace as a community. Instead, with eyes lowered, we are backing into a new millennium, with little serious attention to the questions, "Where shall we be, and where will we be in a position to go, from the year 2001 on?" Twenty years ago, the situation was different. In the late 1960s, many writers kept alive the practice of reflecting on and debating the prospect of human society and culture in the next century and the coming millennium. Some of the writers who participated in that debate analyzed the current trends and extrapolated them over future decades, so arriving at long-range social and political forecasts, even though these were subject to qualification. But what strikes us most, looking back, is the failure of these writers to forecast important changes that were to take place after they wrote, but before their target date, not least the revival of fundamentalist religion, at home and abroad.

Social forecasting is of course notoriously chancy. Even in the field of meteorology, detailed predictions are not practicable for more than a few days ahead; and, if social or political forecasting is even harder, that should

come as no surprise. The strength of well-formed "horizons of expectation" is not that they generate accurate forecasts, to serve as a theoretical
basis for the practical politics of the future: Bertrand de Jouvenel has,
indeed, explained clearly and exactly why our capacity for *prévision sociale*
is so limited. The most that we can hope to foresee is the limits within
which "available" human futures lie. Available futures are not just those
that we can passively forecast, but those that we can actively create: for
these de Jouvenel coined a new name—"futuribles". They are futures
which do not simply happen *of themselves,* but can be *made to* happen, if
we meanwhile adopt wise attitudes and policies.

How are we to recognize and select "wise attitudes and policies"? A well
formulated approach to the future—a realistic range of available futuribles, within reasonable horizons of expectation—does not depend on
finding ways to quantify and extrapolate current trends: that we may leave
to enthusiastic weather forecasters, stock exchange chartists, or econome-
trists. Rather, the questions are, "What intellectual *posture* should we adopt
in confronting the future? What eye can we develop for significant aspects
of the years ahead? And what capacity do we have to change our ideas about
the available futures?" Those who refuse to think coherently about the
future, correspondingly, only expose themselves to worse, leaving the
field clear to unrealistic, irrational prophets.

Ideally, social or political thought is always framed by realistic horizons
of expectation; but a people's actual horizons will frequently be
*un*realistic. Thus, in Oliver Cromwell's time, many educated Englishmen
believed that God would bring the order of things to an end in the 1650s;
and they looked in the *Book of Revelations* for allusions to 17th-century
England as uncritically as any Texan fundamentalist looks today for signs
of an imminent rapture of the saved. The fact that the end of the world did
not occur on schedule deeply shocked many of the Commonwealth
worthies; but in the meanwhile they discussed policies and plans within
delusory horizons of expectation. Some of them even argued that the Jews
should be readmitted to England, on the grounds that God could make
ready His Apocalypse, and build a New Jerusalem on English soil, only after
the conversion of the Jews. When Ronald Reagan dipped into *Revelations*
in the 1984 Presidential campaign and included among his expectations a
coming Armageddon, therefore, listeners with an ear for history heard in
his words some disturbing echoes of the 1650s.

The historical agnosticism and short-term thinking of the 1980s reflect
a general sense that, today, the historical horizon is unusually hard to focus
on, and is shrouded in fog and darkness. Experience in the last quarter-
century has convinced people that the 21st century will resemble the 20th

even less than the 20th century has resembled the 19th. We are now at the end of an era not just in a calendrical sense—leaving behind a thousand years starting with a "1", and entering a thousand years that will start with "2"—but in a deeper, historical sense. The political supremacy of Europe has ended, and the hegemony of European ideas is ending too. For two hundred years, people in Western Europe and North America were content to believe that theirs was the modern age: that their way of farming and manufacturing was the "modern" one, along with their medical skills, that they had "modern" scientific and philosophical ideas, and lived in the relative security of "modern" nation states. They tackled all their practical and intellectual problems in distinctive "modern" ways; and, in a dozen fields, their life embodied rational ways of testing our procedures and institutions, not available to people in the tyrannous societies and super- stitious cultures that existed before the age of "modernity".

Twenty years ago many writers still retained this faith. Their confident extrapolation for decades ahead—their readiness to take mid-20th-century social tendencies and cultural trends as likely to continue unchanged for another 40 or 50 years—is evidence of that. They did not display the unease and sense of historical *dis*continuity which people in many fields claim to be experiencing today. When they proclaimed "the end of ideology", they show a belief that, in the last 300 years, modern philosophy and science had succeeded (in John Locke's famous phrase) in "clearing away the underbrush that stands in the way of knowledge." In their view, if we could only prevent ideological and theological issues from confusing matters, both the intellectual and the practical means of improving the human lot were ready to hand.

Today, the program of Modernity—even the very *concept*—no longer carries anything like the same conviction. If an historical era is ending, it is the era of Modernity itself. Rather than our being free to assume that the tide of Modernity still flows strongly, and that its momentum will carry us into a new and better world, our present position is less comfortable. What looked in the 19th century like an irresistible river has disappeared in the sand, and we seem to have run aground. Far from extrapolating confidently into the social and cultural future, we are now stranded and uncertain of our location. The very project of Modernity thus seems to have lost momentum, and we need to fashion a successor program.

To form reasonable and realistic "horizons of expectation" today, we must therefore begin by reconstructing an account of the circumstances in which the Modern project was conceived, the philosophical, scientific, social, and historical assumptions on which it rested, and the subsequent sequence of episodes that has led to our present quandary. When are we to think of the "modern" era as originating? What ideas or assumptions, about nature or society, have lain at the foundation of the "modern" program for human improvement? And how has the Western imagination come to outgrow these ideas and assumptions? Those are the central questions we need to tackle in this book.

CHAPTER ONE

What Is the Problem About Modernity?

Dating the Start of Modernity

Statements like "The modern age has come to an end" are easier to resonate to than to understand. We can see why people set such store on the demise of modernity—a demise that is supposedly unavoidable, if it has not already happened—only if we first ask what they mean by the word "modern", and just when do they think that Modernity began.

Raise these questions, and ambiguity takes over. Some people date the origin of modernity to the year 1436, with Gutenberg's adoption of moveable type; some to A.D. 1520, and Luther's rebellion against Church authority; others to 1648, and the end of the Thirty Years' War; others to the American or French Revolution of 1776 or 1789; while modern times start for a few only in 1895, with Freud's *Interpretation of Dreams* and the rise of "modernism" in the fine arts and literature. How we ourselves are to feel about the prospects of Modernity—whether we join those who are despondent at its end and say goodbye to it with regret, or those who view its departure with satisfaction and look forward with pleasure to the coming of "post-modern" times—depends on what we see as the heart and core of the "modern", and what key events in our eyes gave rise to the "modern" world.

In one sense, the idea of Modernity "coming to an end" is paradoxical. For advertisers of consumer goods, to be modern is just to be new (to be the latest thing, *le dernier cri*), superseding all similar things. Most of us are living in a consumption economy, which never tires of novelty, and its motto—*semper aliquid novi*—was already familiar to Paul of Tarsus. In this sense, the future brings us new (and "more modern") things one after the other, so that Modernity is the inexhaustible cornucopia of novelty. The

Modern age can have a stop, then, only in some quite other sense, which marks off an identifiable period of history, beginning in or around 1436 or 1648 or 1895, and now showing signs of completion. The critical question is, "What marks define the beginning and end of *Modernity?*"

The end of Modernity is closer to us than the beginning, and may be easier to spot; so let us look at the groups who write or speak about the coming, "post-modern" period in various fields of human activity, and decipher the signs that herald the end of Modernity for them. Recently, this debate has been most articulate in architecture. For thirty years after the Second World War, the modern style of Mies van der Rohe and his followers, with its anonymous, timeless, indistinguishable buildings, dominated large-scale public architecture worldwide. In the 1970s, a new generation of architects and designers, led by Robert Venturi in the United States, with colleagues in half-a-dozen European countries, fought against this featureless and minimal modern style, and reintroduced into architecture elements of decoration, local color, historical reference, and even fantasy that Mies would have objected to on intellectual as well as aesthetic grounds. These designers have been so productive that by now a noted German historian of architecture, Heinrich Klotz, has actually written a fullscale *History of Post-Modern Architecture.*

The debate about "post-modern" architecture is vocal, intriguing, and well publicized, but for our purposes it is rather marginal. When Venturi and his colleagues argue that the age of "modern" architecture is past, and must yield to a new "post-modern" style of building, their target of criticism is not modernity as a whole, but the particular movement in 20th-century art and design known as "modernism". Those who study the origins of the modernist style often trace it back to the late 19th century, particularly to the Glasgow architect-engineer, Charles Rennie Mackintosh: so, in architecture, we are concerned with a story only ninety years old—far less than historians have in mind, when they contrast modern with ancient and medieval history. Yet, for our purpose, architecture is neither irrelevant nor uninteresting: in some curious and unexpected ways modernist art and architecture, from 1900 on, picked up and gave new life to ideas and methods originating in the modern thought and practice of the 17th century. But, whatever else is or is not clear, the *Modernity* around which controversy rages today clearly started long before 1890.

Even the controversy about "post-Modernity" precedes the revolution in architecture begun by Venturi. The "post-modern" is the topic of a set of essays in social, economic and political criticism by Peter Drucker, dating from as early as 1957 and published in 1965 in a book, *Landmarks for Tomorrow.* Drucker pointed out radical differences between current economic, social, and political conditions and those typically associated with the term "Modernity", and concluded that it is quite misleading to apply that term to "the way we live nowadays". He argued that, instead of assuming that the nations of the world can continue with business as usual, we must see that the nation-state, which claims unqualified sovereignty, is no longer the self-sustaining political unit that it was in the 17th and 18th centuries. The times that we live in demand institutions of new and more functional kinds: institutions that overlap national boundaries and serve *trans*national social and economic needs.

If the central topics of the debate about Modernity are the political claims of the modern nation-state, so that the end of Modernity is linked with the eclipse of national sovereignty, we must look for the beginning of that era in the 16th and 17th centuries. On this measure, the modern era began with the creation of separate, independent sovereign states, each of them organized around a particular nation, with its own language and culture, maintaining a government that was legitimated as expressing the national will, or national traditions, or interests. That brings us closer to what contemporary historians call the "early modern" period, and gives us three hundred or more years of elbow room to maneuver in. Before the mid-16th century, the organization of states around nations was the exception, not the rule: before 1550, the general foundation of political obligation was still feudal fealty, not national loyalty. In this sense, the starting date for Modernity belongs where many historians already put it: somewhere in the period from 1600 to 1650.

This date for the start of Modernity also fits the preoccupations of other contemporary critics. The 1960s and '70s saw the renewal of an attack on the mechanistic "inhumanity" of Newtonian Science launched 150 years earlier by William Blake in England, and Friedrich Schiller in Germany. By the mid '60s, people argued, it was time to push Blake and Schiller's critiques through to a political completion. Blake had warned that industry would destroy the country, and turn it into a waste land of satanic mills, but the economic power and political clout of big business now meant that this process was unchecked. With Barry Commoner as a spokesman for biology, and Rachel Carson's *Silent Spring* as a rhetorical manifesto, people in the 1970s fought for "ecology" and "environmental protection", so as to defend the natural world against human despoilers and violators.

The satanic mills and factories about which Blake complained were products of the late 18th and 19th centuries: water or steam power were needed to run the machines that made these new methods of production more efficient than cottage industry had ever been. By this standard, the beginnings of Modernity thus go back to around 1800. Newton's classical *Mathematical Principles of Natural Philosophy* was published in 1687, but his theory of dynamics and planetary motion was of no direct use to engineers. Machinery and "manufactories" waited until the effective development of the steam engine, after 1750. Taking the rise of industry as the mark of Modernity, then, places the start of the modern age on either side of the year 1800, at the time of the Industrial Revolution.

By contrast, if we see Newton's creation of modern science as the start of Modernity, the starting date is in the 1680s; or—to the extent that Newton completed intellectual tasks that were framed by Galileo in scientific terms, and as methodological issues by Descartes—back in the 1630s. This is where Modernity begins for many purposes: British and American universities begin their courses on modern philosophy with Descartes' *Meditations* and *Discourse on Method,* while their courses on the history of science present Galileo as the founder of modern science. The critics are far from unanimous in their objections to modernism and Modernity, and in their chronologies of the modern era, but for most of them the chronology eventually reaches back to the early decades of the 17th century.

If critics of Modernity cannot agree on when the Modern Age began, the same is also true of its supporters. The German philosopher Jürgen Habermas pokes fun at the loose way in which some writers throw the phrase "post-modern" around, and laughs at them as "posties". For him, the modern era began when, inspired by the French Revolution, Immanuel Kant showed how impartial, universal moral standards can be applied to judge intentions and policies in the political realm. In Kant, the French Enlightenment's social ideals found philosophical expression; and, ever since, progressive politics has been directed by the impartial demands of Kantian equity. By destroying the *ancien régime,* the French Revolution opened the road to democracy and political participation, and its moral legacy is as powerful today as it was in the late 18th century. For Habermas, then, the starting point is the last quarter of the 18th century, more specifically the year 1776 or 1789.

That date, however, is only a stepping stone to an earlier beginning. Kant's work did not come out of a blue sky. His emphasis on universal moral maxims extends into ethics an ideal of "rationality" that had been formulated by Descartes, in logic and natural philosophy, more than a century before. Once again, "Modernity" is the historical phase that begins with Galileo's and Descartes' commitment to new, rational methods of inquiry; and any suggestion that Modernity today is over and done with is suspect, being at least reactionary, and very likely irrationalist, too. Contemporary appeals to the "post-modern" may thus serve only as additional obstacles to further emancipatory change.

Other writers value Modernity in other ways, and for other reasons. Old-time progressive politics rested on a long-term faith that science is the proven road to human health and welfare, and this faith shaped the technological agenda for half-a-dozen World Fairs. This dream still carries conviction for many people today: what underlies their continued trust in science and industry is their commitment to the conception of "rationality" that was established among European natural philosophers in the 17th century, and promised intellectual certainty and harmony. The scientific blessings of our age (above all, those in medicine) were not widely available before the late 19th century, but these blessings were happy outcomes of scientific inquiries that have made continuous progress ever since Galileo and Descartes, and so were the long-term products of the 17th-century revolutions undertaken in physics by Galileo, Kepler, and Newton, and in philosophy by Descartes, Locke, and Leibniz.

Modern science and technology can thus be seen as the source either of blessings, or of problems, or both. In either case, their intellectual origin makes the 1630s the most plausible starting date for Modernity. Then, it seems, scientific inquiries became "rational"—thanks to Galileo in astronomy and mechanics, and to Descartes in logic and epistemology. Thirty years later, this commitment to "rationality" was extended into the practical realm, when the political and diplomatic system of the European States was reorganized on the basis of *nations*. From then on, at least in theory, the warrant for a sovereign monarch's exercise of power lay less in the fact of an inherited feudal title than in the will of the people who consented to his rule: once this became the recognized basis of state authority, politics could also be analyzed in the new "rational" terms.

Despite all the ambiguities surrounding the idea of Modernity, and the varied dates that different people give for its origin, the confusions and disagreements hide an underlying consensus. Throughout the current controversy—whether about the modern and the post-modern in art and architecture, the virtues of modern science, or the defects of modern technology—the arguments rest on shared assumptions about rationality. All parties to the debate agree that the self-styled "new philosophers" of the 17th century were responsible for new ways of thinking about nature and society. They committed the modern world to thinking about nature in a new and "scientific" way, and to use more "rational" methods to deal with the problems of human life and society. Their work was therefore a

turning point in European history, and deserves to be marked off as the
true starting point of Modernity.

In this respect, other disciplines and activities thus take a cue from
philosophy and natural science. Questions about the birth and death of
Modernity, or the beginning and end of the Modern Age, are most urgent
in those key fields. Physicists and biologists are aware that the scope and
methods of science today differ markedly from those of Lavoisier's or
Newton's time; but the development of quantum electrodynamics out of
Maxwell's electromagnetism, or of biomolecular genetics from Bernard's
physiology, involves (in their eyes) no discontinuity comparable to that
which occurred in the 1630s. Such 20th-century sciences as quantum
mechanics, ecology and psychoanalysis take us a long way from the axioms
of 17th-century "natural philosophy"—so much so that a few writers are
tempted to call these contemporary disciplines "post-modern sciences".
But this phrase does not mark the break with earlier "modern" science that
is implied in Venturi's substitution of "post-modern" for "modernist"
architecture. The changes of intellectual method or standpoint *within*
20th-century natural science in no way mean that molecular biology, for
example, has *broken with* the ideas of Claude Bernard or Charles Darwin.

Philosophy, by contrast, now faces a more drastic situation. People
working in the natural sciences share in more or less agreed-upon tasks,
but the agenda of philosophy has always been contested: its credentials
have never been agreed upon, even by its classic authors. That self-doubt
was never more striking or severe than in our own century. John Dewey's
1929 Gifford Lectures on *The Quest for Certainty* claimed that the debate
in philosophy had rested, ever since the 1630s, on too passive a view of the
human mind, and on inappropriate demands for geometrical certainty. In
the 1940s Ludwig Wittgenstein argued that endemic confusion over the
"grammar" of language leads to vacuous speculations: far from being
profound, philosophy thus distracts us from the truly important issues.
Edmund Husserl and Martin Heidegger wrote no less caustically about the
philosophical enterprise; while Richard Rorty, surveying the debate from
the late 1970s, concluded that philosophers have little left to do except to
join in a personal conversation about the world as they see it, from all of
their individual points of view. Reading Rorty's essays, we carry off the
image of a party of ex-soldiers disabled in the intellectual wars, sharing,
over a glass of wine, memories of "old, forgotten, far-off things, and battles
long ago."

Given so problematic an agenda, what are philosophers to do? Must they
now regard all philosophy as a kind of autobiography; or can they piece
together an alternative program, out of the wreckage left by their parents'

and grandparents' demolition work? The recent critique here gives us some first useful clues. When doubts are raised about the legitimacy of philosophy, what is called in question is still the tradition founded by René Descartes at the very beginning of Modernity. Though Wittgenstein opens his *Philosophical Investigations* with a passage from Augustine and also discusses some positions from Plato, his main thrust (like Dewey's and Heidegger's) is directed at a "theory-centered" *style* of philosophizing— i.e., one that poses problems, and seeks solutions, stated in timeless, universal terms—and it was just that philosophical style, whose charms were linked to the quest for certainty, that defined the agenda of "modern" philosophy, from 1650 on.

Beginning with Descartes, the "theory-centered" style of philosophy is (in a word) *modern* philosophy, while conversely "modern" philosophy is more or less entirely *theory-centered* philosophy. In philosophy more than elsewhere, then, one can argue that Modernity is over and done with. Whereas in natural science the continued evolution of modern ideas and methods has bred a new generation of ideas and methods that can escape criticisms that are fatal to 17th-century ideas about scientific method, in philosophy there is no way left in which this can happen. After the destructive work of Dewey, Heidegger, Wittgenstein, and Rorty, philosophy has limited options. These boil down to three possibilities: It can cling to the discredited research program of a purely theoretical (i.e. "modern") philosophy, which will end by driving it out of business; it can look for new and less exclusively theoretical ways of working, and develop the methods needed for a more practical (*"post*-modern") agenda; or it can return to its pre-17th-century traditions, and try to recover the lost (*"pre*-modern") topics that were sidetracked by Descartes, but can be usefully taken up for the future.

If the cases of science and philosophy are any general guide to the issues underlying the contemporary critique of the "modern" age, or underlying the recent doubts about the value of Modernity, they confirm that the epoch whose end we supposedly see today began some time in the first half of the 17th century. In a dozen areas, the modes of life and thought in modern Europe from 1700 on (modern science and medicine, engineering and institutions) were assumed to be more *rational* than those typical of medieval Europe, or those found in less developed societies and cultures today. Further, it was assumed that uniquely rational procedures exist for handling the intellectual and practical problems of any field of study, procedures which are available to anyone who sets superstition and mythology aside, and attacks those problems in ways free of local prejudice and transient fashion. These assumptions were not confined to philosophers, but were shared by people in all walks of life, and lay deep in our "modern" ways of thinking about the world.

In the last few years, those assumptions have come under damaging fire. As a result, the critique of Modernity has broadened into a critique of Rationality itself. Faced with questions about rationality, Rorty takes what he calls a "frankly ethnocentric" position: every culture is entitled to judge matters of rationality by its own lights. In a similar spirit, Alasdair MacIntyre requires us to look behind all questions of abstract "rationality" and inquire *whose* conception of rationality is operative in any situation. If the adoption of "rational" modes of thought and practice was the crucial new feature of Modernity, then the dividing line between Medieval and Modern times rests more on our philosophical assumptions than we had supposed. Now that rationality too is open to challenge, the traditional picture of a medieval world dominated by theology yielding to a modern world committed to rationality must be reconsidered.

Evidently, *something* important happened early in the 17th century, as a result of which—for good or for ill, and probably for both—society and culture in Western Europe and North America developed in a different direction from that which they would otherwise have followed. But this still requires us to ask, first, what the events were that were so crucial to the creation of modern Europe; secondly, how these events influenced the ways in which Europeans lived and thought later in the century; and, lastly, how they shaped the development of Modernity right up to our own time—not least, our horizons of expectation for the future.

Most scholars agree on one point. The "modern" commitment to rationality in human affairs was a product of those intellectual changes in the mid-17th-century whose protagonists were Galileo in physics and astronomy, and René Descartes in mathematics and epistemology. Beyond this point, different people go on in different directions. Some focus on the merits of these changes, some on their damaging by-products, while a few attempt to strike a balance between the costs and benefits of the new attitudes. What is rarely questioned is the *timing* of the changeover: the significant changes are usually placed between the prime of Galileo in the early 1600s, and the appearance of Newton's *Principia* in 1687.

As the old song warns, however, what everyone is liable to assume "ain't necessarily so." Too often, what everyone *believes*, nobody *knows*. Until recently, people assumed that Scottish tartans were woven to old designs handed on from generation to generation within a Highland clan, and it was a shock when the historians found that they were invented by an enterprising 18th-century textile merchant from South of the Border. Until recently, again, historians of science believed that William Harvey discovered the circulation of blood, by refuting Galen's theory that the blood "ebbed and flowed" in the veins: a little first-hand research showed Donald Fleming that Galen, too, believed in a unidirectional blood circulation, and that Harvey refined his theory rather than refuting it. The unanimity of earlier historians, it seemed, had been the result of their borrowing from each other's narratives instead of returning to the original texts.

As we have just seen, age-old traditions are sometimes conjured into existence long after the event, and the circumstances of their creation throw as much light on the times in which they were invented and accepted as they do on the times to which they ostensibly refer. As a result, all we can safely conclude from this initial survey of the debate between the moderns and the post-moderns is that, for much of the 20th century, people in Western Europe and North America generally accepted two statements about the origins of Modernity and the modern era: viz., that the modern age began in the 17th century, and that the transition from medieval to modern modes of thought and practice rested on the adoption of rational methods in all serious fields of intellectual inquiry—by Galileo Galilei in physics, by René Descartes in epistemology—with their example soon being followed in political theory by Thomas Hobbes.

These general beliefs are the foundation stones of what we may call the *standard account* or *received view* of Modernity. But the existence of a consensus is one thing: the soundness of this view, the reliability of the historical assumptions on which it depends, are something else. Those questions are sufficiently open to doubt to justify our starting our inquiries, here, by looking again more closely at the actual credentials, and the historical basis, of the standard account.

The Standard Account and Its Defects

Those of us who grew up in England in the 1930s and '40s had little doubt what Modernity was, and we were clear about its merits. It was our good luck to be born into the modern world, rather than some earlier, benighted time. We were better fed, more comfortable, and healthier than our ancestors. Even more, we were free to think and say what we liked, and follow our ideas in any direction that youthful curiosity pointed us. For us, Modernity was unquestionably "a Good Thing"; and we only hoped that, for the sake of the rest of humanity, the whole world would soon become as "modern" as us.

In those two decades we also shared in the received wisdom about the beginning of Modernity. We were told that by A.D. 1600 most of Europe, notably the Protestant countries of Northern Europe, had reached a new level of prosperity and material comfort. The development of trade, the growth of cities, and the invention of printed books, had made literacy as widespread in the prosperous laity as it had earlier been among priests, monks, and other ecclesiastics. A secular culture emerged, characteristic of the educated laity rather than of the Church. Lay scholars read and thought for themselves, no longer recognized the Church's right to tell them what to believe, and began to judge all doctrines by their inherent plausibility. Turning away from medieval scholasticism, 17th-century thinkers developed new ideas based on their first-hand experience.

The rise of a lay culture cleared the ground for a definitive break with the Middle Ages, in both the intellectual and the practical realms. The intellectual revolution was launched by Galileo Galilei, and by René Descartes. It had two aspects: it was a *scientific* revolution, because it led to striking innovations in physics and astronomy, and it was the birth of a new method in *philosophy,* since it established a research tradition in theory of knowledge and philosophy of mind that has lasted right up to our own times. In fact, the founding documents of modern thought—Galileo's *Dialogues concerning the Two Principal World Systems* and Descartes' *Discourse on Method*—both dated from the same decade: that of the 1630s.

We were taught that this 17th-century insistence on the power of *rationality,* along with the rejection of tradition and superstition—the two were not clearly distinguished—reshaped European life and society generally. After a brief flowering in Classical Greece, natural science had made little progress for two thousand years, because people either did not understand, or were distracted from, the systematic use of "scientific method". Earlier ideas of Nature were thus refined spasmodically and haphazardly, for lack of recognized ways to improve scientific thought systematically and methodically. Once the "new philosophers" (notably, Galileo, Bacon, and Descartes) had brought to light and clarified the conditions for intellectual progress in science, ideas of Nature became progressively more rational and realistic. Meanwhile, alongside the new empirical sciences of nature, philosophy was being emancipated from the tutelage of theology, thus setting aside earlier errors and prejudices, and making a fresh start. What Descartes had done for scientific argument in the *Discourse on Method,* he did for general philosophy in his *Meditations.* He carried the analysis back to primitive elements in experience that were, in principle, available to reflective thinkers in any culture, and at all times. As a result, philosophy became a field of "pure" inquiry, open to all clear-headed, reflective, self-critical thinkers.

The 1930s view of Modernity put less emphasis on technology or the practical arts. Initially, the 17th-century revolution in natural science and philosophy had no direct effect on medicine or engineering: the new scientists helped design a few devices, such as vacuum pumps, ship's chronometers, and microscopes; but, as Bacon had foreseen, it was a long time before the theoretical light of 17th century science yielded an equal harvest of practical fruit. (In the event, it took until after 1850.) However, though hopes of technological improvement were deferred, they were none-the-less guaranteed. Given enough time, a sound theory of nature could not help generating practical dividends.

Finally (we learned) the splits within Christendom, and the growing power of the laity, allowed European nations to insist on their sovereign authority to manage their social and political lives, which the medieval Papacy had usurped and the Counter-Reformation Church still coveted. By the year 1630, the Holy Roman Empire was an empty shell of an institution: from now on, European politics focused singlemindedly on the acts of sovereign Nation States. So understood, loyalty and political obligation referred to one state at a time. A few monarchs, like Charles I of England, claimed to be unchallenged embodiments of their nations' sovereignty; but every country had a right to order its affairs, free of interference by outsiders, notably ecclesiastical outsiders. All challenges to sovereign authority arose from within the nation-state in question: for instance, from members of a new, mercantile class, who sought a larger share in the exercise of that national sovereignty. True: in the 1640s, tranquil old England had seen a Civil War, which led to the execution of Charles I. But this (we were told) was a teething trouble of the new age: it sprang from Charles' obstinacy in pressing anachronistic claims. As late as the 1640s, the structure of the Nation-State was not yet clear: the new patterns of society and loyalty took their definitive form only after 1660. Meanwhile, the emancipatory power of reason generated a ferment of enthusiasms that still had to be worked through and outgrown.

One way or another, then, a combination of sensory experience with mathematical reasoning, Newton's science with Descartes' philosophy, combined to construct a world of physical theory and technical practice of which we in the England of the 1930s were the happy inheritors. Right up to the 1950s, indeed, this optimistic line remained appealing, and the authenticity of the historical narrative was rarely questioned. Even now, historians of early modern England still treat the early 17th century as the transition point from medieval to modern times. If this means that William Shakespeare is not a truly modern but a late-medieval dramatist, that leaves them unmoved. In their eyes, this view of Shakespeare is no stranger than John Maynard Keynes' description of Isaac Newton, on the tercentennial of his birth in 1942, as being not merely the first genius of modern science, but also "the last of the Magi".

Looking back at the "received view" of Modernity after fifty years, my inclination is to retort, "Don't believe a word of it!" From the start, that whole story was one-sided and over-optimistic, and veered into self-congratulation. True, it is easy enough to criticize your own former beliefs harshly, so I must try not to exaggerate. In some respects, the standard account is still correct; but we need to balance these truths against its major errors of history and interpretation. These defects become more evident with each year that goes by. The originality of the 17th-century scientists' work in mechanics and astronomy—that of Galileo and Kepler, Descartes, Huygens, and above all Newton—is as real and important as ever. But any assumption that this success was the outcome of substituting a rationally self-justifying method for the medieval reliance on tradition and super-stition misses all the light and shade in a complex sequence of events. On the frontier between philosophy and the sciences, many things have changed since 1950: these changes undermine earlier assumptions that the logical recipe for making discoveries about nature lies in a universal scientific method. The worst defects in the standard account, however, are not matters of philosophy, but of straight historical fact. The historical assumptions on which it rested are no longer credible.

The received view took it for granted that the political, economic, social, and intellectual condition of Western Europe radically improved from 1600 on, in ways that encouraged the development of new political institutions, and more rational methods of inquiry. This assumption is increasingly open to challenge. Specifically, in the 1930s we assumed that 17th-century philosophy and science were the products of prosperity, and that belief no longer bears scrutiny. Far from the years 1605–1650 being prosperous or comfortable, they are now seen as having been among the most uncomfortable, and even frantic, years in all European history. Instead of regarding Modern Science and Philosophy as the products of leisure, therefore, we will do better to turn the received view upside down, and treat them as responses to a contemporary crisis.

We also assumed that, after 1600, the yoke of religion was lighter than before; whereas the theological situation was in fact less onerous in the mid-16th century than it became from 1620 to 1660. Despite his radical ideas, Nicholaus Copernicus in the 1530s or 1540s did not suffer the rigid Church discipline that Galileo was exposed to a hundred years later. After the Council of Trent, the confrontation between the Protestant and Cath-olic heirs to historic Christianity took on a fresh intolerance. This set "papists" and "heretics" at one another's throats, and made the Thirty

Years' War, from 1618 to 1648, a particularly bloody and brutal conflict. In any event, the cultural break with the Middle Ages did not need to wait for the 17th century: it had taken place a good 100 or 150 years earlier. When we compare the spirit of 17th-century thinkers, and the content of their ideas, with the emancipatory ideas of 16th-century writers, indeed, we may even find 17th-century innovations in science and philosophy beginning to look less like revolutionary advances, and more like a defensive counter-revolution.

As a first constructive step toward a better account of the origins of Modernity, let us see why these assumptions no longer carry the same conviction among general historians today that they did in the 1930s. Over the last thirty years, modern historians have reached a unanimous verdict about the social and economic condition of Europe from 1610 to 1660. In the 16th century, Europe enjoyed a largely unbroken economic expansion, building up its capital holdings from the silver in the holds of the treasure ships from Spain's South American colonies: in the 17th century, the prosperity came to a grinding halt. It was followed by years of alternating depression and uncertainty. In early 17th-century Europe, life was so far from being comfortable that, over much of the continent from 1615 to 1650, people had a fair chance of having their throats cut and their houses burned down by strangers who merely disliked their religion. Far from this being a time of prosperity and reasonableness, it now looks like a scene from Lebanon in the 1980s. As many historians put it, from 1620 on the state of Europe was one of general crisis.

The picture of early 17th-century Europe as in "general crisis" was made explicit in the 1950s by the French historian, Roland Mousnier, but it has since been developed by historians of many backgrounds, and from countries as far apart as Scandinavia and Italy, the U.S.A. and the Soviet Union. Naturally, they give different interpretations of the crisis, but the basic facts are not in dispute. By 1600, the political dominance of Spain was ending, France was divided along religious lines, England was drifting into civil war. In Central Europe, the fragmented states of Germany were tearing one another apart, the Catholic princes being kept in line by Austria, and the Protestants reinforced by Sweden. Economic expansion was replaced by depression: there was a grave slump from 1619 to 1622. International trade fell away and unemployment was general, so creating a pool of mercenaries available for hire in the Thirty Years' War, and all these misfortunes were aggravated by a worldwide worsening of the climate, with unusually high levels of carbon in the atmosphere. (This was the time of the Little Ice Age—as described in Virginia Woolf's novel *Orlando*—when the River Thames froze over at London, and whole oxen were roasted on the ice.)

As Spain lost its undisputed command of the South Atlantic, the inflow of silver became unreliable, and the growth of Europe's capital base was checked. There were recurrences of the plague: France was specially hard hit in 1630–32 and 1647–49, while the Great Plague of 1665 in England was only the last in a sequence of violent outbreaks. Meanwhile, a series of cool, wet summers had severe effects on food production. With 80 to 90 percent of the population dependent on farming, this led to widespread suffering and rural depopulation. In marginal upland areas above all (we are told) there was, from 1615 on, a steady fall in grain yields, and entire villages were abandoned, to swell the disease-ridden city slums. Amid these catastrophes, the United Provinces of the Netherlands (Holland, as we know it) stands out as the sole exception, enjoying a Golden Age at a time when the rest of Europe went through a particularly bad patch.

Despite this unanimity among general historians, surprisingly few writers on science and philosophy in the 17th century take that verdict into account. Instead, they continue to treat the reputed prosperity and relaxation of the early 17th century as an obvious and familiar fact. Consult Volume IV of *The New Cambridge Modern History,* covering the late 16th and early 17th century, and you will discover that every essay but one considers how the Religious Wars, notably the Thirty Years' War, affected their subjects. The single exception is the essay on the history of 17th-century science, which ignores these brutal conflicts and treats the agenda of natural science as having arisen autonomously, out of its internal arguments alone.

The second of our earlier assumptions has no more historical basis. Any idea that ecclesiastical constraints and controls were relaxed in the 17th century is misconceived: if anything, the truth was more nearly the opposite. Rejecting all the Protestant reformers' attempts to change the institutions and practices of Christianity from within, the Papacy chose direct confrontation, and denounced the Protestants as schismatic. This policy was launched in the late 16th century after the Council of Trent, but culminated after 1618, with the bloodshed of the Thirty Years' War. From then on, backsliders met with no mercy. Theological commitments were not less rigorous and demanding, but more. There was less chance for critical discussion of doctrine, not more. For the first time, the need to close ranks and defend Catholicism against the Protestant heretics was an occasion for elevating key doctrines out of reach of reappraisal, even by the most sympathetic and convinced believers. The distinction between "doctrines" and "dogmas" was invented by the Council of Trent: Counter-Reformation Catholicism was thus dogmatic, in a way that the pre-Reformation Christianity of, say, an Aquinas could never have been. Theological pressure on scientists and other intellectual innovators did not weaken in the first half of the 17th century: rather, it *intensified*. Nor was this the case on the Catholic side of the fence exclusively: on the Protestant side, equally, many Calvinists and Lutherans were just as rigorous and dogmatic as any Jesuit or Jansenist.

The third assumption is at best a half-truth. In the 17th century, the spread of education and literacy among lay people gave their learning an increasing influence over European culture, and so helped destroy the Church's earlier monopoly in science and scholarship. In many countries, it effectively drove the ecclesiastical culture away from the center of the national scene. But this change was no novelty. Already, by 1600, printed books had been available for over a century. Any suggestion that modern *literature*—in contrast to modern science or philosophy—was significantly influential only after 1600 will not bear examination. In this respect, Galileo and Descartes were late products of changes that were already well under way in Western Europe by 1520, and in Italy a good time before. The cultural world of the 1630s, embodied in men like Blaise Pascal and Jean Racine, John Donne and Thomas Browne, had its distinctive character. But, when we place that mid-17th-century culture beside that of the 16th-century humanists—such writers as Desiderius Erasmus or François Rabelais, William Shakespeare, Michel de Montaigne, or Francis Bacon—we can scarcely go on arguing that the lay culture of Modernity was a product of the 17th century alone.

Printing opened the classical tradition of learning to lay readers, and so was an important source of Modernity. But its fruits began long before Protestants and Catholics reached their later hostility, and the acrimony of the Council of Trent overlaid and distracted attention from the less polemical concerns of the 16th century. If anything, the transition from the 1500s to the 1600s (from *Pantagruel* to *Pilgrim's Progress,* from the *Essais* of Montaigne to Descartes' *Meditations,* and from Shakespeare to Racine) saw a narrowing in the focus of preoccupations, and a closing in of intellectual horizons, not least the "horizon of expectations." As late as the first years of the 17th century, Francis Bacon looked forward to a future for humanity whose time-scale had no clear bounds. Forty years later, serious thinkers in England shared the belief of the Commonwealth worthies, that God's World was in its last days and "the End of the World" was literally "at hand"—to be completed by an Apocalypse, probably in or around the year 1657. When Andrew Marvell wrote, at least half in fun, in his *Ode to his Coy Mistress*,

> Had we but World enough and Time.
> This coyness, Lady, were no crime ...
> But at my back I always hear
> Time's wingèd chariot hurrying near,

his readers understood all his allusions to "the Conversion of the Jews" and the rest as echoes of the fashionable concern with the prophecies in the *Book of Revelations*.

In addition to reconsidering the historical assumptions underlying the received view, which depicted the 17th century as a time when the conditions of work in the sciences strikingly improved, we also need to look again at the deeper belief that 17th-century science and philosophy developed an original concern for rationality and the claims of Reason. This belief is misleading in two ways. Rather than expanding the scope for rational or reasonable debate, 17th-century scientists narrowed it. To Aristotle, both Theory and Practice were open to rational analysis, in ways that differed from one field of study to another. He recognized that the kinds of argument relevant to different issues depend on the nature of those issues, and differ in degrees of formality or certainty: what is "reasonable" in clinical medicine is judged in different terms from what is "logical" in geometrical theory. Seventeenth-century philosophers and scientists, by contrast, followed the example of Plato. They limited "rationality" to theoretical arguments that achieve a quasi-geometrical certainty or necessity: for them, theoretical physics was thus a field for rational study and debate, in a way that ethics and law were not. Instead of pursuing a concern with "reasonable" procedures of all kinds, Descartes and his successors hoped eventually to bring all subjects into the ambit of some formal theory: as a result, being impressed only by formally valid demonstrations, they ended by changing the very language of Reason—notably, key words like "reason", "rational", and "rationality"—in subtle but influential ways.

Nor were the founders of modern science theologically lukewarm or even agnostic—let alone atheist. Isaac Newton found it gratifying that his physics could "work with considering men for belief in a Deity." But he did so, not just because he put a fanciful interpretation on his work, but because one goal of his intellectual project was to justify his Arian views on theology: i.e., his "Arianism," as had been taught by Arius, the major opponent of Athanasius, who made the doctrine of the Trinity orthodox at the Council of Nicaea in the 4th century A.D. In this, he was by no means unusual among 17th-century scientists. Robert Boyle, too, liked to think of his scientific work as serving a pious purpose, by demonstrating God's Action in Nature (this made him, as he said, a "Christian virtuoso"), while Gottfried Wilhelm Leibniz placed theological constraints on the patterns of explanation within physics quite as stringent as any that a medieval theologian might have demanded.

To hint at a point that will be of importance to us later: one aim of 17th-century philosophers was to frame all their questions in terms that rendered them *independent of context;* while our own procedure will be the opposite—to *recontextualize* the questions these philosophers took most pride in decontextualizing. The view that modern science relied from the very start on rational arguments, divorced from all questions of metaphysics or theology, again assumed that the tests of "rationality" carry over from one context or situation to another, just as they stand: i.e., that we can know without further examination what arguments are rational in any field, or at any time, by reapplying those that are familiar in our own experience. Here, by contrast, instead of assuming that we know in advance what questions 16th- or 17th-century writers saw as "rational" at the time, or what kinds of arguments carried weight with them then, we shall need evidence of what was *in fact* at stake in their inquiries.

Our examination of the standard account of Modernity began with a review of its underlying historical and philosophical assumptions, many of which, we hinted, were exaggerated, or even downright false. In the light of this review, where does that received view stand? Clearly, it is time to give up any assumption that the 17th century was a time—the first time— when lay scholars in Europe were prosperous, comfortable, and free enough from ecclesiastical pressure to have original ideas; and it is also time to reconstruct our account of the transition from the medieval to the modern world on a more realistic basis. There must be some better way to draw the line between these two periods, and so avoid the confusions built into our present conception of Modernity. One item on our agenda is thus to outline a revised narrative that can avoid this confusion, and so supersede the standard account.

But that is only one of two complementary tasks. Since the 1950s, when Roland Mousnier wrote about the "general crisis" of the early 17th century, it should be obvious that Galileo and Descartes did not work in prosperous or comfortable times. Even in the 1920s or '30s, however, enough was known to show (if people cared to ask) that the standard account did not hold water. The statistics of recession and depression in the years after

1618 were investigated and published in detail only in the last twenty years, but no writer of the 1930s could plead ignorance of the trial of Galileo, the Thirty Years' War, or the Renaissance Humanism of, for instance, Erasmus and Rabelais, Montaigne, and Shakespeare. The time has therefore come for us to ask why the twin myths of "rational" Modernity and "modern" Rationality, which continue to carry conviction for many people even in our own day, won such an eager response among philosophers and historians of science after 1920. Like any historical tradition, the standard account of Modernity is the narrative of a past episode *reflected in* a more recent mirror: as such, it can be a source of insight both about the episode itself, and about the writers who held up this particular retrospective mirror.

Both sides of that relation claim our attention here. If we are to reach a balanced assessment of the claims of Modernity, we must keep these two tasks in proportion. On the one hand, we can justly criticize 20th-century assumptions about Modernity, only if we take more seriously the actual historical facts about the origins of the modern period. On the other hand, we can pose our historical questions about the period more exactly only if we make allowance for the special perspectives—even, the distortions— that were imposed on the received view by the faulty historical and philosophical assumptions looked at in this first review. As we learn to correct our historical account of Modernity, we may keep at least half an eye on our own historiographical mirror, and so come to understand better the nature of its special perspectives. Conversely, as we set out to eliminate the distortions from that mirror, we may keep in mind whatever discoveries come to light along the way, to show in just what contexts and circumstances the features typical of "modern" life or thought, society or culture, actually made their first appearance in the history of Western Europe and North America.

The Modernity of the Renaissance

The first step in developing our revised narrative of the origins of Modernity must be to return and look again at the Renaissance. As a historical period, the Renaissance gives tidy-minded chronologists some trouble. It saw the first seeds of many "modern" developments, but made few radical changes in the political and institutional forms of "medieval" Europe, and certainly did not abandon them. In the familiar tripartite chronology of European history—ancient, medieval, and modern—the Renaissance falls somewhere on the boundary between the second and third divisions. As a result, historians who rely on that traditional division must treat it either as a phenomenon of "late medieval" times, or else as a premature anticipation of the "modern" age.

Does it matter which we choose? The Renaissance was evidently a transitional phase, in which the seeds of Modernity germinated and grew, without reaching the point at which they were a threat, or worse, to the accepted structures of political society. Many of the leading figures of late Renaissance culture, from Leonardo (1452–1519) up to Shakespeare (1564–1616), worked in situations that retained much of their medieval character, without having fully developed the marks of Modernity proper. This fact can be in no way surprising; and, for our part, we may readily assume some degree of overlap between the "late medieval" and "early modern" history of Europe. Our choice of terms *matters,* then, only if we *let* it matter; and one curious feature of advocates of the received view is their *insistence* on deferring the start of Modernity until well after 1600. (Taking Galileo as their landmark figure for the start of modern science, for example, they call the work of his scientific precursors "medieval" mechanics.) This insistence tends to distract attention from, and even conceals, one major change in the direction of intellectual and artistic, literary and scientific work that occurred in the early years of the 17th century: a change which we shall recognize as one of the crucial steps, for the purposes of our revised narrative.

When we today read authors born in the 15th century, such as Desiderius Erasmus (b. 1467) and François Rabelais (b. 1494), it may take time and effort for us to grasp their "modernity"; but nobody questions the ability of such writers as Michel de Montaigne (b. 1533) and William Shakespeare (b. 1564) to speak across the centuries in ways we feel upon our pulses. Instead of focusing exclusively on the early 17th century, here we may therefore ask if the modern world and modern culture did not have two distinct origins, rather than one single origin, the first (literary or humanistic phase) being a century before the second. If we follow this suggestion, and carry the origins of Modernity back to the late Renaissance authors of Northern Europe in the 16th century, we shall find the *second,* scientific and philosophical phase, from 1630 on, leading many Europeans to turn their backs on the most powerful themes of the *first,* the literary or humanistic phase. After 1600, the focus of intellectual attention turned away from the humane preoccupations of the late 16th century, and moved in directions more rigorous, or even dogmatic, than those the Renaissance writers pursued. Something needs explaining here. To begin with, how far did the later scientists and philosophers positively *reject* the values of the earlier humanistic scholars, and how far did they merely take them for granted? Further, to the extent that they truly turned their backs on those values, how far did the birth of modern philosophy and the exact sciences involve something of an actual *counter*-Renaissance?

Many historians of science or philosophy will find such questions heretical, but they are nowhere near as unfamiliar to historians of ideas. There are good precedents for the suggestion that the 17th century saw a reversal of Renaissance values. Writing about 16th-century Italian intellectual history, for example, Eugenio Battisti found in the conservatism of the Council of Trent what he called an *antirinascimento;* while Hiram Haydn described the literary and intellectual changes in 17th-century England as a "counter-Renaissance". Historians of science, by contrast, take far less seriously the idea that 17th-century rationalists beat a strategic retreat from the achievements of Renaissance humanism, or that their theories rested in part on a destructive critique of its central values. Nor does this idea figure prominently in standard histories of philosophy: Indeed, few of the historians involved even consider the possibility of a connection between the 17th-century change in cultural direction and the wider economic and social crisis of the time.

If we compare the research agenda of philosophy after the 1640s with what it was a century before, however, we find notable changes. Before 1600, theoretical inquiries were balanced against discussions of concrete, practical issues, such as the specific conditions on which it is morally acceptable for a sovereign to launch a war, or for a subject to kill a tyrant. From 1600 on, by contrast, most philosophers are committed to questions of abstract, universal theory, to the exclusion of such concrete issues. There is a shift from a style of philosophy that keeps equally in view issues of local, timebound practice, and universal, timeless theory, to one that accepts matters of universal, timeless theory as being entitled to an exclusive place on the agenda of "philosophy".

Turning back to the Renaissance, then, what are the foci of concern for educated 16th-century laymen in countries like France and Holland? How do they carry further the work of earlier Renaissance scholars and artists in 15th-century Italy, and of later scholars in Northern Europe? In describing these concerns, we must use a word that today has misleading implications, if not for Europeans, then at least for many Americans. The lay culture of Europe in the 16th century was broadly humanistic, so it is natural for us to refer to the writers of the time as "Renaissance humanists"; but, given the present-day fundamentalist Christians' use of the catchall term "secular humanism" as a vogue phrase, some readers may assume that Renaissance humanists must have been hostile to Christianity, and possibly antireligious, if not actually atheists.

Far from this being the case, the major figures of the time in fact saw themselves by their own conscientious lights as sincerely religious. Erasmus wrote an essay, *In Praise of Folly,* which ridiculed dogmatism; yet he combined his loyalty to the traditional Church with being one of Martin Luther's most valued correspondents. Nothing would have pleased him more than to persuade his German friend not to press reforming zeal to the point of no return. (As a friendly critic, he remarked, he had often found quiet and private contrivance from within to be more efficacious than a public confrontation; but Luther's blood was up, and Erasmus could not persuade him.) Michel de Montaigne, who was a child when Erasmus died in the 1530s, criticized claims to theological certainty in a similar vein, as being presumptuous and dogmatic. Yet he too saw himself as being a good Catholic and, on a visit to Rome, felt entitled to ask for an audience with the Pope. The fundamentalists' "secular humanism" is, in fact, a bugaboo. In the 15th and 16th centuries, the emergence of real-life humanism, and the rise of the Humanities as an academic field, took place *inside* a European culture that was still dominantly Christian: indeed, the humanists made major contributions to Reform, not just such Protestant humanists as John Calvin, but also those within the body of the Roman Church.

True, from Erasmus to Montaigne, the writings of the Renaissance humanists displayed an urbane open-mindedness and skeptical tolerance that were novel features of this new lay culture. Their ways of thinking were not subject to the demands of pastoral or ecclesiastical duty: they regarded human affairs in a clear-eyed, non-judgmental light that led to honest practical doubt about the value of "theory" for human experience—whether in theology, natural philosophy, metaphysics, or ethics. In spirit, their critique was not hostile to the practice of religion, just so long as this was informed by a proper feeling for the limits to the practical and intellectual powers of human beings. Rather, it discouraged intellectual dogmatism of kinds that elevated disputes over liturgy or doctrine to a level at which they might become matters of political dispute—or even of life and death.

The humanists had special reasons to deplore, condemn, and try to head off the religious warfare that was picking up intensity throughout the 16th century, as antagonism between the two branches of Western Christianity deepened. Human modesty alone (they argued) should teach reflective Christians how limited is their ability to reach unquestioned Truth or unqualified Certainty over all matters of doctrine. As Etienne Pasquier foresaw, the risk was that, pressed into the service of worldly political interests, doctrinal issues would become fighting matters: in the 1560s, he was already deploring *name calling* between the two sides of the debate—with "papists" denouncing "heretics", and *vice versa*—and he foretold the disasters to which such name calling would lead.

The theological modesty of the humanists owed much, of course, to the recovery of classical learning and literature. Much of Greek and Latin learning was already available to medieval scholars and lawyers: in law and ethics, logic and rhetoric, medicine and philosophy, clerical scholars in the 13th and 14th centuries reconstructed the frameworks of ideas developed in antiquity, notably by Aristotle, and they had a serious grasp of Plato before him, and of the Stoics, Cicero, and Quintilian after him. Being ecclesiastics in Holy Orders, these medieval scholars were less concerned with the historians, Thucydides and Livy, let alone with the Athenian playwrights, whether tragedians like Aeschylus and Sophocles, or writers of comedies like Aristophanes. They had some acquaintance with Latin lyric and epic poetry, from Horace and Virgil to Ovid and Catullus: they were less familiar with the Greek and Roman texts on personalities and politics, or with the memoirs and reflections of the later Latin writers— except, of course, for the *Confessions* of St. Augustine.

The reason is not hard to see. In modern times, novelists and poets find their grist in the very diversity of human affairs; but, for medieval scholars, this variety had little significance. Human beings were sinful and fallible in ways that later readers found fascinating; but medieval clerics and teachers saw these failings as making humans *less,* not *more,* interesting to write about. What merit was there in spelling out (let alone in celebrating) all the variants of human sinfulness or fallibility? Augustine's *Confessions* are autobiographical in form, but their theme is still *confessional:* he revels in telling us what a wild young man he was, to put in a better light the Divine Grace that gave him the opportunity to repent, and save his soul.

With the Renaissance, the rest of ancient literature and learning was available to lay readers. This included the last neglected school of Greek philosophy, that of Epicurus, which surfaced with the recovery of Lucretius's poem, *De Rerum Natura.* It included also history and drama, memoirs and recollections—notably, from Pliny, Suetonius, and Marcus Aurelius—as well as political biographies like those in Plutarch's *Lives.* The poetry of classical antiquity also acquired a new importance for lay readers, first in the Italian city states with Dante and Ariosto, later in Northern or Western Europe as well. Following Georges Sarton, many recent historians of science deplore the dominance of Aristotle over medieval philosophy, for reasons that are now anachronistic. Medieval scholars and educators owed one crucial thing to Aristotle's *Ethics, Politics,* and *Rhetoric:* his sensitivity to the "circumstantial" character of practical issues, as they figure in problems of medical diagnosis, legal liability, or moral responsibility. The recovery of ancient history and literature only intensified their feeling for the kaleidoscopic diversity and contextual dependence of human affairs. All the varieties of fallibility, formerly ignored, began to be celebrated as charmingly limitless consequences of human character and personality. Rather than deplore these failings, as moral casuists might do, lay readers were interested in recognizing what made human conduct admirable or deplorable, noble or selfish, inspiring or laughable. The ground was first prepared for redirecting the arts of narrative (which earlier had played a part in case law or moral theology) into the "novel of character" and other new literary genres.

Renaissance scholars were quite as concerned with circumstantial questions of practice in medicine, law, or morals, as with any timeless, universal matters of philosophical theory. In their eyes, the rhetorical analysis of arguments, which focused on the presentation of cases and the character of audiences, was as worthwhile—indeed, as philosophical—as the formal analysis of their inner logic: Rhetoric and Logic were, to them, complementary disciplines. Reflecting on the detailed nature and circumstances of concrete human actions—considering their morality as "cases"—also shared top billing with abstract issues of ethical theory: in their eyes, casuistry and formal ethics were likewise complementary. Many 16th-century readers were fascinated by theoretical speculations, some of them with overtones of neo-Platonism, or "natural magic". But this speculative streak went hand in hand with a taste for the variety of concrete experience, for empirical studies of natural phenomena (such as magnetism), and for the different branches of natural history.

The results had a certain higgledy-piggledy confusion, including the irresoluble disagreement and inconsistency that led Socrates long ago to despair of a rational consensus about the world of nature. In the Europe of the 16th century, as in classical Athens, some scholars condemned as irrational *con*fusion what others welcomed as intellectual *pro*fusion. For the moment, then—Montaigne argued—it was best to suspend judgment about matters of general theory, and to concentrate on accumulating a rich perspective, both on the natural world and on human affairs, as we encounter them in our actual experience. This respect for the rational possibilities of human experience was one chief merit of the Renaissance humanists, but they also had a delicate feeling for the *limits* of human experience. They declared that, to those whose trust in experience gives courage to observe and reflect on the variety of conduct and motive, "Nothing human is foreign", and they set out to do this in rich detail, which was new at the time, and has rarely been equaled: the political analyses of Niccolò Machiavelli and the dramas of William Shakespeare are among our permanent inheritances as a result. In the 14th century, the accepted ways of thinking had still constrained new ideas of human character and motives: in the last decades of the 16th century, they no longer placed limits on the creator of Othello and Hamlet, Shylock and Portia, Juliet and Lady Macbeth.

The reports of European explorers deepened the humanists' curiosity about human motives and actions. The 16th century saw a growing taste for the exotic, and a fascination with alternative ways of life, that was to be a counterpoint to much later philosophical argument. (As late as the 18th century, Montesquieu and Samuel Johnson still found it helpful to present unusual ideas by attributing them to people in a far-off land like Abyssinia or Persia.) Access to the diversity of cultures put to a test their commitment to an honest reporting of first-hand experience. Exotic populations can be viewed as primitive, savage, or marginally human, their ways of thinking and living as heretical, pagan, or chaotic: that option is always available to those with minds made up in advance. Instead, we could alternatively add these fresh and exotic discoveries to the pool of testimony about Humanity and human life, and so enlarge our sympathy to a point at which the accepted framework of understanding could accommodate the riches of ethnography: that second choice was typical of lay humanists in 16th-century Europe. But this dividing line never set ecclesiastics and secular writers against one another. When, for example, on reaching South America, the *conquistadores* set out to enslave the native population, it was Father Bartolomeo de las Casas who argued for the humanity of the indigenous Americans, and petitioned the Pope to put them out of reach of the slave trade. When posted to Beijing at the turn of the 17th century, yet another priest, the Jesuit Father Matteo Ricci, adopted the life and manners of a Mandarin, and taught Christianity to a Chinese flock in terms that spoke to their condition, rather than condemning it. As for Montaigne, though his journeying reached barely beyond his trip to Rome, he too was happy to collect ethnographic reports, and add to his repertory of personal experience reflections on topics like nudity and cannibalism, which had hitherto been seen as merely scandalous.

Within philosophy itself, the humanists' respect for complexity and diversity worked out differently. Naturalists rejoiced in the profusion of God's Creation, but those who looked for comprehensive systems of physical theory in human experience faced disappointment. Given the very varied ideas that circulated in the 16th-century intellectual world, no one could ever bring matters of physics to a convincing confrontation, and everyone was free to believe what he liked. In natural philosophy, many of the humanists—once again, like Socrates—were driven to adopt attitudes of outright skepticism. In this respect, the position taken by Montaigne in his longest and most openly philosophical essay—viz., the *Apology of Raimond Sebond*—is typical, if at times extreme. Surveying the wide variety of doctrines that 16th-century writers used to explain natural phenomena of Nature, as Socrates had surveyed his predecessors in Elea and Ionia, Montaigne saw attempts to reach theoretical consensus about nature as being the result of human presumption or self-deception. This skepticism about the possibilities of Science went far beyond the ideas of his young admirer and imitator, Francis Bacon. Bacon kept open a long-term hope of reaching agreement about the world of nature. Even so, his methods of observation, and their use in developing new theories, remained close to everyday experience: they fell far short of authorizing the mathematical constructions so typical of 17th-century physics, at the hands of Galileo and Descartes in the 1630s or '40s, or in the striking creations of Isaac Newton from the 1660s on.

In calling 16th-century humanism "skeptical", we must again guard against misunderstanding. Since Descartes, philosophers have thought of skepticism as destructive nay-saying: the skeptic *denies* the things that other philosophers *assert*. This is a fair account of the skepticism that René Descartes himself launched, introducing his method of "systematic doubt": his goal was indeed to pull the rug out from under claims to certainty that lack formal guarantees. Humanist skeptics took a totally different position: they no more wished to *deny* general philosophical theses than to *assert* them. Like the two classical philosophers to whom Montaigne compares himself, Pyrrho and Sextus, the humanists saw philosophical *questions* as reaching beyond the scope of experience in an indefensible way. Faced with abstract, universal, timeless theoretical propositions, they saw no sufficient basis in experience, either for asserting, or for denying them.

In theology or philosophy, you may (with due intellectual modesty) adopt as personal working positions the ideas of your inherited culture; but you cannot deny others the right to adopt different working positions for themselves, let alone pretend that your experience "proves" the truth of one such set of opinions, and the necessary falsity of all the others. The 16th-century followers of classical skepticism never claimed to *refute* rival philosophical positions: such views do not lend themselves either to proof or to refutation. Rather, what they had to offer was a new way of understanding human life and motives: like Socrates long ago, and Wittgenstein in our own time, they taught readers to recognize how philosophical theories overreach the limits of human rationality.

In writing about ethics and poetics, Aristotle exhorted us not to aim at certainty, necessity, or generality beyond "the nature of the case". The skeptics placed similar limits on appeals to experience. We need not be ashamed to limit our ambitions to the reach of humanity: such modesty does us credit. Meantime, the range of particular everyday phenomena, on which human experience gives solid testimony, is unlimited in the realm of human affairs, and in natural history. There may be no rational way to convert to our point of view people who honestly hold other positions, but we cannot short-circuit such disagreements. Instead, we should live with them, as further evidence of the diversity of human life. Later on, these differences may be resolved by further shared experience, which allows different schools to converge. In advance of this experience, we must accept this diversity of views in a spirit of toleration. Tolerating the resulting plurality, ambiguity, or the lack of certainty is no error, let alone a sin. Honest reflection shows that it is part of the price that we inevitably pay for being human beings, and not gods.

Retreat from the Renaissance

During the 17th century, these humanist insights were lost. True, the founders of the Royal Society of London used Francis Bacon's modest claims for natural science in their public propaganda in the 1660s, and in their requests to Charles II for financial support, though in their actual practice they often ignored the constraints that Bacon placed on the uses of theory. In four fundamental ways, however, 17th-century philosophers set aside the long-standing preoccupations of Renaissance humanism. In particular, they disclaimed any serious interest in four different kinds of practical knowledge: the oral, the particular, the local, and the timely.

From the Oral to the Written

Before 1600, both rhetoric and logic were seen as legitimate fields of philosophy. The external conditions on which "arguments"—i.e. public utterances—carry conviction with any given audience were accepted as on a par with the internal steps relied on in the relevant "arguments"—i.e., strings of statements. It was assumed that new ways of formulating theoretical arguments might be found in fields that were as yet merely empirical; but no one questioned the right of rhetoric to stand alongside logic in the canon of philosophy; nor was rhetoric treated as a second-class—and necessarily inferior—field.

This pre-Cartesian position contrasts sharply with that which has been taken for granted throughout the history of modern philosophy. In the philosophical debate that was started by Descartes, everyone read questions about the *soundness* or *validity* of "arguments" as referring not to public utterances before particular audiences, but to written chains of statements whose validity rested on their internal relations. For modern philosophers, the rhetorical question, "Who addressed this argument to whom, in what forum, and using what examples?," is no longer a matter for philosophy. From their point of view, the rational merit of arguments can no more rest on facts about their human reception than the merit of a geometrical proof rested, for Plato, on the accuracy of the accompanying diagrams, even if drawn by a master draftsman. The research program of modern philosophy thus set aside all questions about *argumentation*— among particular people in specific situations, dealing with concrete cases, where varied things were at stake—in favor of *proofs* that could be set down in writing, and judged as written.

This move had historical parallels. In antiquity, Plato condemned the Sophists' use of rhetoric, as "making the worse argument appear the better." Aristotle replied to this libel: he treated questions about the conditions on which, and the circumstances in which, arguments carry conviction as ones that philosophers can address with a clear conscience. Right up to the 16th century, philosophers discussed them without any sense that these questions were *non*-rational, let alone *anti*-rational; but the 17th century undid this good work. It reinstated Plato's libel against rhetoric so successfully that colloquial uses of the word "rhetoric" have ever since been insulting, hinting that rhetorical issues have to do only with using dishonest tricks in oral debate. (To this day, serious students of rhetoric have to explain that the term is not necessarily deprecatory.) After the 1630s, the tradition of Modern Philosophy in Western Europe concentrated on formal analysis of chains of written statements, rather than on the circumstantial merits and defects of persuasive utterances. Within that tradition, *formal logic was in, rhetoric was out.*

From the Particular to the Universal

There was a parallel shift in the scope of philosophical reference. In the Middle Ages and the Renaissance, moral theologians and philosophers handled moral issues using case analyses like those that still have a place in Anglo-American common case law. In doing so, they followed the procedures that Aristotle recommended in the *Nicomachean Ethics.* "The Good," Aristotle said, "has no universal form, regardless of the subject

matter or situation: sound moral judgment always respects the detailed
circumstances of specific kinds of cases." Their insights into the particularity of human action nourished the practice of Catholic and Anglican
casuistry right up to the 17th century: even Descartes, while expressing the
hope that ethics might eventually achieve the standing of a formal theory,
acknowledged the provisional adequacy of this inherited moral experience. In the 1640s, however, Antoine Arnaud, a close friend of the mathematician Blaise Pascal, was indicted in the ecclesiastical court at Paris on
a charge of heresy, at the insistence of the Jesuits: in his defense, Pascal
published a series of anonymous *Provincial Letters.* His chosen target was
the method used by the Jesuit casuists, based on analysis of specific,
concrete "cases of conscience" (*casus conscientiae*). The sarcasm of his
letters ridiculed the Jesuits ferociously, and brought the whole enterprise
of "case ethics" into lasting discredit.

Within the practice of medicine and law, the pragmatic demands of daily
practice still carried weight, and the analysis of particular cases retained
intellectual respectability. But, from now on, casuistry met the same
comprehensive scorn from moral philosophers as rhetoric did from the
logicians. After the 1650s, Henry More and the Cambridge Platonists made
ethics a field for general abstract theory, divorced from concrete problems
of moral practice; and, since then, modern philosophers have generally
assumed that—like God and Freedom, or Mind and Matter—the Good and
the Just conform to timeless and universal principles. They view as unphilosophical or dishonest those writers who focus on particular cases, or
on types of cases limited by specific conditions. (Let theologians weave
casuistical nets: moral philosophers must work on a more general and
abstract plane.) As a result, philosophers again limited their own scope: the
careful examination of "particular practical cases" was ruled out of ethics
by definition. Modern moral philosophy was concerned not with minute
"case studies" or particular moral discriminations, but rather with the
comprehensive general principles of ethical theory. In a phrase, *general
principles were in, particular cases were out.*

From the Local to the General

Over the third issue—viz., the *local*—a similar contrast held good. The
16th-century humanists found sources of material in ethnography, geography, and history, in none of which geometrical methods of analysis have
much power. Ethnographers collect facts about such things as the judicial
practices in various local jurisdictions, and anthropologists like Clifford
Geertz then discuss them in such books as his *Local Knowledge.* Early in

the *Discourse on Method,* by contrast, Descartes confesses that he had had a youthful fascination with ethnography and history, but he takes credit for having overcome it:

> History is like foreign travel. It broadens the mind, but it does not deepen it.

Ethnographers are unmoved by inconsistencies among the legal customs of different peoples; but philosophers have to bring to light the general principles that hold in a given field of study—or, preferably, in all fields. Descartes saw the curiosity that inspires historians and ethnographers as a pardonable human trait; but he taught that philosophical understanding never comes from accumulating experience of particular individuals and specific cases. The demands of rationality impose on philosophy a need to seek out abstract, general ideas and principles, by which particulars can be connected together.

Descartes' reaction again has historical parallels. Plato had seen different *mal*functioning cities, like Tolstoy's "unhappy families", as displaying specific pathologies. Political historians are free to study these differences, if that is their taste: by contrast, the philosopher's task is to seek out general principles of "political health" lying behind local idiosyncrasies, so as to throw light on the things that make a city healthy or *well*functioning. Aristotle took a broader view of political philosophy. Human life does not lend itself to abstract generalizations. The variety in political affairs is, in his view, an inescapable aspect of civic life, and, as such, it is also proper grist for the philosopher's mill. So matters remained up to the 16th century. When modern philosophers dismissed ethnography and history as irrelevant to truly "philosophical" inquiry, they excluded from their enterprise a whole realm of questions that had previously been recognized as legitimate topics of inquiry. From then on, *abstract axioms were in, concrete diversity was out.*

From the Timely to the Timeless

Finally, like medieval theologians, Renaissance humanists gave equal weight to concrete issues of legal, medical, or confessional practice, and to abstract issues of theory. All problems in the practice of law and medicine are "timely". They refer to specific moments in time—now not later, today not yesterday. In them, "time is of the essence"; and they are decided, in Aristotle's phrase, *pros ton kairon,* "as occasion requires". A navigator's decision to change course 10° to starboard is as rational as the steps in a mathematical deduction; yet the rationality of this decision rests not on formal computations alone, but on when it is effected. The relevant sums may have been performed impeccably; but, if the resulting action is unduly delayed, the decision will become "irrational".

Questions about the timeliness of decisions and actions, utterances and arguments, had been staple topics for earlier philosophy. For 16th-century scholars, the very model of a "rational enterprise" was not Science but Law. Jurisprudence brings to light, not merely the link between "practical rationality" and "timeliness", but the significance of local diversity, the relevance of particularity, and the rhetorical power of oral reasoning: by comparison, all projects for a universal natural philosophy struck the humanists as problematic. A hundred years later, the shoe was on the other foot. For Descartes and his successors, timely questions were no concern of philosophy: instead, their aim was to bring to light permanent structures underlying all the changeable phenomena of Nature.

From the start, then, transient human affairs took second place for modern philosophers, and they sidelined matters of practical relevance and timeliness, as not being genuinely "philosophical." From the 1630s on, students of jurisprudence might continue to look to philosophy as a source of intellectual methods; but within philosophy law and medicine played only marginal parts. Philosophers had no interest in factors that held good in different ways at different times. From Descartes' time on, attention was focused on timeless principles that hold good at all times equally: *the permanent was in, the transitory was out.*

These four changes of mind—from oral to written, local to general, particular to universal, timely to timeless—were distinct; but, taken in an historical context, they had much in common, and their joint outcome exceeded what any of them would have produced by itself. All of them reflected a historical shift from *practical* philosophy, whose issues arose out of clinical medicine, juridical procedure, moral case analysis, or the rhetorical force of oral reasoning, to a *theoretical* conception of philosophy: the effects of this shift were so deep and long-lasting that the revival of practical philosophy in our own day has taken many people by surprise.

It is no accident that diagnostics and due process, case ethics and rhetoric, topics and poetics, were sidelined and called in question at the same time. In practical disciplines, questions of rational adequacy are timely not timeless, concrete not abstract, local not general, particular not universal. They are the concern of people whose work is centered in practical and pastoral activities, and 17th-century philosophers were *theory-centered,* not *practical-minded.* Procedures for handling specific types of problems, or limited classes of cases, have never been a central concern of modern philosophy: rather, it has concentrated on abstract, timeless methods of deriving general solutions to universal problems. Thus, from 1630 on, the focus of philosophical inquiries has ignored the particular, concrete, timely and local details of everyday human affairs: instead, it has shifted to a higher, stratospheric plane, on which nature and ethics conform to abstract, timeless, general, and universal theories.

———————

Why did the focus of intellectual preoccupations in Europe change so drastically *at just that time*? How should we explain this turning away, after 1630, from the oral, local, transient, particular aspects of life and language, and the new emphasis on written arguments, general ideas, and abstract, timeless principles? Some of the relevant factors, such as the rise of a lay culture, we have already discussed. In the Middle Ages, the chief vehicle of medieval religious teaching was oral preaching, and this supported an interest in rhetoric. Once the printed page supplemented or replaced the spoken word, lay scholars could read all the Scriptures and Commentaries for themselves, so they focussed more on the criticism of written arguments. Lay readers were less involved in pastoral care than their ecclesiastical forerunners: they debated ethical theory, but had no responsibility for "the cure of souls." The 16th-century humanists had continued to discuss the issues of practical philosophy; but, like a true intelligentsia, philosophers in the 17th century discussed theoretical issues from the sidelines.

More is surely needed to explain why, after centuries of practical philosophy in an Aristotelian vein, the new philosophy demanded not just closer attention to issues of theory, but the outright expulsion from philosophy of all practical concerns. Where are we to find this "more"? Here, above all, the historians of philosophy need to take more seriously recent work on the economic and social history of the early 17th century. By now, the discrepancy between the received account of Modernity, in which science and philosophy were products of 17th-century prosperity and comfort, and the general historians' view that the years after 1610 were years of social disorder and economic retreat, is too gross to be ignored. Our own inquiry began from that discrepancy, and it is time to look at it directly, inquiring, "In what ways did the changed intellectual focus in early 17th-century Europe reflect the wider social and economic crisis of the time?"

John Dewey and Richard Rorty both concluded that philosophy turned into its "modern" dead end as a result of the work of René Descartes; yet neither philosopher, oddly, troubled to ask why the Quest for Certainty was so enticing not a century or so earlier or later, but *at just this time*. For them, it was enough to diagnose the errors that Modern Philosophy fell victim to: why that affliction struck philosophy as and when it did, they did not think it necessary to ask. By ignoring such historical issues, however, their own arguments exemplify the continuing split between rhetoric and logic—a feature of the very position they claimed to reject. The question, "Why did educated people in the mid-17th century find the Quest for Certainty so attractive and convincing?," is itself a rhetorical question of the kind that Descartes ruled out of philosophy: a question about the *audience* for philosophy in that particular context. It asks why the Cartesian Error—if it was an error—carried special conviction with people from 1640 on, in a way it did not do in the High Middle Ages, and no longer does today.

That question can hardly be irrelevant to philosophy, especially now. If Wittgenstein is right, the philosopher's task is precisely to show why we are tempted into these intellectual "dead ends." If that task takes research into social and intellectual history, so be it. The claim that all truly philosophical problems must be stated in terms independent of any historical situation, and solved by methods equally free of all contextual references, is one of the rationalist claims typical of modern philosophy from 1640 to 1950, rather than of philosophy in either its medieval or its post-Wittgensteinian form. The central question of our own inquiry escapes that objection. It has to do, frankly, with the history of ideas: the fact that René Descartes might call it unphilosophical is beside the point. Rather, this fact illustrates once again the central phenomenon that concerns us here: viz., the 17th-century rejection of local, timely, *practical* issues, and substitution of a philosophical research program whose focus was exclusively general, timeless, and *theoretical*.

From Humanists to Rationalists

To sharpen up the point, let us put Montaigne and Descartes face to face. Written in the 1570s and 1580s, Michel de Montaigne's *Essais* present a fully fledged humanist philosophy. In his one philosophical essay, the *Apology of Raimond Sebond,* Montaigne makes out a powerful case for classical skepticism, as the way to escape a presumptuous dogmatism. His other essays explore different aspects of human experience: there, he draws on his first-hand recollections, the testimony of neighbors and friends, or the evidence he extracts from classical literature or from the narratives of contemporary historians and ethnographers.

Once accustomed to Montaigne's personal style and idiom, many late 20th-century readers find him more congenial than his successors in the

17th century. Reading what Michel de Montaigne and Francis Bacon have to say about a hundred topics from human experience—for example, the claims of friendship, cannibalism, nudity, or the conventions of dress—we find their language as familiar in our time as it was to their original readers between 1580 and the early 1600s. Neither Montaigne nor Bacon harps on the theological rights and wrongs of his views: the *Apology* is the only essay which even skirts near to theology. Both of them discuss life as they find it, and write about it in a nondoctrinal spirit.

It is not (to repeat) that either author was "irreligious": Montaigne was a practicing Catholic, and Bacon went to Anglican service as often as convention demanded. Still less did they belong to any *anti*religious party. They were men of their times, and lived like men of their times; but, given the nature of those times, they did not find it indispensable, either to be forever invoking the name of God, or to voice a continual anxiety about their personal salvation. In this, Augustine's *Confessions* contrast with Montaigne's *Essais*. Montaigne passes wry comments on his own everyday behavior: on his unhealthy habit of eating greedily, so that he bites his tongue and even his fingers. But he does not bare or beat his breast, as though this habit required him publicly to confess his Sins. Quite the reverse: his aim was to set aside pretense and attitudinizing, self-aggrandizement or ostentatious self-reproach, and to provide an unvarnished picture of his experience of life, and attitudes of mind.

Montaigne's point of view contrasts sharply, also, with that of René Descartes or Isaac Newton. The intellectual modesty of the humanists led thinkers like Bacon and Montaigne to adopt a cool, nonjudgmental tone that makes them congenial to us, and to put a distance between their religious affiliation and their philosophical or literary reflections on experience. By contrast, the 17th-century founders of modern science and philosophy had theological commitments which shaped their whole enterprise. Repeatedly, Descartes and Newton express concern about the religious orthodoxy of their ideas: we understand the force of their scientific speculations fully, only if we take those commitments into account. Yet it is not that Montaigne's and Descartes' interests were so far apart that they ended at cross purposes, "passing like ships in the dark." On the contrary, in his final essay, *Of Experience,* Montaigne confronted head-on the chief philosophical problems that Descartes was to address fifty years later; and he drew reasons from his own experience to reject *in advance* the conclusions that Descartes argued for in general, abstract terms in the *Meditations.*

Montaigne is scornful about attempts to separate mental activities from bodily changes: "He who wants to detach his soul, let him do it . . . when his body is ill, to free it from the contagion; at other times, on the contrary, let the soul assist and favor the body and not refuse to take part in its natural pleasures." Elsewhere, he writes:

> Since it is the privilege of the mind to rescue itself from old age, I advise mine to do so as strongly as I can. Let it grow green, let it flourish meanwhile, if it can, like mistletoe on a dead tree. But I fear it is a traitor. It has such a tight brotherly bond with the body that it abandons me at every turn to follow the body in its need. I take it aside and flatter it, I work on it, all for nothing. In vain I try to turn it aside from this bond, I offer it Seneca and Catullus, and the ladies and the royal dances; if its companion has the colic, it seems to have it too. Even the activities that are peculiarly its own cannot then be aroused; they evidently smack of a cold in the head. There is no sprightliness in [the mind's] productions if there is none in the body at the same time.

He is especially hard on philosophers who use the contrast between Mind and Body to justify despising bodily experience. Philosophers are drawn to dualism, he suggests, only when they are uncomfortable with their own corporeal natures:

> Philosophy is very childish, to my mind, when she gets up on her hind legs and preaches to us that it is a barbarous alliance to marry the divine with the earthly, the reasonable with the unreasonable, the severe with the indulgent, the honorable with the dishonorable; that sensual pleasure is a brutish thing unworthy of being enjoyed by the wise man.

What reason might a modern philosopher have to scorn the flesh? Facing this question, we may look at the personality differences between the Renaissance humanists and the rationalist thinkers who succeeded them. Once again, there is a striking difference between Montaigne and Descartes. The ladies of the French Court—so we are told—kept one of Montaigne's later essays in their boudoirs (the one with the curious title, *On some verses of Virgil*) and read it for pleasure. This essay reflects on his sexual experience, and deplores the habit of social prudery:

> What has the sexual act, so natural, so necessary, and so just, done to mankind, for us not to dare talk about it without shame and for us to exclude it from serious and decent conversation? We boldly pronounce the words "kill," "rob," "betray"; and this one we do not dare pronounce, except between our teeth. Does this mean that the

less we breathe of it in words, the more we have the right to swell our thoughts with it?

For himself, he says, "I have ordered myself to dare to say all that I dare to do, and I dislike even thoughts that are unpublishable."

He is open about his enjoyment of sexual relations ("Never was a man more impertinently genital in his approaches") though they are most agreeable, he insists, when love-making is an expression of real affection. He reflects on the embarrassments of impotence. In later years, he says—he died in his fifties—it is harder, faced with an unforeseen chance to make love to a beautiful woman, to make sure that he has a satisfactory erection:

> He who can await, the morning after, without dying of shame, the disdain of those fair eyes that have witnessed his limpness and impertinence, ["Her silent looks made eloquent reproach"—OVID] has never felt the satisfaction and pride of having conquered them and put circles around them by the vigorous exercise of a busy and active night.

Far from blaming this failing on his body, however, he acknowledges that the weakness springs from ambiguity of desire as much as from physical frailty, and readily accepts personal responsibility for the fact that his body seems on occasion to let him down:

> Each one of my parts makes me myself just as much as every other one. And no other makes me more properly a man than this one.

Some will find it frivolous to interpret Montaigne's attitude to sex as throwing light on his *philosophy:* they may even find his reflections morally offensive, and accuse him of being excessively preoccupied with the topic. In reply, we may note that, in length, the *Virgil* essay is only one-twentieth (5 percent) of the *Essais:* in the other 95 percent, he reflects on other experiences with the same candor and hatred of pretension. We may turn the question back on the objectors, and ask, "What has René Descartes to say about these topics? Could he have adopted as relaxed an attitude to his sexual experience as Montaigne?" That question answers itself. By the time of Descartes, the habits of social prudery that Montaigne deplored were back in the saddle. The Court ladies would hardly have treated the works of Descartes as pillow books: far from sexuality being a topic about which he wrote explicitly, we can reconstruct his attitudes only by inference: by decoding words in his texts as euphemisms for sexual topics, and by seeing if the course of his life gives us a clue to those attitudes.

Looking for euphemisms, we may start with the word, "passions": particularly in Descartes' last major book, written for Queen Christina of Sweden, the *Treatise on the Passions.* Clearly, in his view, we need not take responsibility for our emotions. Feelings are not something *we do:* They are what *our bodies do to us.* Mental life comprised for Descartes, above all, rational calculation, intuitive ideas, intellectual deliberations, and sensory inputs: we can accept responsibility for the validity of our calculations, but not the emotions that disturb or confuse our inferences. Taken at its face value, then, Descartes' position implies that a philosopher can *disclaim* all responsibility for his erections, unless he has a *good reason* for deciding to have one.

Nothing in Descartes' published treatises on philosophy approaches Montaigne's candor or ease, and the story of his life suggests that he felt some embarrassment over sexuality. He reportedly took his housekeeper as a lover, and she in due course bore him a daughter. The child's early death grieved him deeply; but he continued to refer to the mother as a servant and the little girl as his "niece." His choice of words is curious. Cardinals were supposed to be celibate, and so had "nieces" or "nephews"; but did Descartes need to be so reticent? Was he moved by puritanism, or snobbery? Was the housekeeper's standing too humble for a member of an upwardly mobile family on its way to the *noblesse de la robe?* Or was his reason less devious? At our distance we have no way of knowing, but this is clear. Montaigne "dared to say all that he dared to do", but in his private life Descartes acted as he did in his professional life where—he noted self-revealingly—*larvatus prodeo* ("I present myself *masked*").

Montaigne and Descartes may have differed in personality, but their intellectual opposition went further. For Montaigne, part of our humanity is to accept responsibility for our bodies, our feelings and the effects of the things we do, given those bodies and feelings; and we must do so, even if we cannot always keep these things under complete control. Elsewhere, he talks about farting, repeating from St. Augustine the story of the man who, by controlling his gut, could fart in time with music. The example is, as a reader finds it, either amusing or *risqué,* but Montaigne uses it to make a serious point—viz., that there is no use laying down a hard and fast line to divide bodily processes ("material") from voluntary activities ("mental"), since there is no way to be sure in advance of experience just which of our bodily functions we can or cannot bring under deliberate self-control. Montaigne lives in the world of Rabelais: neither writer is constrained by "respectability"; but, by Descartes' time, we are halfway to George Bernard Shaw's *Pygmalion,* in which Eliza Doolittle's father complains at having to wear a suit and behave in ways that an honest working man is not obliged to do. The social issue hides an intellectual point. There is more to the issue of Mind and Body than appears on the surface: how we handle it is not just a matter of theory: since the stakes involve "self-command", it raises moral or social issues. The changes in intellectual attitude and philosophical theory from 1580 to 1640 thus go hand-in-hand with wider changes in attitude to acceptable and unacceptable conduct. By the 1640s, the rationalists do not just limit rationality to the senses and the intellect—what psychologists now call "cognition": they also reflect the first inroads of the "respectability" that was so influential over the next two-and-a-half centuries.

Is this comment relevant to the history of science or philosophy? Do we not handle intellectual problems independently of social attitudes, and *vice versa*? In separating rationality and logic from rhetoric and the emotions, we are unwittingly committed to the basic agenda of modern philosophy. Epistemology involves not just intellectual, but also moral issues. Abstract concepts and formal arguments, intuitive ideas and propositions are not the only grist for a philosopher's mill: rather, he can attend to the whole of human experience, in varied, concrete detail. These are the lessons we learnt from the humanists, and they are a long way from a rationalism that sets emotion apart from reason, and plunges us into moral escapism. Treating the feelings as mere effects of causal processes takes them out of our hands, and relieves us of responsibility: all we are rationally responsible for (it seems) is *thinking* correctly.

Both Montaigne and Descartes were strong individualists. Both men saw the first step in the getting of wisdom as lying in self-examination. Descartes' *Discourse on Method* and *Meditations,* as much as Montaigne's *Essais,* were meant to serve as a model of clear-headed self-reporting. But their individualism takes them in different directions. In Descartes, there is already a flavor of "solipsism"—the sense that every individual, as a psychological subject, is (so to say) trapped inside his own head, while the scope of his reflections is limited to sensory inputs and other data that reach his Mind and make him the individual he is. Fifty years earlier, Montaigne also wrote *as an individual,* but always assumed that his own experience was typical of human experience generally, if there were no special reason to think otherwise in some particular case. There was thus no hint of solipsism in Montaigne's reading of experience: he did not hesitate to rely on other people's reports, but developed his own account of friendship, cripples, or whatever, in ways that move freely in a world composed of many distinct, independent persons.

The early 17th century thus saw a narrowing of scope for freedom of discussion and imagination that operated on a social plane, with the onset of a new insistence on "respectability" in thought or behavior, and also on a personal plane. There, it took the form of an alienation quite familiar to the late 20th century, which expressed itself as *solipsism* in intellectual matters, and as *narcissism* in emotional life. For Montaigne, "(life) experience" is the practical experience that each human individual accumulates through dealing with many coequal others: for Descartes, "(mind) experience" is raw material from which each individual builds a cognitive map of the intelligible world "in the head". In the 1580s, it did not occur to Michel de Montaigne that he was "locked into his brain". The multiplicity of people in the world, with idiosyncratic viewpoints and life stories, was not a threat. Everyone recognized that each individual's fate was, ultimately, personal—as the madrigalist put it, "Only we die in earnest, that's no jest!"—but people still dealt with each other equally, as separate individuals. Their thoughts were not yet banished, even for theoretical purposes, within the prison walls of Descartes' solipsistic Mind, or Newton's inner *sensorium*.

The contrast, between the practical modesty and the intellectual freedom of Renaissance humanism, and the theoretical ambitions and intellectual constraints of 17th-century rationalism, plays a central part in our revised narrative of the origins of Modernity. By taking the origin of Modernity back to the 1500s, we are freed from the emphasis on Galileo's and Descartes' unique rationality, which was a feature of the standard account in the 1920s and '30s. The opening gambit of modern philosophy becomes, not the decontextualized rationalism of Descartes' *Discourse* and *Meditations,* but Montaigne's restatement of classical skepticism in the *Apology,* with all its anticipations of Wittgenstein. It is Montaigne, not Descartes, who plays White: Descartes' arguments are Black's reply to this move. Montaigne claimed in the *Apology* that "unless some one thing is found of which we are *completely* certain, we can be certain about nothing": he believed that there is no general truth about which certainty is possible, and concluded that we can claim certainty about nothing. Both Descartes and Pascal were fascinated by Montaigne. As a young man, Descartes studied the *Essais* at La Flèche: the College library had a fine copy, with annotations some scholars think are his own first reactions. As Black, Descartes answered Montaigne's gambit by setting himself the task of locating the "one thing" for which certainty is needed. He found this in the *cogito*—arguing, "I have mental experiences, so I know my own existence for certain." In spite of all the skeptical limits of human finitude, it seemed to him, about that at least we could be completely certain.

By carrying Modernity back to a time before Galileo and Descartes, and giving the Renaissance humanists credit for originality—even "Modernity"—we open up all kinds of new possibilities. Above all, we can set aside any last lingering impression that such writers as Erasmus, Shakespeare, and Montaigne were still (in a sense) "late medievals", since they lived and worked before the breakthrough to the "modern" world, which began with the creation of the exact sciences. The 16th-century humanists were the founders of the modern Humanities just as surely as the 17th-century natural philosophers were founders of modern Science and Philosophy: for instance, the ways of describing human cultures implicit in Book VI of Aristotle's *Ethics,* and reintroduced in our day by Clifford Geertz as "thick description", were already put to use in Montaigne's omnivorous ethnography. Indeed, the contrast between humanism and rationalism—between the accumulation of concrete details of practical experience, and the analysis of an abstract core of theoretical concepts—is a ringing pre-echo of the debate on *The Two Cultures* provoked by C. P. Snow's Rede Lecture to the University of Cambridge.

On its first appearance, Snow's argument read like a discussion of social and educational institutions in 20th-century Britain; but his thesis had overtones from intellectual history. From the time of Benjamin Jowett at Oxford, the administrative élite of Britain sharpened its teeth (or claws) on texts in the "more humane" forms of literature: *literae humaniores,* in the silver Latin of the Oxford syllabus. The university training given to engineers, doctors, and other technical experts, by contrast, focussed instead on the exact sciences. The two groups looked for their *formation professionelle* to different historical backgrounds. Higher civil servants were trained on Plato or Thucydides, later on Shakespeare or Namier, and knew little of the intellectual techniques that engineers and physicians inherited from the more exact traditions of Isaac Newton and Claude Bernard. If the Two Cultures are still estranged, then, this is no local peculiarity of 20th-century Britain: it is a reminder that Modernity had two distinct starting points, a humanistic one grounded in classical literature, and a scientific one rooted in 17th-century natural philosophy.

What has yet to be explained is why these two traditions were not seen from the beginning as complementary, rather than in competition. Whatever was gained by Galileo, Descartes, and Newton's excursions into natural philosophy, something was also lost through the abandonment of Erasmus and Rabelais, Shakespeare and Montaigne. It is not just that the rich vigor of Shakespeare overshadowed all the tortuous imagery of the metaphysical poets, or the prosaic *longueur* of Dryden or Pope. Quite as much, it is that the humane attitudes of openness, relaxation, and bawdiness which were still permissible in the time of Rabelais and Montaigne, were driven underground not long after 1600. By the standards of intellectual history, the change we are concerned with here was uncommonly rapid. Completed in the 1580s, Michel de Montaigne's *Essais* were still best-sellers in the early 17th century: finished in the 1630s, René Descartes' *Discourse* and *Meditations* soon dominated philosophical debate. If we are to give a revised account of the step from the first, humanist phase of Modernity to the second, rationalist phase, we shall thus be dealing with a mere fifty years.

The question "Why did this transition take place *just when* it did?" thus brings in its train the further question "Why did it happen *so fast*?" The crucial thing to look at is not Montaigne and Descartes as individual writers or human beings: it is the climate of opinion that let readers be skeptically tolerant of uncertainty, ambiguity, and diversity of opinion in the 1580s and '90s, but turned so far around that, by the 1640s or '50s, a skeptical tolerance was no longer viewed as respectable. Shifting our focus to this climate of opinion, we may ask what happened between 1590 and 1640 to turn the clock back, and why by the mid-17th century most writers were more dogmatic than the 16th-century humanists had ever been. Why did people in the 1640s no longer regard Montaigne's tolerance as compatible with sincere religious belief? In particular, why did they spend so much energy, from then on, trying to give their beliefs "provably certain" foundations? In the 1580s and '90s, skeptical acceptance of ambiguity and a readiness to live with uncertainty were still viable intellectual policies: by 1640, this was no longer the case. Intellectual options opened up by Erasmus and Rabelais, Montaigne and Bacon, were set aside, and for a remarkably long time these options were taken seriously only by consciously "heterodox" thinkers.

The rationalists hoped to elevate questions of epistemology, natural philosophy, and metaphysics out of reach of contextual analysis, but their attempt to decontextualize philosophy and natural science had its own social and historical context, which demands examination here. The call for "certain foundations" to our beliefs has lost its original appeal in the 20th century, if only because more was at stake in the rationalist Quest for Certainty than is acknowledged in standard histories of science and philosophy, or than is at stake today in philosophy, now that we find ourselves back where the humanists left us. To see how this change came about, let us now return to the situation in which all these things took place, and ask: "If European attitudes underwent such a drastic transformation between 1590 and 1640, what happened to precipitate that change?"

CHAPTER TWO

The 17th-Century Counter-Renaissance

Henry of Navarre and the Crisis of Belief

We must not underestimate the size of this task. It is not always obvious how deeply our current ways of thinking, notably about science and philosophy, are still shaped by the assumptions of the rationalists. Suppose, for instance, that we turn to the entry in the standard French reference book, *La Grande Encyclopédie,* on "Descartes, René", written by Louis Liard and Paul Tannéry. This entry begins as follows:

> For a biography of Descartes, almost all you need is two dates and two place names: his birth, on March 31, 1596, at La Haye, in Touraine, and his death at Stockholm, on February 11, 1650. His life is above all that of an intellect [*ésprit*]; his true life story is the history of his thoughts; the outward events of his existence have interest only for the light they can throw on the inner events of his genius.

In thinking about Descartes, the authors tell us, we can abstract from their historical context not just the various philosophical positions he discusses, and the different arguments he presents, but also his entire intellectual development.

René Descartes' father used to call him *mon petit philosophe*. His mother died while he was an infant, and from his early years he was a deeply reflective child. So, the authors assure us, we can totally grasp the development of his ideas, if we simply reconstruct the inner events of his genius: we do not need to refer to the outward events of his life, since these did not essentially influence the history of his thoughts. That was a purely internal process.

If this view of Descartes' intellectual development were the whole story, it would be unfair to criticize Dewey and Rorty for failing to ask why the dead end into which he supposedly led philosophy—the Quest for Certainty—carried such conviction with him, and was so attractive to his readers. On the *Grande Encyclopédie* view, Descartes' meditations might have occurred to any reflective thinker with the clear perceptions that young René himself possessed. Where he was at school, what he did during his first dozen years after college, and what else was happening in the larger world during all that time: such facts as these are merely incidental. So what more is there to ask?

The consistency of this account of Descartes' life is at first sight impressive. If philosophical problems have the same meaning and force always and everywhere, if the most effective way of stating and solving them is to "decontextualize" them, what does it matter where or when a philosopher was alive and active? On second thoughts, however, the idea that we can always decontextualize philosophical issues is a substantial assumption. What if that were true only in certain circumstances, with qualifications, or conditionally? We can hardly leave the entire context of Descartes' ideas wholly unexamined: might not something turn up in his life and times, which did more than throw incidental sidelights on his intellectual development? What you do not take the trouble to look for, you are unlikely to find. Faced with questions about Descartes' life and times, most historians of philosophy look the other way.

Those historians may think our whole enterprise pointless, but we can return here to the questions: "Why do cultural changes occur when they do? What kinds of occurrence are capable of initiating them? And what particular event led to an abandonment of 16th-century humanism?" In carrying our revised narrative to the next stage, we may take our courage in both hands, and interpret these questions directly and naïvely. One event in fact presents itself, whose impact across the whole of the European scene is well-documented, and whose relevance to our present problem is not hard to establish. It is the assassination of King Henri IV of France, better known in English as Henry of Navarre. To suggest that this event *caused* the shift from humanism to more rigorous, dogmatic modes of thought would be an exaggeration: it will be enough to see it as *emblematic* of changes that were ready to begin, or had already begun. Henry's murder may or may not have been "epoch-making"; but, at least, we can take it as "epoch-marking."

The year is 1610; the date is May 14; the time is early afternoon; the place the rue de La Ferronnerie in Paris. Henry had spent six weeks in Paris, making preparations for the year's military operations against the Spanish in Belgium, Navarre, and Italy. Spain had been the dominant political and economic power in Europe for more than a century. By the time of Henry's grandson, Louis XIV, it had largely lost its dominance to France; but in 1610 it was still a real threat to Henry's French Kingdom. Aside from a main line of confrontation along the Pyrenees, the Spanish Habsburgs still held large territories in the Netherlands to the North of France, as well as Milan and Northern Italy to the South East, and the line of the "Spanish Road" down the Rhine valley, joining Italy to Holland; so it was not unreasonable for Henry of Navarre to plan a show of military force against this Spanish encirclement.

What happened next is well described by Henri's recent English biographer, David Buisseret:

> Early in the afternoon of 14 May, he took his carriage to go and see Sully at the Arsenal. The carriage had a long bench seat, and Henri sat in the middle of it, with Epernon on his right and the duc de Montpazon on his left; La Force and Laverdin were also there. The day was fine, and the carriage's awnings were taken down, so that the king and his friends could see the decorations in the streets of Paris, ready for the ceremonial entry of Marie de Medici—newly crowned queen—the following day.
>
> On leaving the Louvre, Henri dismissed the Captain of the Guard, Charles de Praslin, so that the carriage was accompanied only by a dozen or so footmen and some horsemen riding behind it. Soon the vehicle was forced to stop in the rue de La Ferronnerie, where the traffic was heavy and the road narrow. Henri, who had forgotten his glasses, was listening to a letter which Epernon was reading to him. Most of the footmen ran on ahead, to take a short cut; one of the coachmen went ahead to clear the traffic, and the other bent down to tie his garter. At that moment a large red-headed man sprang up alongside the coach, leaned across Epernon, and stabbed the king three times. The first blow grazed a rib, the second pierced his lung and cut the aorta, and the third was lost in Montpazon's cloak. Neither Montpazon nor Epernon reacted fast enough to attempt to parry any of the blows; poor Henri, blood gushing from his mouth, soon lost consciousness.

The coach turned back to the Louvre, but by the time it arrived Henri was dead. News of the assassination at once fanned out, across France and throughout Europe, as fast as horsemen and messengers could carry it. Wherever it arrived, it provoked confusion and dismay.

Like the murder of President John Kennedy in November, 1963, the assassination of Henri IV was immediately seen as a historical turning point. There had been earlier unsuccessful attempts on his life, and his predecessor, the last Valois King, Henri III, had also died at the hands of an assassin. Though not exactly unexpected, Henri's murder came as the final confirmation of people's worst fears. His disappearance from the scene dashed the last hope of escaping from irresoluble conflicts.

To see what was at stake for France, and for those who were happy to have Henri IV out of the way, let us reconstruct the background to his murder. In his person, Henry embodied the crucial problems of his time, both political and religious. For most of the 16th century, the kings of France belonged to the Catholic family of Francis I, Count of Angoulême and Duke of Valois, whose son, Henri II, married the formidable Catherine de Medici. Henri II died in 1559 from a wound at a jousting tourney, but by then the Valois dynasty seemed established: Henri and Catherine had had three sons, to be successive heirs to the throne. But the family was unfortunate. Francis II was barely fifteen at his father's death, and died the very next year. Charles IX, a child of ten in 1560, ruled until 1574 under the domination of his mother and the two devout Catholic brothers, Henri duc de Guise, and Cardinal Louis of Lorraine. As for the youngest, Henri III, his authority was partly undercut by resentment at his reliance on homosexual favorites, partly by his inability to decide whether to go on tolerating the rebellious arrogance of the duc de Guise, or else to take an independent direction. Finally exasperated by the Guise brothers, he contrived in 1588 to have them murdered; but this in turn infuriated the extremists of the *Sainte Ligue,* or Catholic League, and he himself was struck down by the fanatical monk, Jacques Clément. In this way, the Valois dynasty came to a premature end.

As matters turned out, the prince with the best claim to the throne, Henri III's acknowledged successor, came from the Protestant family of Bourbon, Counts of Béarn and Navarre, in the foothills of the Pyrenees. Henry of Navarre's upbringing was divided between his parents' castle at Pau, in Béarn, and the Royal Court in Paris. In his youth, he had reason to learn how the conflict between the French Protestants and Catholics was damaging the nation. The bitterest lesson came in 1572, soon after his marriage at the age of 18 to Catherine's daughter, Marguerite de Valois. With Charles IX's connivance, supporters of the Guises slaughtered many of the Protestant gentry who had come to Paris for the wedding, in the notorious "Massacre of Saint Bartholomew". From that time on, Henry's religious loyalties were ambiguous. After the Massacre, he became a nominal Catholic, if only to save his life, but he soon escaped from Paris and resumed leadership of the Protestants in the South and West of the country.

Succeeding to the throne in 1589, Henry was unable to control Paris, where the Catholic League was strong. In 1593, he formally renounced Protestantism, and was welcomed to Paris by the Archbishop of Bourges. Some people find his diplomatic comment, *Paris vaut une Messe*—"If the price of Paris is going to Mass, it is worth paying"—intolerably cynical: to him, it was unavoidable and realistic; without converting he could not handle the nation's problems. Once he was securely established, he soon showed his determination to reduce the role of religion in politics; and with the Edict of Nantes (1598) he codified and regularized the position of his Protestant citizens.

Rather than let his new Catholicism be a reason for persecuting his former fellow Protestants, he did his best to stabilize relations between the two religious parties, and guarantee civil liberties to the substantial minority of Protestant "Huguenots." By the standards of the time, it was an act of courage and foresight: not surprisingly, it met with domestic opposition, and he found it hard to get it endorsed by the various regional *parlements,* notably that in Paris itself. The supporters of the Catholic League, in particular, continued to suspect him of duplicity, to the point of spreading a rumor that his project for a campaign against the Spanish possessions in Italy concealed a secret plan to seize Rome, and install a Protestant Pope. (His eventual assassin, in 1610, had been a frustrated candidate to the Jesuit order, François Ravaillac.)

Centuries later, it is hard to see why for so long people resisted the notion that a loyal citizen of France might be a devout Protestant rather than a Catholic, or the other way around. Yet, if we are to feel the full force of the present narrative, we must try to understand this fact. From the start, the rise of French Protestantism had political overtones. To the indignation of the Catholic nobility and peasantry, Martin Luther and John Calvin won widespread support among professional people and artisans in Western and Central Europe: Calvin established a Protestant republic in the city state of Geneva. In the mid-16th century, local rulers made religion an excuse for extending their political power, and a series of politico-religious conflicts in Central Europe was temporarily haulted by the Treaty of Augsburg in 1555. This authorized each ruler to impose his chosen religion on his own subjects, in accordance with the formula, *cuius regio eius religio.*

This arrangement was acceptable in the fractured and fragmented counties, duchies, and kingdoms of Central Europe, where people of deep theological commitments need not move far to find, either a ruler who shared their convictions, or a tolerant free city like Frankfort-am-Main. But the French Kingdom was an extensive, long-unified territory, of much the extent of today's France, which relishes the natural boundaries of its self-styled "hexagon." For France, internal migration was not the answer. Either the Catholics might suppress the Protestant heresy, as the Guises and the Catholic League proposed; or the Protestant Huguenots might become a dominant majority; or a compromise solution was needed that decoupled national loyalties from religious affiliations.

Henry of Navarre aimed at the third solution. In his time (to repeat) it was a daring innovation, open only to a ruler who combined personal self-confidence with an urbane and relaxed tolerance. Henri IV's attitude to practical politics reminds one of Michel de Montaigne's attitude in the intellectual realm. This is no coincidence: the two men were trusted colleagues. Montaigne supposedly ran confidential missions on Henry's behalf in his negotiations with the Protestant and Catholic leaders: they may even have been members of the same secret society. Henry no more let doctrinal dogmatism outrun political pragmatism than Montaigne let philosophical dogmatism override the testimony of familiar experience. Both men placed modest experiential claims above the fanatical demands of doctrinal loyalty, and so were (in the true sense) "skeptics."

Henry's skepticism (like Montaigne's) was no "negative dogmatism", which systematically refuses to accept whatever is not totally certain. Rather, it was the modest skepticism of those who respect everyone's right to opinions arrived at by honest reflection on first-hand experience. If, in their reading and reflection, serious minded Frenchmen found good reason in their hearts to join with others of the Protestant persuasion— what Catholics called the *religion prétendue reformée*—did it make them any less loyal and trustworthy French citizens? If the Kingdom of France operated on the traditional principles of "monarch" and "subject," need a new-found religious conviction weaken the loyalty of a French Huguenot to his legitimate sovereign? France might be seen as the King's personal inheritance, to which he was entitled by genealogy—so that the unity of the country was imposed by feudal title; or it could be seen as the home of the French nation, which owed allegiance to the rulers who embodied the best traditions of France—so that its unity was that of the Nation. Either way, as Henry saw it, the prudent and far-sighted policy was one of religious toleration: imposing religious conformity could only damage both the Kingdom and the Nation.

We can see now how much was at stake in Henry's noble experiment: to this day, Frenchmen have not forgotten what he tried to do. Even now, two centuries after the Revolution of 1789, the French speak of Henri IV with affection, and recognize that his policies were shaped by equity and goodwill. Conversely, they celebrate Ravaillac in cabaret turns, as a model of clownish irritability. They contrast the autocratic claims of Henri IV's successors, for the next century and a half, with his openness and tolerance: he is credited with wanting for his subjects "a chicken in every pot." Henri's reputation as a lover also remains green: in this, he outshines even John Kennedy, and is still known today as *le vert galant*—"the evergreen ladies' man". In his lifetime, it was only the fanatics who questioned the sincerity of his intentions for France; and the reputation he won around 1600 has survived unscathed through four hundred years.

In May 1610, all this was put in peril. At a time when the European monarchs were picking sides in the name of religious loyalty, Henry tried to show that one might govern a large kingdom while accepting the loyalty of citizens of different religions. (Another surprising exception was Poland, whose 1555 Constitution guaranteed Protestants religious toleration.) In England, successive monarchs of different religions had persecuted their opponents as nonconformists—Protestants as victims under Queen Mary and Philip of Spain, unreconstructed Catholics under Elizabeth I—but Henry hoped to build in France a kingdom which held the balance between Catholic and Protestant subjects.

The Catholic League continued to invoke religious uniformity as the core of national unity, with the battle cry, *un roi, une loi, une foi* ("one King, one law, one faith"). But their claim that the guarantee of national unity was to persecute or forcibly convert religious minorities had not been put to the test of experience. In France, it would impose hardship on a substantial fraction of Henry's loyal subjects, not least his fellow Béarnais, and it would end by destroying the very loyalties it was meant to strengthen. So, Henry preferred to take the chance of demonstrating that a single large nation, or kingdom, that found room for citizens of more than one religion, would not thereby destroy its citizens' loyalty or the cohesion of its society.

After Henry's death, the Edict of Nantes was not repealed at once, but its provisions were progressively whittled down or disregarded. As the years passed, the religious dissension he had tried so hard to prevent reasserted itself. After a few years, the aging Philippe Duplessis Mornay, one of Henry's earliest and most faithful supporters among the Protestant notables, wrote to the young King Louis XIII, protesting the loyalty of himself and his fellow Huguenots, but deploring the revival of religious conflict and begging relief from the disabilities to which Protestants were more and more subjected. The screws were tightened gradually, by the political Cardinals, Richelieu for Louis XIII and Mazarin for the young Louis XIV, though the Edict was not finally revoked until 1685. It was the events of 1789 that finally confirmed the prudence and farsightedness of Henry's policies. The violent overthrow of the Bourbons in the French Revolution was a product, not least, of the accumulated wrongs of the long-suffering Huguenots.

Henri IV's assassination struck a mortal blow to the hopes of those, who, in France and elsewhere, looked to toleration as a way of defusing denominational rivalry. It came as a shock to Catholic traditionalists as well. While the Duc de Guise lived, Catholic opposition to King Henri III was a threat to the kingdom: Henri de Guise's ancestry was close enough to the Valois to make him a plausible Pretender. After Henri IV came to the throne, the Catholic League continued to struggle, more in the hope of pressuring the King than with any intention of displacing him. Henry's highly public conversion to Catholicism, and his desire to keep the Pope's support, left him open to persuasion. After a failed attempt on his life in 1594, the *parlement* of Paris expelled the Jesuits from much of the country. In 1603, Henry lifted the suspension, and authorized them to set up several colleges and schools. With continuing pressure, the Catholics hoped, more might be achieved, and the Protestants' entrenched rights might be further weakened.

Under Henry's protection, the Protestants' struggle shifted, as he intended, away from the military into the political realm. Ravaillac's dagger put an end to the improvement. Many Catholics had denounced Henri IV in harsh rhetorical terms, but Ravaillac played for keeps. Was he "a lone killer", or was he the instrument of a conspiracy? Did Henry's companion in the carriage, the duc d'Epernon, defend the King less than assiduously? With Ravaillac as with Lee Harvey Oswald, many in France still find it hard to believe that he was a solitary and embittered fanatic, who killed the King without encouragement from others. Given the affection of the French for Henri IV, suspicions of a conspiracy have remained alive ever since; but, with Ravaillac as with Oswald, evidence of any conspiracy was well concealed, and no one else's name has been convincingly linked to Ravaillac's act.

For the moment, all but a band of fanatical Leaguers were appalled. Even those who disapproved of Henri's protection of the Huguenots had not wished his death. The scene in the Cathedral at Reims, when news of the murder came to the city, is typical of a wider reaction:

> The Canons in the chapter house were unable to speak, some of them being full of tears and sobs, the rest gripped with depression. The people of Reims appeared pale, cast down, their expressions all changed, for, having lost the King, they reckoned that France itself was lost.

The same scene was repeated across the country, and there was a flood of printed pamphlets, many anonymous, lamenting, deploring, or accusing. On the evidence of printing press output we can say that, for fifty years before and fifty after, no event in France provoked more than a fraction of this public response.

In practical terms, Henry's murder carried to people in France and Europe the simple message, "A policy of religious toleration was tried, and failed." For the next forty years, in all the major powers of Europe, the tide flowed the other way. In England, Charles I wanted to arrange an accommodation between the Anglican Church and the Church of Rome, but most Anglicans were firmly anti-Papist and their views were shared by the Puritans and Presbyterians. In Spain and Austria, meanwhile, the Habsburgs, despite sizeable Protestant communities among their mine workers and craftsmen, as well as in the Czech nobility, were more and more committed to leading the Catholic cause. In fragmented Germany, political and religious rivalries persisted locally, ready to be aggravated by outside powers. Even in liberal Poland, to which Faustus Socinus had fled from Italy to set up an early Unitarian Church at Rakow, the King was persuaded to cancel the Protestants' constitutional protection in the 1630s and reimpose Catholic domination. Then, only Holland survived as a haven of tolerance, to which Unitarians and other unpopular sects could retreat for protection.

With all the larger states lined up in this religious confrontation, the fragmentation of Germany made it a crucial target. In this situation, even a minor dynastic dispute could easily threaten the balance of power. From 1607 to 1610, the focus was on a small group of territories that lay across the Rhine, upstream from its entry into Holland, the duchy of Jülich-Cleves Berg. The death of its ruler left an ambiguous succession, to which both Protestant and Catholic princes had plausible claims. Henry was anxious to prevent Leopold, the Habsburg Archduke of Austria, seizing such a strategically vital area, and was tempted to intervene on the Protestant side. (This proposal may have helped to fuel Ravaillac's anger.) But only in 1618 did the general war that had been threatening ever since Henri's death ignite across central Europe.

For thirty years, in a series of brutal and destructive military campaigns, shifting alliances of outside powers used the territory of Germany and Bohemia as a gladiatorial ring in which to fight out their political rivalries and doctrinal disagreements, most often by proxy, and turned the Czech and German lands into a charnel house. Just after Henry of Navarre's assassination, it was too easily assumed that his death had proved a policy of religious toleration unviable. Twenty years later, the first Austrian

military thrusts into Germany had been blunted, and the interposition of
the Swedish army led to deadlock across the battlefront. By then, no one
could argue that this attempt to impose uniformity of religion was an
improvement on Henri IV's policy; but, by that time, no one could see a
way out of the conflict into which they had been drawn, and the war
dragged on. Across the whole of central Europe, from the mid-1620s to
1648, rival militias and military forces consisting largely of mercenaries
fought to and fro, again and again, over the same disputed territories.

The longer the bloodshed continued, the more paradoxical the state of
Europe became. Whether for pay or from conviction, there were many
who would kill and burn in the name of theological doctrines that no one
could give any conclusive reasons for accepting. The intellectual debate
between Protestant Reformers and their Counter-Reformation opponents
had collapsed, and there was no alternative to the sword and the torch. Yet,
the more brutal the warfare became, the more firmly convinced the
proponents of each religious system were that their doctrines *must be*
proved correct, and that their opponents were stupid, malicious, or both.
For many of those involved, it ceased to be crucial what their theological
beliefs were, or where they were rooted in experience, as 16th-century
theologians would have demanded. All that mattered, by this stage, was for
supporters of Religious Truth to believe, devoutly, in *belief itself.* For them,
as for Tertullian long ago, the difficulty of squaring a doctrine with
experience was just one more reason for accepting this doctrine that much
the more strongly.

As José Antonio Maravall has shown, both the Spanish and the wider
Baroque culture reflected the internal incoherences and stresses within
mid-17th-century Catholicism, and helped to make its artistic expression
histrionic and grotesque—if only as a way of resisting the temptations to
disbelief. Most baroque of all, at the first climax of the Thirty Years' War,
with the Catholic victory of the Austrian armies at the Battle of the White
Mountain, near Prague, in 1620, a beautiful small church was constructed
in Rome in honor of the Holy Mother of the Prince of Peace, and named
Santa Maria della Vittoria. Within it was assembled the most ambiguous
piece of sculpture ever created: *The Ecstasy of Saint Theresa* by Bernini.
Above a row of benefactors—or voyeurs—Saint Theresa is surrounded by
Divine radiance, and lifted up toward an angel, or cherub. As any adult
onlooker recognizes, the ecstatic expression on the Saint's face is meant
to be spiritual, but its content is plainly sexual.

In this blood-drenched situation, what could good intellectuals do? So
long as humane Renaissance values retained their power for Montaigne in
the private sphere, or for Henry of Navarre in the public sphere, there was

hope that the reasoned discussion of shared experiences among honest individuals might lead to a meeting of minds, or, at the least, to a civilized agreement to differ. By 1620, people in positions of political power and theological authority in Europe no longer saw Montaigne's pluralism as a viable intellectual option, any more than Henry's tolerance was for them a practical option. The humanists' readiness to live with uncertainty, ambiguity, and differences of opinion had done nothing (in their view) to prevent religious conflict from getting out of hand: *ergo* (they inferred) it had helped *cause* the worsening state of affairs. If skepticism let one down, certainty was more urgent. It might not be obvious what one was supposed to be certain about, but *un*certainty had become *un*acceptable.

By the 1630s, no one could see an end to the warfare in Germany, and negotiations for peace threatened to be as protracted as the fighting itself—as happened in our time in Vietnam also. Failing any effective political way of getting the sectarians to stop killing each other, was there no other possible way ahead? Might not philosophers discover, for instance, a new and more rational basis for establishing a framework of concepts and beliefs capable of achieving the agreed certainty that the skeptics had said was impossible? If uncertainty, ambiguity, and the acceptance of pluralism led, in practice, only to an intensification of the religious war, the time had come to discover some *rational method* for demonstrating the essential correctness or incorrectness of philosophical, scientific, or theological doctrines. The relevance of Henri IV's assassination to the intellectual origins of Modernity is, therefore, not as remote as we may suppose. Could such an event by itself "cause" the changes of emphasis apparent in Europe from 1590 to 1640? Surely not: to assert baldly that Henry of Navarre's murder was a "necessary and sufficient condition" for the adoption of the rationalist research program of Cartesian philosophy or Newtonian physics would be absurd. But a case can be made out for a weaker claim. The eclipse of Montaigne's philosophical reputation, and the political consequences of Henri IV's murder, are linked by a common thread: the dissatisfaction with skepticism which led people, in turn, into an unwillingness to suspend the search for provable doctrines, an active distrust of disbelievers, and finally to *belief in belief itself*.

If Europeans were to avoid falling into a skeptical morass, they had, it seemed, to find *something* to be "certain" about. The longer fighting continued, the less plausible it was that Protestants would admit the "certainty" of Catholic doctrines, let alone that devout Catholics would concede the "certainty" of Protestant heresies. The only other place to look for "certain foundations of belief" lay in the epistemological proofs that

Montaigne had ruled out. On reflection, perhaps, human experience might turn out to embody clarities and certainties that Montaigne and the skeptics had overlooked. Henry's murder was not an immediate occasion to renew the philosophical dialogue, but it helped to bring the desperation of the time into sharper focus, and provided a natural context in which the Quest for Certainty could take shape.

1610–1611: Young René and the Henriade

It is one thing to concede that Henry of Navarre's murder might have had drastic intellectual consequences: it is quite another to show that it in fact had such effects, or that René Descartes, who framed the agenda of modern philosophy and physical science, was personally aware of that tragedy. Those who accept the standard account of Descartes' life and work will, in any case, regard such speculations as out of the question: on their view, his philosophy was conceived and must be understood as the pure product of a reflective mind untouched by external events.

We are not yet in a position to challenge head-on the assumptions of the *Grande Encyclopédie* biography, but we already have reason to raise our eyebrows. Had we not compared Henri IV with Michel de Montaigne, the reasons for the retreat from Renaissance humanism, and the eclipse of philosophical skepticism, might have remained totally obscure: as for a link between Henry's assassination and the development of Descartes' philosophy (or, at least, its reception) we certainly shall not find one if we do not look for it. In this respect, the standard account of Descartes is circular and self-confirming. On its face, it stops us from looking for the very evidence that might call it in question. What that evidence might be, is our next question.

In 1603 (to recall) Henri IV authorized the Jesuits to resume their preaching throughout France, and to set up a chain of new academies for talented boys of the professional and noble classes. For many years, the distinguished scholars, writers, and administrators of France studied at these Jesuit colleges. By the terms of this agreement, Henry also deeded to the Society of Jesus as the site for the first College one of his family properties at La Flèche, not far from Le Mans. (With typical irony, he chose the *château* where he was reputedly conceived.) Finally, he agreed that after his death and that of his second wife, Marie de Medici, their hearts should be enshrined in the College Chapel at La Flèche. At the time, there was no reason to expect this clause to be activated for many years; but, meanwhile, it demonstrated his seriousness of purpose.

Twentieth-century people, who have their own expectations about the proper disposal of human bodies, may find this last clause gruesome. Aside from post-mortem examinations and organ transplants, we expect them to be preserved respectfully and intact: those of Kings and Queens (if anything) with greater delicacy than those of commoners. But there was a well-established medieval system of ideas about the embodiment of kingship in the corporeal forms of individual monarchs, and provisions such as Henry conceded were not unusual in the royal families of Europe. In 1603 or 1610, then, people found nothing objectionable in disposing of Henry's heart in this way, nor were they too scrupulous to put this term into effect. On hearing of Henry's death, the Jesuits claimed his heart. It was taken from Paris to La Flèche by stages: there, in a silver chalice, it was enshrined in the Chapel early in June, at an elaborate ceremony mingling grief with pride, and attended by the whole College community. Among those on hand at the ceremony was the talented but frail student from La Haye en Touraine, René Descartes.

The fact that at a young, impressionable age Descartes was present on this occasion proves nothing by itself; though it confirms that, for Descartes, Henry's death was no "news item" that might cross his mind, without particularly attracting his attention. But there was more to the occasion. Many people still suspected the Jesuits of being behind the assassination, so the good Fathers of La Flèche took care not to let this fact cloud their students' minds. Instead, they made Henry's death an object lesson for instructional and devotional ends. On the anniversary of the enshrinement, as further testimony of their affection and respect for the King, they staged another *Henriade,* as the first of a series of annual celebrations of Henri IV's memory. For the first *Henriade* in 1611, the best students at the College wrote scholarly exercises extolling the dead King's virtues. A pyramid 45 feet high was built at the College, in which the chalice with Henri IV's heart was demonstrated to visitors; and the students' essays and poems were displayed around a nearby arch. For three days, the College was open to visitors from the surrounding region: recitations and speeches were staged for their edification.

After the ceremony, all the exercises were collected together, and published by a local printer, Jacques Rezé, and bound in a thick vellum, with a title page reading:

In Anniversarium
Henrici Magni
Obitus Diem

*

Lacrymae Collegii
Flexiensis Regii
Societatis Iesu

["On the aniversary/ of Henry the Great's/ day of death/*/ the tears of the College/ Royal at La Flèche/ of the Society of Jesus."] Several copies of the *In Anniversarium* are still available today. One is in the Houghton Library at Harvard, others are in Jesuit houses, while the Paris *Bibliothèque Nationale* lists a copy in its *catalogue des anonymes,* or catalogue of anonymous works. Nevertheless, for curious reasons, the *Bibliothèque Nationale* copy was, until recently, not readily accessible. Confiscated after the Revolution from the Priory of the Jacobin Friars in the rue St. Honoré, it was catalogued at first under "Y", for "Latin Verse", a heading under which few might look for it. When the *Bibliothèque* was recatalogued, in 1855, it was then given a new call number in the more appropriate category, "Lb^{35}"—"Historical materials relating to the reign of Henri IV." At that time, however, the call number entered on the card in the *catalogue des anonymes* was incorrect: anyone who asked for the book by that number was brought a mid-19th-century German lecture on Henri IV's supposed plan to unseat the Pope. Going through this task as recently as 1986, it took me time and persistence to find the right call number, correct the card, and reconstruct the history of this error. Meanwhile, this particular copy of the *In Anniversarium* seems not to have been available for scholarly use since its accession to the Library, some time between 1792 and 1803.

Most of the exercises in the book are in Latin, a smaller number in Greek, a few—which are less bound by the forms of classical rhetoric than those in the ancient languages—in French. The initial exercises in Latin use standard rhetorical forms, and praise the King in exaggerated and empty terms. We can imagine the Fathers' instructions: "Georges is to praise the King for his magnanimity; Charles is to compare him with Alexander the Great; [etc.]" There is a shorter collection in Greek at the end of the book; but in the middle we find twenty-five pages in French, which display a liveliness, vigor, and originality (even an eccentricity) that catch the attention.

The author of the first item in French, a sonnet, is schizophrenic. He is meant to write about Henry of Navarre, but the center of his mind is occupied by something else: a thrilling new report of Galileo Galilei's discovery of four previously unknown heavenly bodies moving around the planet Jupiter. The year 1610 had not only been the year of Henry's murder.

It also saw the publication, in January, of Galileo's book on the Moon and the Planets, reporting observations using his new astronomical telescope. Europeans had for long assumed that the heavenly bodies were perfect. They knew no Moon but the Earth's, and did not realize that other planets might have "moons" of their own. Galileo's reports were a shock, a thrill, or both, depending on a reader's temperament. In the year 1610, it was still twenty years before Galileo's damaging comparison of the Ptolemaic and Copernican world systems plunged him into confrontation with Church authority, and brought him public disgrace and house arrest outside Florence. For the moment, when his exciting new book, *Sidereus Nuncius* (*The Starry Messenger*) reached them at La Flèche not long before work was to begin on the *Henriade,* the Jesuits, with their intellectual curiosity, had no reason to keep it out of the hands of their pupils.

The sonnet from the 1611 text reads in the original:

Sonnet
sur la mort du roy
Henry le Grand, et sur
la descouuerte de quelques nouuelles Planettes,
or Estoiles errantes autour de Iupiter, faicte
l'Annee d'icelle par Galilée Galilée, celebre
Mathematicien du grand Duc de Florence

La France auoit des-ja reſpandu tant de pleurs
Pour la mort de son Roy, que l'Empire de l'onde
Gros de flots ravageoit à la Terre ſes fleurs,
D'un Deluge ſecond menaçât tout le Monde.

L'ors que l'Aſtre du iour, qui va faiſant la ronde
Autour de l'vnivers, meu de proches malheurs,
Qui haſtoient deuers nous leur courſe vagabonde,
Luy parla de la ſorte, au fort de ſes douleurs.

FRANCE, de qui les pleurs, pour la mort de ton Prince,
Nuisent par leur excez à tout autre Prouince,
Ceſſe de t'affliger ſur ſon vuide Tombeau,

Car Dieu l'ayant tiré tout entier de la Terre,
Au Ciel de Iupiter maintenant il etclaire
Pour servir aux mortels de coeleſte flambeau.

[Sonnet
on the death of the king
Henry the Great, and on
the discovery of some new Planets,
or Stars wandering around Jupiter, made
this Year by Galileo Galilei, famous
Mathematician of the Grand Duke of Florence

France had already scattered so many tears
For the death of her King, that the Realm of the wave
Big with deluges ravaged her flowers from the Earth,
Threatening the whole World with a second Flood.

When the Day Star, which makes the circuit
Around the Universe, moved by impending sorrows,
Which were speeding their wandering course towards us
Spoke to her of Fate, above her distress.

FRANCE, whose tears, for the death of thy Prince,
Are injuring with their excess every other Region,
Desist from grieving over his empty Tomb,

For, God having lifted him all above the Earth,
In the Heaven of Jupiter he now shines
To serve to mortals as a heavenly torch.]

Is this attempt to link Galileo's discovery of Jupiter's moons to the grief of
the French at the loss of their King somewhat carpentered? Is there
something artificial about the poetic conceit that Henri IV now gazes down
on his bereaved Kingdom from the Heavens, as a New Star? We may give
the author an "A" for ingenuity, if not for emotional depth. Still, in a
juvenile writer, at most 17 years of age, emotional depth is perhaps too
much to ask. In his account of the *Henriade,* Fr Camille de Rochemonteix
brushed the poem aside as overblown and odd (*boursoufflé et bizarre*).
This comment might be fitting, if the sonnet had been by one of his
grown-up Jesuit colleagues; but as a judgment on a teenage student's
scholastic exercise it is unjust. If we look again at the sonnet, another
tantalizing question suggests itself. René Descartes was among the talented
young students at La Flèche at this time, and would surely be expected to
contribute to the *Henriade.* As we look through the book, it is tempting to
ask whether this sonnet might not turn out to have been the first printed
work by the young Descartes.

One cannot put the point beyond doubt. Given anonymous exercises,
without independent evidence of authorship, it is equally possible that

Descartes wrote, rather, the longer exercise that follows the sonnet and includes physiological speculations of kinds he may well have devised. But Descartes does tell us that his most extraordinary experience at the College was his first encounter with Galileo's ideas. With his confessed passion for Galileo, and for vernacular poetry, is it likely that the poem is by another unknown college contemporary?

Descartes' authorship of this sonnet is not, of course, crucial to our understanding of Modernity. What matters is that, during young René's formative years at La Flèche, Henri's assassination was not just a fact of common knowledge, but a preoccupation of the College community. Starting from this point, we can begin to chip away at the foundations of the *Grande Encyclopédie* account of Descartes' intellectual development. The claim that a philosopher's arguments can be wholly explained with only minimal attention to his historical circumstances, we may answer, is not *self-validating*: instead, it needs to be reconsidered.

Notice how Descartes spent the first ten years after he left College, and it adds more weight to the opposite scale. Just as Henri IV's murder was no passing item of news, irrelevant to his development, so too with the other catastrophic event of his lifetime. When the Thirty Years' War broke out in 1618, Descartes was in his early twenties; when it at last ended in 1648, he had two years to live; his whole mature life was spent under its shadow. An introverted, self-preoccupied person, who turned his back on the world and set out to do nothing but write on abstract philosophy, might possibly shut out of his mind all trace of an historical disaster that other Europeans (notably, in Germany) recall with dread and horror to this day. That is *just possible*; but then another damaging question arises. Is it, after all, flattering to the young Descartes to emphasize, as the *Grande Encyclopédie* authors do, his singlemindedness and totally pure *ésprit*? Are we to see him as the sort of indifferent, hard-hearted person who could ignore the suffering produced by the Thirty Years' War? Surely, his philosophical thought and writing are not meritorious merely because he turns his back on the central tragedy of his time?

Descartes was, in fact, no more indifferent to the Thirty Years' War than to Henri IV's assassination. During the first dozen years of the War, he took any chance of following its progress in person. After one year at Law School in Poitiers, he went to Holland, and signed on as a gentleman observer studying Prince Maurits of Nassau's new military techniques: to get closer to the fighting, he next joined the Duke of Bavaria's staff, and accompanied his army on its campaigns. When he retired from the life of a peripatetic young gentlemen and settled down in Holland in the early 1630s, to work up his ideas about epistemology and natural philosophy, he was far from being the disembodied, decontextualized *ésprit* depicted in the *Grande Encyclopédie*. Rather, he was a mature, well-informed man, whose formative years had exposed him at first hand to the two cardinal events of the early 17th century.

With this background, Descartes' reaction to Montaigne's skepticism is easier to understand. The force of the skeptical case in the "Apology", and the candid exuberance characteristic of the *Essais,* swept him away. But he could not share Montaigne's tolerance of ambiguity, unclarity, lack of certainty, or the diversity of contrary human opinions. The more that the political situation in France and Europe collapsed, the more pressing was the need to find a way to escape the doctrinal contradictions that had been a prime occasion for the religious wars, and were—whatever the political realities—the pretext for continuing them. Rather than see Descartes' works as the creations of a man on whose genius the events of his time throw little light, let us "recontextualize" the intellectual ideas and methods that the standard account of modern philosophy takes such care to "decontextualize."

The point of doing this will become evident, when we shift attention away from Descartes personally, and consider the wider *reception* of his ideas. Then, we shall see how far the climate of thought had changed since 1590. At the height of Montaigne's popularity, Descartes' attempt to avoid Montaigne's skepticism, by finding a "single certain thing" that made other certainties possible—in his case, the *cogito*—might have met criticism as failing to answer the powerful arguments for classical skepticism. Fifty years later, for a generation whose central experience was the Thirty Years' War, and a social destruction that had apparently become entirely out of hand, the joint appeal of geometrical certainty and "clear and distinct" ideas helped his program to carry a new conviction.

1610–1611: John Donne Grieves for Cosmopolis

Henry's assassination caused no less despondency abroad than it did in France itself. The Pope was distressed to hear of it, with good reason. He of all men understood that the hopes of preserving the shreds of peace between the rival camps in Europe rested on Henry's moderation and the ambiguous situation of France, where opposing the Habsburgs of Spain was more urgent than any anti-Protestant crusade.

When the French ambassador brought the news to James I in London, the King's older son, Henry Prince of Wales, surrendered to his grief and wept openly. Prince Henry had regarded his namesake, the King of France, as a second father, and looked forward to having his guidance later, when he succeeded James on the English throne. Now, the diplomatic situation in Europe had taken an irreversible turn for the worse: devastated by the news, Prince Henry retired to his bed and did not resume his normal life and duties for several days. Nor were matters improved when the Prince himself died, a few months later, at the age of 19—possibly of typhoid—and the succession passed to his more obstinate, less talented brother, the future Charles I. At the time, as today, people wondered whether, if they had survived, Kings Henri IV of France and Henry IX of England might not have been able, in alliance, to save Europe from the catastrophes of the next forty years.

One English author reacted to Henry's murder at once, and produced in 1611 two complex and problematical poems: John Donne. Hiram Haydn picks on Donne as one representative of his "counter-Renaissance". This is appropriate, for John Donne was a highly conservative figure, in whose personal life the religious conflicts of the time were played out, in some tragic ways. *The Oxford Companion to English Literature* tells us in its biographical note that Donne

> was born into a devout Catholic family, his uncle Jasper Heywood being the leader of the Jesuit mission in England.... Educated at home by Catholic tutors, Donne went at the age of 11 [in 1583] to Hart Hall, Oxford, favoured by Catholics because it had no chapel, so that recusancy attracted less notice ... In 1593 his younger brother Henry died in prison after being arrested for harbouring a Catholic priest. Somewhere about this time Donne apparently renounced his Catholic faith ....

The next twenty years of his life, from 1595 to 1615, were unsettled. He was, in turn, a gentleman volunteer on expeditions against Spain under the command of the Earl of Essex and Sir Walter Raleigh; secretary to Sir Thomas Egerton; a Member of Parliament under Egerton's patronage; and disgraced (even imprisoned) for eloping with Lady Egerton's heiress and niece, Ann More. Lacking steady employment, he served as travelling companion and confidential secretary to a series of patrons, and he was courting support from Sir Robert Drury, a Suffolk landowner, at the time of Henri IV's death in 1610. Finally, to restore his reputation, he entered the Anglican Church in 1615, and there found rapid promotion.

In England, Henry's murder was viewed as another "dirty trick" by the Jesuits, who would defend it if challenged, with casuistical arguments about the moral legitimacy of tyrannicide. (Not that many people in 1610 seriously considered Henri IV as a *tyrant*!) The first of Donne's two long

1611 poems is thus a strange diatribe against the Jesuits that purports to
describe a secret meeting in Hell, at which Ignatius Loyola conspires with
his colleagues in the inferno to disrupt human affairs: its title is *Ignatius
his Conclave*. This poem is so odd that many scholars ignore it: some of
the standard editions of Donne's *Collected Poems* even omit it. Donne's
conservative point of view is clear from the fact that Loyola's conspirators
in Hell include a whole tribe of "innovators"—this category includes, not
least, Copernicus and the other new astronomers. As Donne regards
Loyola's Jesuitical followers as "disturbing the peace" of honest, God-
fearing England, he regards the astronomical novelties of Copernicus or
Kepler as designed to overturn the ideas of decent harmless people, and
so condemns their authors as trouble-makers.

The attitude to intellectual innovation that finds bilious expression in
Ignatius his Conclave reappears in more elegiac mood in Donne's other
poem from 1611, one of two so-called "Anniversaries", with the title, *An
Anatomy of the World*. On its first appearance, Donne's *Anatomy* was
damagingly criticized, both for the exaggerated tone of its language, and
for its nauseating flattery of the young girl whose death is the occasion for
poem. This was the Drurys' daughter, Elizabeth, who had recently died,
before Donne ever had a chance to meet her. He celebrates all the
supposed virtues of maiden womanhood, going in sequence through all
the respects in which, in Donne's own time, the whole world seemed to
be in universal decay, and treating her death as emblematic of growing
chaos. This exaggerated idolization of Elizabeth Drury, however, is not the
point: his agenda lay elsewhere. Her death gave him a chance to enumerate
all the things he deplores in his own time. His subject is not the dead girl.
It is (as his subtitle says) "the Frailty and Decay of the whole World."

One central passage refers to the physical and astronomical ideas of the
"new philosophers"; and this is often quoted, by historians who fail to
recognize Donne's conservative irony, as anticipating the discoveries that
will establish themselves as glories of the "scientific revolution." In citing
it, it will help us to see more clearly the thrust of John Donne's criticisms,
if we put these familiar lines into a slightly larger context, by adding a few
lines before and after the most familiar ones. With this addition, lines 203
to 218 (out of 474) read as follows:

> And now the Springs and Sommers which we see,
> Like sonnes of women after fifty bee.
> And new Philosophy cals all in doubt,
> The Element of fire is quite put out;
> The Sun is lost, and th'earth, and no mans wit

Can well direct him, where to looke for it.
And freely men confesse, that this world's spent,
When in the Planets, and the Firmament
They seeke so many new; they see that this
Is crumbled out againe to his Atomis.
'Tis all in peeces, all cohaerance gone;
All just supply, and all Relation:
Prince, Subject, Father, Sonne, are things forgot,
For every man alone thinkes he hath got
To be a Phoenix, and that there can bee
None of that kinde, of which he is, but hee.

There is no hint here that Donne *recommends* these new ideas. On the contrary, he regards the revival of atomism as destroying the organic unity of Nature, and symbolizing the decay into which the Order of Nature is falling. Nor is his concern with the decay of Nature only theoretical. In those years, people in England were aware that the country's climate was deteriorating: that too was a sign that the frame of things was out of joint, probably irreversibly. Donne's younger contemporary, Thomas Browne (who was born in 1605 and survived Cromwell's Commonwealth, to be knighted by King Charles II after the Restoration) voiced a belief that is implicit in Donne's poem, and became explicit among educated Englishmen in the 1640s and '50s. The "general decay" was a sign that "the greater part of Time is run than is to come"; so that the End of the World could be looked for in the lifetime of men now walking the Earth. Far from assuming that God fashioned Nature to operate by unchanging Laws, people now looked out for portents of a coming Apocalypse.

To capture the full sense of the last six lines of the passage quoted, we must look carefully at the punctuation. At line 209—"crumbled out againe to his Atomis"—Donne comes to a stop. What has gone before is the evidence of "decay in nature". Now, he drives home the political and moral implications of the decay. "'Tis all in pieces, all cohaerence gone." He is no longer talking about physics and astronomy: what is now lost to the World, with the organic unity that used to characterize the *cosmos,* is people's sense of family cohesion and political obligation. Who still thinks of himself as Subject to Prince, or Son to Father? Society is now *narcissistic.* Every individual sees himself as unique and inimitable, and reinvents his pattern of life, like a Phoenix. In the old days, people were relied on to share the values of community and family, and to respect the legitimate demands of their station. Now, the moral fabric of family and society have fallen apart so completely that people think—and behave—as though they

were merely social "atoms" lacking the intrinsic relations of a truly coherent society.

The very meter in which John Donne writes *An Anatomy of the World*
(his drooping iambics) marks the poem as an Elegy for cosmic and social
decline: these iambic pentameters reappear 50 years on, in John Milton's
Paradise Lost. Between Donne in 1610 and Milton in the 1660s, England
saw Oliver Cromwell and his colleagues trying to build a Commonwealth
that would introduce the Justice of God to the world of human affairs. After
the Stuart Restoration, those like Milton himself, who had in 1650 been
more than half convinced that the Commonwealth might succeed, were
marked by a sense of loss Christopher Hill has recently chronicled in his
striking book, *The Experience of Defeat.* Nor did Milton exhaust the
emotional power of this metrical scheme. After the First World War,
William Butler Yeats captured the same sense of loss once again, in his
poem, *The Second Coming.* Those who see 1914 to 1945 as a period of
European history comparable to the Thirty Years' War find Yeats' echoes
of Donne quite remarkable. Their sentiments are so close that we could
even telescope the two texts:

> 'Tis all in pieces, all Cohaerance gone,
> All just supply, and all Relation:

> Things fall apart; the center cannot hold;
> Mere anarchy is loosed upon the world .. ;
> The best lack all conviction, while the worst
> Are full of passionate intensity;

> For every man alone thinkes he hath got
> To be a Phoenix, and that there can bee
> None of that kinde, of which he is, but hee.

In Donne's *Anatomy,* we recognize the authentic *conservative* voice. With
the antennae of an author who picks up the "feel" of his time, Donne voices
regret that the world is out of hand in not one, but a dozen ways. His
concern is not just the warfare between Protestant and Catholic zealots,
though by 1610 this threatens to become unmanageable, as it did after
1618. Nor is his concern merely the decay of political loyalty and allegiance, the growth of the cities, or the eclipse of social relationships built
on the older rural pattern—as shown by the rising number of "masterless"
men, outside the traditional networks—though this aggravates the general
alienation. Nor is he solely concerned with the narcissism of his time,
though he deplores "extreme individualism" as vocally as Robert Bellah
does today. His target is not even the doubts about traditional astronomy

and physics that Copernicus's successors are spreading, though this skepticism does corrode the earlier confidence in Providence and the Human Reason. What shines through this passage in John Donne's poem is, rather, his sorrow and alarm at the apparent fact that *all these different things are happening at the same time.*

From Donne's standpoint, current experience with the weather, the discoveries of astronomers, new ideas about the structure of matter, a lost sense of political loyalty and family duty, and even the widespread fragmentation of self, are not just so many separate and distinct things. In underlining the interconnectedness of psychological and political issues with those that are cosmological and physical, he represents them to us as *aspects of a single whole.* The ideas of Copernicus and Kepler are not merely exciting new ways of thinking about (say) the motion of planets or the structure of ice. More corrosively, from John Donne's point of view, they undermine the entire accepted *Cosmopolis.*

This word "cosmopolis" calls for comment. In Classical Greece and before, people recognized that the World into which humans are born, and with which they have to deal, embodies two distinct kinds of "order." There is an Order of Nature, evidenced in the annual cycle of the seasons, and in the monthly changes of the tides. Practical activities (agriculture and navigation, for example) depend for their success on human ability to achieve command of this order, though this influence is at best marginal. The traditional Greek word for that first kind of order was *cosmos:* to say that the astronomical universe (*ouranos*) was a *cosmos* was to record that celestial events happen, not randomly, but in a natural order. There is also another Order, that of Society, as evidenced in the organization of irrigation systems, the administration of cities, and other collective enterprises. There everything ostensibly happens under human control, though the greed of tyrants and the interests of conflicting groups create rifts in the social·fabric that challenge the imagination of men of goodwill. The Greek·word for this second kind of order was *polis:* to say that a community (*koinoneia*) formed a *polis* was to recognize that its practices and organization had the overall coherence that qualified it—in both the ancient and modern senses of the term—as a "political" unit.

From the beginnings of large-scale human society, people wondered about the links between *cosmos* and *polis,* the Order of Nature and that of Society. Many cultures dreamed of an overall harmony between the order of the heavens and the order of human society. For example, in Classical China, people spoke of the country as the Celestial Kingdom, while rulers relied for their authority on the Mandate of Heaven; as early as 750 B.C., likewise, one of the state institutions in Babylonia was the forecasting service, whose duty it was to track regular celestial events, and warn of unforeseen "omens" like lunar and solar eclipses that would cause public alarm if the authorities did not foretell them. (The prophet Isaiah calls the Babylonian forecasters "monthly prognosticators.") Plato's *Republic,* too, argues in theoretical terms that, if we recognize the existence of a "rational" order in the planetary system, it can strengthen our confidence in the possibility of achieving a similarly "rational" order in the ways in which human states and societies can be run.

Later, when Alexander the Great broadened the Greek horizon beyond its former preoccupation with single cities, we find Stoic philosophers fusing the "natural" and "social" orders into a single unit. Everything in the world (they argued) manifests in varied ways an "order" which expresses the Reason that binds all things together. Social and natural regularities alike are aspects of the same overall *cosmos + polis* — i.e. *cosmopolis.* The practical idea that human affairs are influenced by, and proceed in step with heavenly affairs, changes into the philosophical idea, that the structure of Nature reinforces a rational Social Order.

From the time of St. Augustine (c. A.D. 430), the idea of cosmopolis played a less central part in Christian theology. Attention now focused on the ways in which human beings *fail* to maintain the moral order, or to achieve their personal ideals within the human world—"sin"; and on the spiritual disciplines by which they can learn to overcome these lapses—"salvation". From this standpoint, the natural order is only a backdrop in front of which the human drama follows its own plot. So conceived, our theories of nature have little to do with general theology, let alone with moral theology. Discussions of cosmology were left to the philosophers, whether Platonists, Aristotelians, or Stoics; and it did not make much theological difference which of these schools one followed.

With the Renaissance, however, the interest of European lay readers in newly recovered classical texts reawoke the concern with cosmology. After Dante, they again discussed the overall structure of the universe, human and natural. Speculations about harmonies between natural and human affairs again became fashionable. In retrospect, many of these "correspondences" now seem fantastic and illusory; but they encouraged a revival of interest in natural science, and prepared a ground for later work by 17th-century "new philosophers." In the 16th century, French intellectual circles developed a sympathy for Stoic ideas: in particular, for the belief that human conduct is "right" only if, in some sense, it is *natural* or *according to Nature.*

In the 1610s, Donne thus reflects on the simultaneous decline of the English weather, the planetary system, the constitution of the material world and the rest, knowing that he can count on his readers to be familiar with such "cosmopolitical" ideas, and so open to his suggestion that the "frailty and decay" in human experience had a larger *cosmic* significance. For the world to be "cohaerent", integrity was required in natural and human realms alike. Its loss could be made good, only by finding ways of reestablishing it in both realms equally. Meanwhile, deterioration was for Donne a character of the entire universe, and many contemporaries shared his dark vision. In extreme cases, the apocalyptic Jacob Boehme in Germany and the Commonwealth sectarians in England were tempted into numerological calculations about the date of the Last Day that had been condemned by orthodox theologians from Augustine on. Still, we can hardly fault those who felt that everything was out of control, and that, after 1610, Europe's loss of all social, political, and spiritual cohesion had moved beyond all remedy.

The more the Counter-Reformation zealots gloried in the slaughter of Protestants at the Battle of the White Mountain, the more the Swedish mercenaries of Protestantism put the Catholic strongholds of Germany and Bohemia to the torch, and their populations to the sword, the more people of moderation and goodwill were, for a whole generation, filled with despair. Such horrors were the day-to-day diet of Europe throughout the years from 1618 to 1648.

1640–1660: The Politics of Certainty

In the conditions of the time, then, the issues of certainty, rational con sensus, and necessity, which the 16th-century skeptics had left as a challenge to philosophy, were far more than matters of theoretical taste or opinion. René Descartes was exposed in person to the consequences of Henri IV's murder, and to the Thirty Years' War that followed, in which Protestant and Catholic armies sought to prove theological supremacy by force of arms. In Henri IV's death John Donne too recognized the collapse of a cosmopolitical framework that had hitherto sustained much of what was best in the life and thought of Europe. People at large were left in bewilderment, sensing that matters were now out of hand. With Henry's tolerant balancing power off the scene, the drive towards general war reached a point at which it was beyond the power of either churchmen or statesmen to control, and the philosophy of skepticism was a luxury that few people felt able to accept.

It is with these circumstances in mind that we can understand why the Quest for Certainty developed the appeal it did, from the 1630s on. The shift within philosophy, away from practical issues to an exclusive concern with the theoretical—by which local, particular, timely, and oral issues surrendered their centrality to issues that were ubiquitous, universal, timeless, and written—was no quirk of Descartes. All the protagonists of modern philosophy promoted theory, devalued practice, and insisted equally on the need to find foundations for knowledge that were clear, distinct, and certain. Facing dogmatic claims by rival theologians, it was hard for onlookers of goodwill to restrict themselves to the cool modesty of an Erasmus or a Montaigne, who would have argued (with Pyrrho and Sextus) that it was a mistake for theologians to claim certainty on either side, and that human candor should lead us to admit that matters of faith are intellectually *un*provable and accordingly *un*certain. The protagonists in the religious wars had no stake in skepticism; nor would they call off their war for Lacedemonian reasons; living in a time of high theological passion, the only other thing thinking people could do was to look for a new way of establishing their central truths and ideas: one that was independent of, and neutral between, particular religious loyalties.

All along, of course—if Dewey and Rorty are right—this was too much to expect. No set of "clear and distinct ideas" could ever be found, whose self-evident correctness showed itself to all reflective thinkers equally: in the long run, they would be forced to be pragmatic, and return to that honest examination of experience in which Montaigne and Bacon had alone been ready to place their trust. Given the historical situation of Europe in the 1630s and '40s, however, to suggest that the rationalist experiment was never worth making would be to betray a lack of sensitivity. It would no doubt have been preferable if Henri IV of France and Henry IX of England had survived, to steer the diplomatic policies of the European states away from the rocks of intolerance onto which they relentlessly drove after 1610. Then a decent feeling for the finitude of human power, which restrained both the intellectual ambitions of Montaigne and the political ambitions of Henry of Navarre, might have retained the respect that it lost in the event. As matters stood, there was no alternative to circumventing the theological dogmatists, by arguing in their own idiom—the idiom of *certainty*.

The 17th-century philosophers' "Quest for Certainty" was no mere proposal to construct abstract and timeless intellectual schemas, dreamed up as objects of pure, detached intellectual study. Instead, it was a timely response to a specific historical challenge—the political, social, and theological chaos embodied in the Thirty Years' War. Read in this way, the projects of Descartes and his successors are no longer arbitrary creations of lonely individuals in separate ivory towers, as the orthodox texts in the history of philosophy suggest. The standard picture of Descartes' philo-sophical development as the unfolding of a pure *ésprit* untouched by the historical events of his time, so graphically presented in the *Grande Encyclopédie,* gives way to what is surely a more lifelike and flattening alternative: that of a young intellectual whose reflections opened up for people in his generation a real hope of *reasoning* their way out of political and theological chaos, at a time when no one else saw anything to do but continue fighting an interminable war.

If the 17th-century were as tranquil as the received view of Modernity implies, an ivory-tower view of 17th-century philosophy might be accept-able. In fact, nobody was indifferent to the turmoil of the time: in the bloody theological deadlock of the Thirty Years' War, philosophical skep-ticism became *less,* and certainty *more,* attractive. In the long term, the hope of finding quasigeometrical ways of resolving basic theological disputes proved a vain one, but that is not the point. Our present task is to explain why, at the time, the rationalist program had an appeal to new generations of readers and thinkers that outshone the modest, skeptical lights of the Renaissance humanists. The *reception* of Descartes' ideas is thus a historical issue, and calls for an answer in equally historical terms: that answer is at hand, if we can take seriously the overpowering effects of the 17th-century religious conflict.

Historians of the early modern period have rightly emphasized the social disorder and economic retreat that are documented features of life in early 17th-century Europe. Yet, while economic and social causes can have intellectual and spiritual effects, the reverse may also happen. Having before us the condition of Iran, Ulster, and Lebanon, in all of which economic rivalries and religious differences have interacted with and reinforced one another, we may take more seriously the ways in which the earlier loss of consensus about theological, cosmological, and other fun-damental beliefs intensified all the other factors in the 17th-century crisis. We can then recognize how hard it was, once Henri IV's political policy of religious toleration was abandoned, to stand by the humanists' intellectual policy of challenging all dogmatic assertions and respecting honest dif-ferences of opinion.

The general crisis of the early 17th century was, in short, not just economic and social, but also intellectual and spiritual: the breakdown of public confidence in the older cosmopolitical consensus. Rather than thinking of the 17th-century philosophers as sleepwalking their way through the turmoil of the times, therefore, we can see modern philosophy as a further product of the same conflict that shaped so many other aspects of human experience between 1610 and 1650.

How far, then, do Descartes' philosophical ideas, as received by his contemporaries and successors, give a fair and balanced view of his own personal position? In one respect at least, this reception was one-sided and unbalanced. The Descartes who set out to place the central areas of human knowledge on "foundations" that are "clear, distinct, and certain", whose ideas are the point of departure for the philosophical rationalism of the modern era—this is the Descartes of the *Meditations*. In his early essays, we see him taking threads from earlier philosophy, and weaving them into a new cloth: first, using the fallibility of the senses to call everything experiential in doubt, and then appealing to the self-evidence of those basic ideas whose clarity and distinctness is not in question. The connection between his existence and his mental experiences—the "single unquestionably certain thing" that he discovers along the way—is, then, the discovery that he appeals to as rebutting Montaigne's denial of certainty in philosophy.

But this was never more than one-half of his intellectual enterprise. Throughout his life, Descartes was also interested in finding empirically adequate but comprehensive theories in physics. That was the ambition toward which his passion for Galileo pointed him after 1610, and which shared the center of his mind with the ambition to construct inherently "certain" and "demonstrable" foundations for metaphysics and the theory of knowledge. The Descartes of the *Meditations* was also the man who wrote the *Discourse on Method,* and the later *Principles of Philosophy.* Ultimately, the lines of thought that emerged in the *Discourse* diverged from the high road of rationalist philosophy, and became a starting point for physical theory—notably, Newton's theory of motion and gravitation. Descartes' first readers and direct successors may have picked up and pursued his initial preoccupation with *certainty;* but we must here keep our minds open to other, more *scientific* aspects of his work.

The *Discourse on Method* proposes a model for intellectual theory that begins by applying algebraic methods to Euclid's geometry, but can be extended to any scientific field that lends itself to formal analysis. Descartes did not send the *Discourse* into the world on its own: instead, he issued it as a preface to three samples, in which he applied his new method to coordinate geometry, meteorology, and optics. Despite all the imaginative power of his *Meditations,* we cannot forget how much labor he spent on theoretical physics, above all in the preparation of his mature *Principles of Philosophy,* the four-part work that reports on his attempt at producing an all-embracing system of theoretical physics. People today find Descartes' physics odd and ill-founded: his reputation as a scientist, like that of Aristotle, suffers because many are put off by unacceptable details. More significant, however, is the lasting influence of his model for the logical structure of theories, which was the required form for all future systems of physics, from Newton on.

Newton issued his *Mathematical Principles of Natural Philosophy* in 1687. It was in three parts, and most of Book II is devoted to a detailed examination of Descartes' theory of planetary motion. In Newton's day, that theory—according to which the planets are carried around the sun by the circulation of "vortices" (eddies) in a weightless interplanetary substance—was the most plausible forerunner of Newton's own account, and was "the one to beat"; but Newton shows that it can fit the known facts about planetary motion, only if we make a dozen highly improbable assumptions about the density of the interplanetary substance, and other crucial points. Still, the fact that Newton thought it worth expounding Descartes' theory at such length is evidence of its significance for him. No one had offered so comprehensive an analysis of the solar system as Descartes had sketched; and Newton's own account was to follow this methodological example.

The method of basing theories on "clear and distinct" concepts thus appealed to Descartes for two distinct kinds of reasons—*instrumental,* as solving problems in the empirical sciences, and *intrinsic,* as a source of "certainty" in a world where skepticism was unchecked. At times, this dual purpose left his priorities unclear. In closing the *Principles of Philosophy,* for instance, Descartes refuses to claim logical or metaphysical certainty for his account of nature. He cannot formally prove that his system of natural philosophy is the one-and-only theory free of contradiction or inconsistency. We are to think of it, rather, as one tentative way of deciphering natural phenomena, and, as such, it has only a *moral* certainty. Still, "moral certainty" is not to be despised. Faced with a script whose sense we do not understand, we are happy to reach a point at which we can interpret its symbols in ways that make sense at all: the more examples an interpretation lets us read without lapsing into unintelligibility, the more confident we are that we have in essentials hit on their actual meaning. Those who recall how Michael Ventris and John Chadwick deciphered the Linear Minoan B script, from Knossos in Crete and Mycenae in Southern Greece, know the force of this argument. The claim that it was an early form of Greek, rather than (e.g.) Lurian or Phoenician or Semitic, became more and more unanswerable as their ability to construe new texts increased.

Given the *Meditations* alone, we may read Descartes as a pure "foundationalist"; but, in the *Principles,* he is clearly working more as a code breaker, or "cryptanalyst". Initially, he hoped to show that we can, after all, find the secure basis for human knowledge of which Montaigne was skeptical. By the time of the *Principles,* irrefutable provability is not so urgent: he is content to decipher natural phenomena in terms that apply generally to phenomena he has not yet had the chance to consider. As such, his account of nature was in direct empirical competition with rival "decipherments"; and, in the event, Newton's account of physical Nature proved to have a more solid cryptanalytical basis.

Hence the ambiguity over Descartes' priorities: in his own mind, and those of his readers and successors, these two sides of his program—foundationalist and cryptanalytical—are not clearly distinct. He may concede in theory that his arguments give his scientific conclusions no more than moral certainty. But (in Galileo's words) he did not doubt that "the Book of Nature is written in mathematical symbols," and he clearly assumed that mathematicians were able to decipher this Book univocally. Presumably, he had not hit on *one possible* way of reading those symbols: if right, his decipherment was *the correct* reading of the Book of Nature. Further, if this method of cryptanalysis was extended to other fields of inquiry, one might then reformulate those sciences, too, in terms of new concepts, whose clarity and distinctness yielded a new theory, with the same "self-guaranteeing" character as Euclid's geometry.

No doubt, all science called for empirical study. But the aim of this empirical work is not, as Francis Bacon had taught, to accumulate a mass of "factual data" without which no future theory can display its merits: rather, it is to assemble the material needed in order to spot the "clear and distinct ideas" that God's creative action has embodied in each fresh field of scientific experience. Descartes does not set out to *prove* that unique "clear and distinct ideas" are available in all fields of experience, nor does he trouble to argue that such ideas confer "Euclidean" status on every new theory: he did not need to establish this afresh in every case—his whole method of arguing relied on it. In taking it as a starting point for the "theoretical" program of modern science, he underestimated the time and effort required to complete the task: there was, in particular, something grandiose in the belief that he could, single-handed, construct the entirety of physics. Yet the achievements of later centuries justify the imaginative reach of his method. All that we now question are his incidental claims that one-and-only-one particular "decipherment" will forever prove *uniquely* correct, and that the "necessary foundations" on which it rests will finally be apparent to any reflective mind.

The two sides of Descartes' intellectual program were respectively to be foundation stones for modern science and for modern philosophy. From

Newton on, by way of Euler to Kant or later, the charms of certainty and uniqueness were as powerful as they were for Descartes. It was not enough to see Newton's theory of motion and gravitation as *one possible* account of terrestrial and celestial mechanics; nor did physicists admit that later generations might justifiably replace Newton's theory by one grounded on different axioms. For the whole 18th century, they tried in all kinds of ways to prove that Newton's own "Axioms or Laws of Motion" provide the only consistent (conceivable, coherent) account of matter in motion, and are indispensable to future natural science, as they stand.

In the long run, of course, this effort failed in mechanics, just as it did in geometry. There is a case for arguing that the geometrical ideas of Euclid rest on the intuitive ideas we use in handling practical tasks in carpentry or thinking about spatial relations in terrestrial experience: the 18th-century writers were keen to prove that Euclid's geometry had unique merits even as *formal mathematics,* but ended by demonstrating the opposite. (If you modify the axiom of parallels, this will not lead to self-contradictions, as would happen if it were, mathematically, a uniquely valid system, but instead generates alternative "geometrical" systems that are—by formal standards—neither better nor worse than Euclid's original.) In the long run, Newton's physics was inevitably compared with that of Einstein in pragmatic rather than epistemological terms: however, in 1687, Einstein's work was two hundred years ahead or more, and at the time the premise of *certainty* was as much of a selling point for the new "natural philosophy" as its empirical power to account for the phenomena of nature.

To sum up: the Cartesian program for philosophy swept aside the "reasonable" uncertainties and hesitations of 16th-century skeptics, in favor of new, mathematical kinds of "rational" certainty and proof. In this, it may (as Dewey and Rorty argue) lead philosophy into a dead end. But, for the time being, that change of attitude—the devaluation of the oral, the particular, the local, the timely, and the concrete—appeared a small price to pay for a formally "rational" theory grounded on abstract, universal, timeless concepts. In a world governed by these intellectual goals, rhetoric was of course subordinate to logic: the validity and truth of "rational" arguments is independent of *who* presents them, *to whom,* or *in what context*—such rhetorical questions can contribute nothing to the impartial establishment of human knowledge. For the first time since Aristotle, logical analysis was separated from, and elevated far above, the study of rhetoric, discourse and argumentation.

This change had far-reaching consequences. Aristotle saw intimate connections between ethics and rhetoric: for him, every ethical position was that of a given kind of person in given circumstances, and in special relations with other specific people: the concrete particularity of a case was "of the essence". Ethics was a field not for theoretical analysis, but for practical wisdom, and it was a mistake to treat it as a universal or abstract science. That is just what 17th-century philosophers had to do, if ethics were to join physics and logic on the *rational* side of the fence, and escape from the chaos of diverse and uncertain opinions. While the irony of Pascal's anonymous tracts destroyed the intellectual claims of "case ethics", Henry More and the Cambridge Platonists took Descartes as inspiration, and attacked the task that Aristotle had condemned as impossible. Practical ethics now took second place: instead, moral philosophy followed the theoretical road of natural philosophy. Rather than pursue the minutiae of moral practice, philosophers concentrated on clarifying and distinguishing the concepts of ethics, and formulating the universal, timeless axioms that (for a rationalist) must lie at the base of any "rational" system of ethics.

In law, again, the practical administration of justice continued to rest on the concrete, limited methods of the common law tradition; but academic jurisprudence developed increasingly formal and theoretical goals. There, scholars did not even wait for Descartes to set an example. As a native of Holland—though by now living in exile in Paris—Grotius wrote his treatise *On the Law of War and Peace* (*De Iure Belli et Pacis*), which was published in 1625. Without abandoning the concrete topics of earlier analyses, he reorganized the general rules of practical law into a system whose principles were the counterparts of Euclid's axioms; and so launched jurisprudence onto the "theory-centered" path it followed in Continental Europe until the early 19th century, when Savigny's critique of legal history obliged scholars to think again about the universality and abstractness of their "principles". Appearing at a crucial moment in a barbarous, uncontrolled war, Grotius' *War and Peace* made an impression, not just on lawyers but on general intellectual debate; and its ripples may have helped to give Descartes, in Holland in the early 1630s, courage to use the model of Euclid in his own account of rationality.

Soon enough, the flight from the particular, concrete, transitory, and practical aspects of human experience became a feature of cultural life in general, and above all of philosophy. Scholars may write of Descartes' concern for the problems of medicine; but he was not concerned with any procedures to be relied on in the timely treatment of particular patients: what interested him were ways of explaining the workings of the body in terms of physical and chemical mechanisms. His physiological interests thus anticipate "biomedical science" more than they do clinical medicine.

In politics, too, an impatience with the particularity and concreteness of ethnography and history encouraged the new style of "political theory" of which Thomas Hobbes' *Leviathan* is paradigmatic. Given our familiarity with its method, it is easy to forget how novel this style of theory was. Like Thucydides in Athens, political philosophers in Renaissance Italy, such as Machiavelli and Guicciardini, based their accounts of politics on reflective analyses of historical experience: they started from a city or a state, a kingdom or republic, as it operated in actual historical fact. Only after 1640 was political theory handled in abstract, general terms, with the individual citizen or subject taken as the unit of analysis—the "atom" or "particle" of politics—so that the problem became to explain the political loyalty of the individual to the State.

The last, crucial field we need to consider is theology. Our revised account allots the move from the first to the second phase of Modernity— from 16th-century humanism to 17th-century rationalism—its specific context: the crisis in European culture, as Counter-Reformation activists led by the Jesuits collided with the intransigent Protestants and their political supporters. How did the formal teachings of the Churches, and the intellectual style of the theological debate, reflect this transition? As the "mathematical and experimental" natural philosophy took root, and as Euclidian geometry became more influential, many people speculated about the theological implications of the new movement, and explored ways of applying its methods in theology. Here, the consequences of the quest for certainty were explicitly political. By the 18th century, the ability to construct formal demonstrations of religious doctrines ("more rigorous than thou") was less a way of carrying intellectual conviction than an instrument of ecclesiastical persuasion and apologetics.

In the High Middle Ages, Christian theology—we say *Christian,* not *Catholic,* to describe the pre-Reformation tradition to which both parties in the later conflict looked back—was more relaxed and adventurous than it became after the late 16th century. Medieval theologians were spared the Vatican monitoring and censorship to which a Hans Küng and a Charles Curran are subjected today. Nicolas Cusanus taught doctrines for which Bruno was to be burned at the stake; Copernicus gave free rein to his imagination in ways no longer permitted to Galileo; Aquinas took up and reanalyzed the positions of Augustine and his other predecessors, and reconciled them not just with each other, but with the texts of such non-Christians as Aristotle and Cicero. In short, the Church operated with an academic freedom that ceased to exist, once the Protestant and Counter-Reformation theologians were joined in confrontation. After the Council of Trent, ecclesiastical censors in Rome started to monitor the work of theologians in the Provincial Churches in a new way; the Holy Office, rooting out "heretics" in ways that are all too familiar, became more widespread and vigorous; and for the first time Catholic teaching hardened into theses (or "dogmas") that were no longer open to critical discussion, even by sympathetic believers, and whose immutable truth it was politically indispensable to assert, for fear of yielding to the heresies of the Protestants. Instead of free-wheeling *Summas,* the 17th century was fed a diet of centrally authorized *Manuals;* and the Roman authorities began to intervene formally in moral theology by laying down general rulings about moral issues, or *responsa,* with the full force of authority. (Here too, the modern image of Catholicism is not an ancient creation, but is of recent political origin.)

With the transition from *Summas* to *Manuals,* from speculative and revisable doctrines to immutable and infallible "dogmas", theology and rationalism entered into an ambiguous alliance. Descartes settled in Holland around 1630 with encouragement from his teachers at La Flèche: he avoided the shadow of censorship by working in Holland, but he tried never to put himself at odds with the Church, in the way the forthright Galileo had done. (It is tempting, if a little unfair, to describe Descartes as a loyal son of the Counter-Reformation: like Yevtuschenko in the USSR, he was ready to hide his true opinions behind a mask—*larvatus prodeo.*) Once his philosophical texts appeared, however, theologians read them with trepidation. They were alarmed to see that he apparently gave a new handle to the "deists" who saw that, on his account of the material universe, God needed only to start it up at the Creation, and could then leave it to operate mechanically without any further Divine Intervention. Galileo's trial had had a traumatic effect on Descartes. Foreseeing the risk of theological criticism, he added to the *Principles* a ritual bow toward *Genesis,* by conceding that the Biblical text was the "true" account of Creation, and arguing that his theory shows only that Nature behaves *just as it would* if it reached its present form by mechanical means.

Descartes' "deist" successors took this bow as a transparent evasion, and the Catholic Church was not much happier about the implications of his natural philosophy. One thing about his ideas, however, was to their taste: his insistence on the need for *certainty.* Once rationalism raised the intellectual stakes, Catholics could not go on playing by older, more relaxed rules: if formal rigor were the order of the day in physics and ethics, theology must follow suit. Confronting Protestant heretics on the one side, and skeptical deists on the other, the theologians decided: "If we can't join them, let us beat them at their own game."

In the Library of the Convent of Ste. Geneviève, near the Pantheon in

Paris, is a manuscript entitled, *Traité sur l'autôrité et de la réception du Concile de Trente en France*. It describes the struggle, after the Council of Trent, to uproot the "pernicious heresies and errors" of Protestantism, and paints a revealing picture of the intellectual position of the Catholic Church in early 18th-century France. The whole argument is an example of history written retrospectively: It begins, "The Council of Trent was summoned to root out the errors of Luther"; and its final pages show how far the demand for "undeniable foundations" had made its way into Catholic theology by 1725. Looking back, the author credits the Council with anachronistic motives, which are intelligible only if already, in the 1570s, it could invoke the principles of a philosophical rationalism that was invented in the 1630s. The ambition of the Counter-Reformation, it tells us, was "to prove invincibly our most fundamental belief."

Montaigne's reaction to these claims can be imagined; yet neither Aquinas nor Erasmus would have been happy about this use of the phrase, "invincible proof". Neither of them claimed that human beings, however wise and inspired, could put matters of faith and doctrine beyond scope of reconsideration and revision. Both of them would be shocked to see that the Christianity they treasured was abandoning its former sense of human finitude, and falling into a dogmatism contrary to human nature as they knew it. Despite all its turmoil and religious divisions, the 16th century had been, by comparison, a time when the voice of sweet reasonableness made itself heard, and was widely valued. From 1610 on, and most of all after 1618, the argument became active, bloody, and strident. Everyone now talked at the top of his voice, and the humanists' quiet discussions of finitude, and the need for toleration, no longer won a hearing. In the circumstances, the best that "men of reason" could do was outshout the theological dogmatists, and find a way of beating them at the game of "invincibly proving" their fundamental beliefs.

Using Euclid's axiomatic method as a Joker with which to trump all the inconclusive arguments of theology was a risky but enticing strategy. We shall never know for sure how far Descartes understood the duplicity of his project, but must not underestimate his skill at self-concealment. *Larvatus prodeo:* from the moment when the Church authorities punished Galileo for speaking his mind, Descartes took care to watch his step, and "masked" he remained to the day of his death. One thing at least is sure. The philosophers who succeeded Descartes caught on to the game, and went on playing it less duplicitously, for just so long as the theoretical approach of modern philosophy—what we are here calling "rationalism"—retained its plausibility and charm.

Evidently, that time is now over. But our historical studies give us two first reassurances that may help to counter the undiluted pessimism about philosophy shown today by critics like Richard Rorty. In the first place, the *practical* aspects of philosophy had a long and vigorous history before Descartes and the rationalists came on the scene, and promise to survive the present crisis within philosophy, untouched by the corrosive effects of 20th-century criticism. In the second place, the 17th-century triumph of rationalism, and the Quest for Certainty to which it gave rise, did not happen out of a clear blue sky, but were intelligible responses to a specific historical crisis. Viewed in context, that is, the rationalist move of *decontextualizing* the problems of science and philosophy, and using the methods of formal logic and geometry as a basis for a rational resolution of physical and epistemological problems, was more than a worthwhile experiment in philosophical method. It was also a smart political move: a rhetorically timely response to the general crisis of 17th-century politics. But the success of this move had its price. The directions in which it pointed intellectual and practical life in Europe, after 1650, led people away from the "sweet reasonableness" of the first phase of Modernity, and required the "provability" of human knowledge in ways that have perpetuated the dogmatism of the Religious Wars.

It is an exaggeration to imply that the second phase of Modernity undid all the good work of the first, or that the 17th-century revolution in philosophy and science was really a *counter-revolution*. Still, the fact remains that this "revolution" was not motivated by purely "progressive" intentions, as we were taught to believe in the 1930s and 1940s—motives that are found, more realistically, in Francis Bacon's writings. Quite as much, the 17th-century revolutions were carried through—and won public support—as ways of establishing hard-line positions of a kind that humanists like Montaigne would have regarded as suspect. The received view of Modernity thus tried, anachronistically, to credit 17th-century philosophers with the toleration, and the concern for human welfare and diversity, that belonged rather to 16th-century humanists: positions that were linked with a skeptical philosophy that rationalist philosophers like Descartes were bound, in public at least, to reject and abhor.

The First Step Back From Rationalism

To summarize our revised narrative so far: on the received view, Modernity began with a 17th-century commitment to "rationality" that was made possible by economic prosperity and reduced pressure from the Church, but a fresh look reveals a more complex story. The key features of the modern age were products not of a single intellectual origin, but of two distinct beginnings. The first was embodied in the Renaissance humanists, from Erasmus on, who lived in times of relative prosperity, and built up a culture of "reasonableness" and religious toleration. The second beginning was embodied in the 17th-century rationalists, starting with Descartes, who reacted to times of economic crisis—when toleration seemed a failure and religion took to the sword—by giving up the modest skepticism of the humanists, and looking for "rational" proofs to underpin our beliefs with a certainty neutral as between all religious positions. When historians dated modernity from the early 17th century, they saw it as the creation of intellectuals who, following Galileo and Descartes, set out to develop rational modes of thought, free of medieval superstition and theological influence: in this, they shared the position of the men whom they saw as the pioneers of Modernity. In a word, the received view of Modernity that was second nature to those of us who grew up in the 1930s and '40s was based on the rationalist assumptions that underlay the original program of the 17th-century "new philosophers", whose works the advocates of the received view so warmly admired.

Descartes was convinced that we can build a secure body of human knowledge, if we scrap our inherited systems of concepts and start again from scratch—with a clean slate—using "rationally validated" methods. That meant, on the one hand, framing one's basic theories around ideas whose merits were clear, distinct and certain: on the other, using only demonstrable arguments, having the necessity of geometrical proofs. In the 1930s, it was assumed that an explicit account of science would do just that: this was the deeper meaning of the term "scientific method." Both the received view of Modernity, and the standard narrative of its origins, were thus rationalist constructions. Far from its being certain or self-evident that all intellectual problems—let alone, practical ones—can be "rationally" resolved in abstraction from their historical contexts, the decontextualization of philosophy was itself historically motivated. We can explain the merits of the rationalist program for people in the 17th century, only by looking at what was "at stake" *there and then* for serious-minded intellectuals like Descartes.

The ivory tower biography of Descartes in the *Grande Encyclopédie* leaves half-a-dozen striking episodes in his life opaque, or accounts for them by praising him for turning his back on the tragedies of his time. Instead of assuming that he was unmoved by Henry IV's assassination, and applauding him for ignoring the Thirty Years' War, we have asked here what personal experience he actually had of those historical episodes. The answers are not only more revealing than any that are implicit in the

Grande Encyclopédie approach, but are more relevant to his intellectual program and philosophical conclusions than rationalist historians allow. The first step back from a commitment to rationalism is to acknowledge that we can never fully *decontextualize* philosophy or science. When we deal with intellectual or practical problems, we can never totally clean the slate, and start from scratch, as Descartes demands when he explains in the *Discourse* how to reach his position of systematic doubt. Rather, we start from where we are; and the best indication that we are handling our problems in a "rational" or "reasonable" way is not the fact that we *reject* all inherited concepts, but the extent to which we use experience to *refine* those inherited concepts.

In his time, Descartes knew, a program of theory-building was more feasible in some fields than in others. For physics, he hoped to provide a complete and final system of basic theoretical ideas. In ethics, the hope of developing a comprehensive analysis was still, he conceded, a dream: meanwhile, we must muddle along with the "provisional" morality taught in our communities and churches. By the 1960s, what was true for him of ethics evidently held good in intellectual fields, too, even in physics. Clear-headed theorizing involves radical rethinking, and so compels us to discard some earlier ideas; but it never goes as far as Descartes claims, in turning a flame-thrower on all inherited ideas. When Isaac Newton wrote his *Principia,* for instance, he used Descartes' axiomatic model of exposition, but his philosophical claims are both more modest, and more experiential, than those of Descartes. His point of departure was not a ground stripped of previous landmarks: he began from everyday, intuitive ideas of weight, force, time, and space, and explained with care how the use of such ideas in his system of dynamics drew upon, but at the same time refined, those everyday ideas.

———————— ◆ ◆ ————————

Why, then, were the years from 1610 to 1650 so exceptional? In the High Middle Ages, a practical-minded Aristotelianism had coëxisted with a theoretical-minded Platonism: why was this balance upset so suddenly and completely after 1600? That question has no single short answer, but one point deserves to be underlined. The religious conflict triggered by the Reformation took place at just the same time when the traditional cosmology—the Sun and Planets moving around a stable, stationary Earth—at last come under sustained attack.

This historical coincidence created an impression. The more acute the differences between Protestant and Catholic zealots, the more dogmatically they denounced one another, and the more urgently did cooler heads embrace the project for a "rational" method to establish truths whose certainty was clear to reflective thinkers of any denomination. Meanwhile, the more vigorously Galileo advocated the new Copernican System—the Earth being just one more planet moving around the Sun—the more pressing was the need for a full renovation of natural philosophy. Even allowing for John Donne's personal conservatism in the face of the challenges to received ideas about Nature and Society, therefore, his alarm in the *Anatomy of the World* was perceptive and not inappropriate. It was all very well for Montaigne to play classical skeptic in the 1580s, and to brush aside all philosophical disagreements on the ground that, in such disputes, "nothing particular" is at stake. But, after 1618, serious-minded intellectuals were free to reply:

"Granted, *nothing in particular* is at stake in our cosmology: what is at stake is *everything in general.*"

The rationalists' ambition to build a "foundation" for knowledge was, thus, not aimed at epistemology alone. They looked not just for a way to give knowledge the certainty that Montaigne and his fellow skeptics denied it: they also wanted to build up a fresh cosmology from scratch. The unique crisis that Donne intuitively recognized in 1611—collapse of cosmology and epistemology simultaneously—evoked from the New Philosophers an equally unique reply: if *everything in general* is under threat at one and the same time, *everything in general* must be restored and underpinned in a brand new way. Natural philosophy itself must be rebuilt on geometrical foundations, if the epistemological foundations of a new cosmology are to be guaranteed.

It was a daring program, but the situation could not (apparently) be dealt with less drastically. From 1650, European thinkers were taken with this appetite for universal and timeless theories. As the program gathered momentum, it overwhelmed Aristotle's warnings about the need to match our expectations to the nature of the case, and to avoid demanding irrelevant kinds of "certainty" or "necessity". Ethics and politics joined physics and epistemology as fields of abstract, general, eternal theory. Like a great Moloch, this appetite for theory consumed all the branches of practical philosophy: case ethics, practical politics, rhetoric, and all. So began an estrangement between philosophy and the humanities—history and ethnography as much as rhetoric and casuistry—that was to continue until just the other day.

———— • ————

Up to this point, our revised narrative of the origins of Modernity has concentrated on *historical* questions about 16th- and 17th-century thought. But, as we foresaw at the outset of this inquiry, our historical narrative generates also a parallel, or *historiographical* analysis. This second story is concerned with the ways in which our *perception* of Science and scientific method has changed since the 1930s, and notably since World War II. Though often referred to as "logical positivism", the view of science in the 1930s and '40s was dominated by rationalism—it shared all the 17th-century assumptions. After 1945, this view survived for some ten years without any real challenge: many people retained from pre-war days the dream of a Unified Science—a system built around pure mathematics, like Russell and Whitehead's *Principia Mathematica,* but encompassing the totality of scientific knowledge. The tide turned in the 1950s. A new generation of philosophers, with previous experience in natural science rather than in pure mathematics or symbolic logic, wrote about science in a new *style:* less exclusively logical, and more open to historical issues.

This novel philosophy of science was a challenge to the orthodoxy of logical empiricism. Chronicling its early years, Theodore Kisiel finds its origin in my 1953 book, *The Philosophy of Science;* but, undoubtedly, the most influential document of the movement was Thomas S. Kuhn's book, *The Structure of Scientific Revolutions,* published in 1962. By a paradox, Kuhn's book appeared as an annex to the *Encyclopedia of Unified Science:* within a project to base Science on formal logic, it was a Trojan Horse. From time to time, Kuhn argued, physicists raze the conceptual structure of their science, and rebuild it on new foundations, from the ground up: in this, he sounds like Descartes, or like the positivists themselves. But the foundation of a newly reconstructed science is not a system of "self-evident" ideas or "formal" axioms: it is the next item in the historical sequence of patterns of explanation ("paradigms") that have shaped successive phases in the history of physics. At the end of the day, then, philosophers of science interested in the foundations of physics can dig no deeper than the current "paradigms" permit.

Not everyone saw at once just what a change this move represented, or how far it stepped back from the context-free questions of Cartesian rationalism, toward the historical candor of the humanist tradition. Let us therefore look for a moment at its outcomes. In analyzing a science, it replaces *axiom systems,* which aspire to universal timeless validity, by *paradigms,* which are the creations of a given age or phase of Science. It also substitutes for the dream of a singular *method,* applied across the board, the fact of plural explanatory *methods,* each of which is limited in scope and lifetime. In place of a *formal* analysis of the logical structure of any scientific theory, as was aimed at by the positivist philosophers of

Vienna in the 1920s, it relies on the *historical* analysis of diverse, variable concepts in different sciences, at different times.

Things had come a long way from the decontextualized philosophy of the *Grande Encyclopédie,* or the formal ambitions of Unified Science; and before long the implications of the new approach were attacked by those who retained a taste for earlier, rationalist ambitions. Rationalists had always feared selling out to history and psychology, and making rational judgments on science hostage to the happenstance of human behavior at one moment or another: inevitably, this would reintroduce the ambiguity and uncertainty that the successors to Descartes struggled to eliminate. A series of books appeared in the late 1960s, criticizing the historical method in philosophy of science for surrendering all of science's claim to objectivity, and treating scientific judgments as matters of local taste.

Once the Kuhnian move had been made, however, the Berlin Wall that kept historians and philosophers of science apart was demolished. After the mid '60s, professional meetings of both groups included sessions on their common interests. Historians relaxed their fear of metaphysical corruption enough to discuss philosophical aspects of earlier science; and philosophers softened their distrust of historical contingency enough to ask how the ideas of "method" or "objectivity", say, have changed from one phase in the history of science to another.

All the same, rationalism died hard. For the next ten years, most philosophers of science were ready to entertain only a limited range of historical questions. The philosophical purpose of historical analysis was confined, in their eyes, to what Imre Lakatos called the "rational reconstruction" of episodes in the development of modern science; and, in these reconstructions, only certain factors *counted as* "rational." The only acceptable historical questions involved the changing "internal" structure of science:. at Karl Popper's insistence, sharp criteria were used to "demarcate" genuinely scientific issues from other, irrelevant, or superstitious questions about ideology and metaphysics. In a rationalist spirit, the "demarcation criteria" were timeless and universal demands of a "critical reason" that operated above or apart from the changes and chances of history. The scientific arguments of earlier times and fields must be judged in the light, not of what was at stake or carried weight for people *at the time,* but of new, 20th-century demands imposed on past science by present day philosophy.

This limitation on our historical interpretations, however, had some problematic consequences. Jürgen Habermas has accustomed us to the idea that all of knowledge is rooted in human interests of some kind; but we must here ask a further question: viz., How far can the "interests" that are served by the pursuit of knowledge be identified once for all, in advance, and in timeless and universal terms? Karl Popper's insistence that the criteria of scientific rationality are universal implies that we can decide, here and now, what it is "scientific" to consider *anywhere and at any time*. According to him, all "scientists" worthy of that name serve the same timeless interests everywhere and always. Others may conclude that we can master the scientific ideas of earlier times fully, only if we look at them in their original contexts. The question thus becomes: Is there any substitute for treating the history of science or philosophy as fields for genuinely *historical* study? The development of science and philosophy need not conform to abstract definitions, read back into the historical record from a 20th-century viewpoint: rather, we must interpret earlier ideas in terms of interests that were *perceived as* "at stake" at he time when they were first debated. Those interests will, no doubt, overlap those that seem "at stake" from our present point of view, but we cannot equate the stakes there-and-then with those here-and-now, without any historical examination.

We must not be too proud to reconstruct the rhetorical contexts in which people decided *for themselves* what was important in each debate. Some of their scientific interests may coincide with ones that are still acceptable to 20th-century philosophers of science: if so, well and good. Others are of kinds that a 20th-century positivist might be ashamed to acknowledge, e.g., the desire to give astronomy its lost "cosmopolitical" significance: in that case, so be it. Anything that people of Leibniz and Newton's calibre *saw as* at stake in their inquiries, surely *was* at stake in their inquiries: rather than tell them their business, we should ask, "Why did the situation there and then make these *un*positivistic interests so weighty and important?"

In these inquiries, our approach to "scientific method" can follow the example of common law or case law, not the model of statute law. We shall discover what carries weight with philosophers and scientists, not by imposing *a priori* definitions of "philosophy" and "science" on their work, but by seeing how their ideas of rationality and reasonableness developed, and were refined, in the course of their working practice.

In one respect, in particular, our revised narrative is more complex than those in the standard histories of philosophy. There, every new philosopher entering the intellectual scene is read as criticizing his predecessors and engaging in argument *on precisely the same ground*. René Descartes advances thesis A, Benedict de Spinoza counters with the thesis B, Gottfried Wilhelm Leibniz caps them both with the position C: it is then for us to judge in retrospect—*sub specie aeternitatis*—which of the three puts forward the strongest arguments for his position. This clash between rival theses generates a debate whose merits and defects are presented as no less "context-free" than the theses themselves.

Yet, in fact, no two philosophers living ten years apart can stand on *precisely* the same ground. Each new philosopher presents theses to an audience that lives, with him, in a situation different from those of his predecessors. Their *contexts* of writing often differ in major respects; and, by ignoring these differences, we impoverish our understanding of the *content* of their ideas. Descartes in the 1630s and '40s, and Leibniz in the 1680s and '90s, lived and wrote in very different historical and rhetorical contexts, and it does no good to our grasp of each man's ideas if we insist on reading them in identical terms. True, some of Leibniz's theses use terms that Descartes had used 50 years before; but, putting forward the theses he did in the way he did, he went beyond what is plain on the surface of his texts, and pursued his argument in directions just as unlike those of Descartes as the historical situation in the 1680s was unlike that in the 1630s.

Once in a while, like the Gods of Olympus, Great Philosophers come down and mingle in the World of Men. Instead of reading philosophical texts always in a timeless and abstract stratosphere, it is better to "recontextualize" the debate, and give Descartes and Leibniz their proper credit for allowing their intellects to be stirred by critical *événements extérieurs* in their respective times. At this point, then, we may take up the historical task again, and carry our revised narrative forward from the years when the Thirty Years' War reached its exhausted close.

CHAPTER THREE

The Modern World View

Fashioning the New "Europe of Nations"

*A*fter 1650, the peoples of Northern and Western Europe faced grave problems of political and intellectual reconstruction. For fifty years, religious fervor and ideological denunciation had undermined the arts of diplomacy, and Europeans had lost the arts of living together in mutual respect. Both sets of arts now had to be restored. Domestically, the years of the Religious Wars saw the power of the landed nobility diluted, as the influence of professional men and city merchants grew. This new historical situation required the countries of Western Europe to develop fresh social structures and modes of solidarity.

Both social tasks had intellectual counterparts. The breakdown of diplomatic communication in the previous half-century was rationalized as a by-product of theological antagonisms: serious-minded men on both sides of the barricades now had to hammer out fresh modes of discussion that would let them circumvent (if not overcome) earlier disagreements. For those who survived into the years after the Religious Wars, the dream of logically necessary arguments whose "certainty" could go beyond the "certitude" of any theological position kept its charm in both modes of reasoning and language. Half a century of confrontation and head-butting made Rationalism look all the more enticing. In the long run, might it not also help to bind up the wounds in Cosmopolis, and restore the lost harmony between the natural and social orders?

In 1600, the principal countries of Europe bore the clear stamp of their feudal pasts. In England, Elizabeth I was still vigorous; in France, Henri IV was reaching the peak of his power; and both rulers at the same time served as their countries' last medieval monarchs, and as their first national sovereigns. By summer 1610, both had departed the scene, precipitating the crisis of the years from 1610 to 1650. After 1650 the dust settled, and there was little doubt that feudalism was now over: in Britain and France as much as in Holland, the sovereign would rule, from now on, not as the feudal inheritor of a country's real estate, but as the symbolic embodiment of the nation itself. The change took some time to become unmistakable; the later Stuart Kings of England, Charles II and James II, compromised their power by trying to ignore it; but, by the 1690s, there was no longer any doubt that the scale had tilted.

The Thirty Years' War dragged to a close in 1648. It ended as a peace of exhaustion, not of conquest. What started as a local conflict among German duchies and mini-states had, by 1630, become a slugging match by proxies for outside superpowers. The Catholic protagonist was the Habsburg Emperor of Austria, Ferdinand III, distantly supported by his kinsmen in Spain; the Protestant leader was King Gustavus Adolphus of Sweden, acting as ambiguous mercenary for the French Kings, Louis XIII and his infant successor, Louis XIV. The result was stalemate. As early as 1638 peace negotiations began in Hamburg; in 1641, the parties to the conflict agreed to talk about a permanent settlement in two cities of Westphalia—Austria and Sweden negotiating in Osnabrück, and France and Austria in Münster—and by summer 1642 the outline treaties had been agreed upon. But the war dragged on for six more years while the last practical details were hammered out. Ferdinand made his final concessions only after the Protestant forces, in their campaign of 1648, overran Bavaria and laid siege to Prague. (The whole story is depressingly familiar to any reader who followed the negotiations to end superpower involvement in Vietnam and Afghanistan.) The Treaties of Münster and Osnabrück, as they finally took shape, are often referred to jointly as "the Peace of Westphalia". Once peace came, a system of sovereign "nation-states" was set up which gave structure to the political and diplomatic affairs of Europe right up to the First World War.

Three decades of war had proved nothing about the relative merits of Catholicism or Protestantism. Spectacular bloodletting changed no minds and transformed no souls. There was forcible conversion: Prague was a Protestant stronghold in 1618, but held the Protestant army at bay for much of 1648. Changes of conviction were another matter. By the end, all the major powers had the best of domestic reasons to back off, provided only that they could avoid appearing "pitiful helpless giants." Ironically, the only person to protest publicly against the treaties was the Pope, Innocent X. His predecessor, Urban VIII, had helped initiate preliminary negotiations in 1638–41, but ten years later Innocent found the terms of the Peace unacceptable. It was not that Innocent positively relished seeing Protestant blood spilled: rather, he recognized that the new system of sovereign nations undercut rights and powers that earlier Popes had exercised without challenge. From now on, instead of secular rulers having to conform to the Church's demands, they could interfere freely in ecclesiastical affairs. In late 1648, he published an indignant brief, in which he complained,

> that the Emperor had given away things that were not his to give: the goods of the church to heretics in perpetuity, freedom of worship to heretics, and a voice in the election of the [Holy Roman] Emperor. It was a peace against all canon law, all councils, all concordats.

Still, the Roman authorities had lost the power to enforce their demands. Even within the Church, the interest of the provinces in protecting their autonomy against the centralizing tendencies of the Curia pressed them into alliances with the local political authorities. Two French Cardinals in turn became the political agents of Louis XIII (Richelieu) and Louis XIV (Mazarin). Without the need to break from Rome formally, Catholicism in France thus became, in their hands, no less "Gallican" than the Church of England was "Anglican."

This was to be the pattern of the future. In the medieval Church, a transnational hierarchy of literate clerics and scholars exercised their moral and spiritual authority over the mainly unlettered rulers of Europe. That authority was now broken. Aside from the sheer increase in power of the nation-states, the rise of a literate and educated laity tilted the balance toward the secular, and against the ecclesiastical powers. From now on, Church affairs were increasingly influenced by national policy. The Peace of Westphalia reestablished the rule agreed on in 1555, in the Treaty of Augsburg, by which each sovereign chose the official religion of his own State. In practice, the choice was still subject to negotiation between a ruler and his subjects, but from now on established religion was the general rule. In the "new" nation of Holland, Protestantism was tempered by a widespread toleration of individual Catholics: elsewhere, temporal rulers required their citizens to toe the general line.

None of this happened overnight. It took time for a fresh pattern of relations, within and among nation-states and between states and their churches, to settle down, become familiar, and shape "commonsense" attitudes. Nobody wanted to see a general reopening of hostilities, but the earlier convulsions still produced aftershocks. The 1650s were a time of transition. In France, Louis XIV came of age in 1651; in Sweden, the 1650s saw serious conflict between the social classes; even in self-contained England, the social fabric of the nation was under severe strain after

Charles I's execution in 1649. The political structure of Modernity took firm shape, and the "Europe of Nations" was at last clearly defined, only after 1660, with the Stuart Restoration in England and the assumption of personal power by Louis XIV in France. Ambiguities remained as late as the 1680s. In England, the Stuart kings tried to reestablish Catholicism in the face of their subjects' opposition: the conflict was resolved by the flight of James II. He was replaced in 1689 by the Dutch Protestant Prince, William of Orange, who ascended the throne jointly with Mary, his wife, who was the daughter of James II.

From 1660 on, then, the states of Europe were preoccupied with the task of overcoming the destructive effects on their social and material fabric of the wars of the previous half-century. As early as 1610, John Donne wrote of traditional loyalties as "things forgot": dying in 1631, he was spared from witnessing King Charles I's death, and the turbulence of the Common-wealth. The longer the conflict went on, the more frayed social relations became. After 1650, the overriding task for the ruling oligarchies was to create some assurance of social coherence: In Theodore Rabb's happy phrase, the central theme of 17th-century Europe was a "struggle for stability". For the purposes of our own inquiry, the corresponding question now is, "How did the late 16th-century struggle for *social and political* stability dovetail, and interact, with the post-Cartesian quest for *scientific and intellectual* certainty and stability?"

The other preoccupation of the Nation-States, from 1650 on, was the continuing problem of religious conformity and toleration. On one side, the creation of established national Churches created expectations about the readiness of citizens to conform to the demands of those Churches: how, then, should secular authority treat the minorities that refused to conform, and remained loyal to other denominations? After thirty years of bloodshed, few people still considered the price of imposing religious conformity worth paying, but the local pressure for conformity remained strong, and religious minorities were everywhere subject to some degree of discrimination or persecution. Different nations handled the twin tasks of redefining social stability, and creating national churches, in different ways. In the 1690s, English papists were exposed to social disabilities and public scorn; but their penalties were less severe than the persecution and condemnation of heretics in the France of Louis XIV and Bishop Bossuet. In Denmark and Holland, or the German States of Hesse and Württemberg, a balance was struck in yet other ways. Despite national and regional differences, these states faced the same problems, and the nation-states of late 17th-century Europe each represented a different variation on a common set of tunes.

At one end of the spectrum, in Austria, continued Lutheranism was seen as disloyalty to the Habsburg dynasty, and the Protestant minority of craftsmen and professionals had to choose between conversion, death, and flight. In France, the Protestant minority was denied the right to work in many professions, and exposed to military attacks that drove them back into their traditional strongholds, deep in the *Massif Central*. Many talented Huguenots with their families escaped abroad across land, or became boat people and headed for England or America. Elsewhere, in the uneasy balance between religions, dissenters were denied political or social opportunities, including the chance to go to a University or to be members of the parliament or legislature. But, in one way or another, a balance was struck between full toleration and full conformity which stopped short of the horrors of a renewed religious war.

If different nations handled the problems of social stability and religious toleration differently, the reasons reflect the earlier traditions and historical memories of the peoples involved. At one extreme, the United Provinces of the Netherlands (Holland) was a "young" country that had expelled the armies of Habsburg Spain barely eighty years earlier. Lacking the constraints of long-standing institutions, its people developed new social forms of confidence, and the Calvinist majority could be unusually tolerant of the Catholic minority. At the opposite extreme, the Habsburgs of Austria and Spain appointed themselves standard-bearers of Catholicism, and equated nonconformity with social disorder. Early in the 16th century, Charles I of Spain (the Emperor Charles V) had faced the *guerra de las comunidades*—an abortive quasi-Cromwellian revolt led by three provincial merchants, Padilla, Bravo, and Maldonado—and had made it the excuse for converting or expelling Muslims, Jews, and Protestants alike. A century later, Spain's declining economic power was leading to a fossilization of its institutions, which continued after a Bourbon dynasty succeeded the Habsburgs. From then on the Habsburgs in Vienna were the leaders of conservative, Counter-Reformation Europe: after the liberal revolts of 1848, the young Franz Josef was as resistant to change as his remote cousin, Charles V, had been three hundred years earlier.

Between these extremes, England and France were type examples of "national" development. In England, Charles I's misguided attempt to act as an autocrat in a country with old parliamentary traditions ensured the initial success of the Republican Commonwealth: so for a decade, under Cromwell, people in England indulged democratic dreams of many kinds. In the meantime, the suspension of censorship over printing encouraged debate both about theological doctrines and political theories, and also about new social institutions. Some of the opinions expressed in this debate struck cautious souls as "turning the world upside down": e.g., the "levelling" proposal to abolish titles of nobility and distinctions of rank in the Church, and egalitarian demands for the redistribution of land and property—even the advocacy of free sexual relations. Those who longed for a return to order and decorum equated republicanism with anarchy, and so prepared people's minds for restoring the monarchy. Still, the power that Parliament had won under Charles I and the Interregnum prevented two later Stuart Kings from exercising royal authority in the autocratic manner of their father, Charles I; a crucial step had been taken toward making *constitutional,* not *absolute,* monarchy the foundation of British political institutions. However, this step rescued England from "absolutism" in only one sense: in another, the "sovereignty" of British constitutional monarchs remained as *absolute* as that of any royal autocracy. It denied any outside body or institution the right to stand in moral judgment over the actions of the British government, as the Popes and Bishops of the Church had regularly done in dealing with the secular rulers of medieval Europe.

Under Cromwell many Englishmen, like Muslim fundamentalists in Iran under the Ayatollah Khomeini, believed that their rulers were doing God's work on Earth. In the eyes of Cromwell's followers, the English were chosen by God, and were being challenged to create God's Kingdom in "England's green and pleasant land". This was the true significance of the Commonwealth. Success in that noble task would permit an Apocalypse in the mid-1650s: frustration of this happy outcome was put down to sinfulness on the part of the citizens. Thus, in Milton's phrase, "Paradise was Lost." After the Restoration, such "vulgar enthusiasms" were laughed at by "the better sort" of people, and cynical views tended to prevail: at the same time, the Established Church played its part by calling down God's blessings on the reestablished rulers of the state, and so confirming the fragile stability of the social order. During the subsequent three hundred years, if we can trust the Anglican clergy, the Lord God has had miraculously few occasions to find moral fault with the actions of the British Government or its agents.

In France, the Peace of Westphalia was followed by some years of turbulence. The landed nobility resented the extreme power accumulated by the Royal agents, Richelieu and Mazarin, and tried to retrieve control by opposing the autocratic policies of Louis XIV and his ministers. Even more, they resented a whittling away of their traditional rights by the admission to Court of upstart professionals—the *noblesse de la robe.* Rumblings of a revolt by the aristocratic *Fronde* had led Mazarin to speed up negotiations for the Peace, but it was unclear for some years if the Royal authorities could regain control of the situation. By the late 1650s, this had been done, and for most of Louis XIV's seventy and more year reign—as also from 1715 on, in the near–sixty-year reign of his great-grandson, Louis XV—France was an *absolute* monarchy in both senses of the term. Unlike the British Stuarts, Louis XIV kept the power of the State in his own hands. He projected his authority as a source of "illumination" that enlightened all the actions of the State, and as the "force" responsible for both stability and change. As King, he was the Sun around which the State's motions turned: even a personal embodiment of the State itself. By his choice, citizens were raised to (or banished from) positions of authority, within an order whose Cartesian rationality and symmetry were as impressive as those of his Palace and Park at Versailles.

For more than a century, Britain and France thus set the examples by which other nations measured themselves. Both countries established stability of a kind that had been rare in Medieval Europe, and was largely absent in the turbulent years of the early 17th century. Both apparently provided successful patterns for others to follow. The greater fragility of the autocratic model was publicly displayed only in 1789, when the Bourbon *ancien régime* was overturned by the French Revolution. Even so, many historians have argued that the monarchy was doomed less by autocracy itself than by the incompetence of Louis XIV's successors. The familiar couplet by Alexander Pope is "classical" in thought as in expression:

> For forms of government let fools contest:
> Whate'er is best administered is best.

Whether monarchical powers were exercised through free decisions of a wise Sovereign, or hedged about by constitutional limits, either way the indispensable goal was the stability of the nation. In England and France, the shadows of earlier catastrophes clouded the public's memory, like half-forgotten nightmares, and the risk of returning to a more turbulent time was more than most people could face. In time, the fact that England was a Protestant nation, France a Catholic one, became less important than their common stakes in domestic stability and diplomatic balance. The English might revile the French as Papists, and the French condemn the English as Heretics, but both sides took care not to push their mutual scorn to destructive levels.

Before long, a stabilizing anti-symmetry began to link the actions of the two nations. In 1685, Louis XIV revoked the last, largely disregarded protections which the Edict of Nantes had given the French Protestants, so removing any formal objection to the policy of rooting the Huguenots out of the Auvergne; but this act at once had international consequences. By tilting the balance against a policy of domestic toleration, Louis made James II's pro-Catholic policies insupportable to English opinion across the Channel. In this way, he not only precipitated James's replacement by William III, but also helped intensify English counter-persecution of the Catholics in Ireland. The Established Churches in England and France both had their national commitments, and any recalcitrant religious minority— whether the Protestants in the Auvergne, or the Catholics in Ireland—was a convenient object of condemnation and punishment in response to any perceived threat from the other nation.

The new European system of states, built around absolute claims to nationhood, needed political balance not just in its diplomatic structure: even more, it depended on stable systems of social relations within each nation. Given a historical situation in which feudalism could no longer provide a general mode of social organization, fashioning the new system of Nation-States meant inventing a new kind of *class* society. The full significance of this change can easily be misunderstood. On the one hand, we must avoid focussing exclusively on economic relations among these "classes": they are important, but only part of the story. On the other hand, we must not treat the 17th-century idea of social *class* as carrying into a new historical period the idea of *rank* or *degree* already familiar in medieval feudal society.

There are deep differences between these ideas. In medieval times, the Sovereign gave subjects who already belonged to the "nobility"—or whom he raised to it—grants of land, or titles of higher or lower degree. For most people, however, the central question was not a horizontal but a vertical one, i.e., the question of one's point of attachment to a network of fealty, of Master and Man: "Who is your Master? Whose Man are you?" In medieval society, the lines of division cut *vertically:* the population was divided into the groups of families and villages that owed duties to a given noble family. Within those groups some persons or families were closer to the nobles, and others had humbler occupations. But, if only for lack of transport, there was no opportunity for countrywide "solidarity" to de-velop among skilled craftsmen or farm laborers *as such.* In the 16th and 17th centuries, the clear threat to social stability and loyalty was seen as the growing number of "masterless men": not merely vagrants, but those people (e.g., printers and charcoal burners) whose ways of life did not attach them securely to the vertical chains of reciprocal obligation that had been constitutive of traditional society.

A strong sense of the "nation" *qua* "nation" began to take shape only in the 16th century, once again in Britain and France. For the first time, the monarch was thought of as holding power, not as the legal possessor of his inherited feudal domains, but as an emblem of the nation or people. King Henri IV of France was remembered with affection for having tried to unite, and serve the interests of the French—as a people and a nation. Queen Elizabeth was similarly valued for her rhetorical ability to speak as the embodiment of England. Conversely, fifty years later in England, the regicides defended their execution of Charles I by claiming that his autocratic, pro-Catholic policies betrayed the people and the nation it was his duty to serve. (This shift in the locus of sovereignty from the person of the Head of State to the "nation" or "people" was a crucial step toward the sovereign "constitution" of the United States.)

Within the nation-states that developed after 1650, merchants and traders had positions of power alongside, and often equal to, those of the traditional landed gentry. With wider literacy and social awareness, people were less concerned with local questions about feudal relations, and more conscious of their positions within the structure of the entire nation. In 1611, Donne rightly saw *feudal* loyalties as "things forgot": after 1650, the fabric of society was strengthened, not by returning to that largely irrelevant feudalism, but by reinforcing its *class* structure. In this way, older assumptions about loyalty to the local family—

> God bless the Squire and his relations,
> and keep us in our proper stations—

yielded to a more refined perception of people's places within a spectrum of "upper", "middle", and "lower" classes—"better or worse kinds of men", and "higher or lower orders". So, for the first time, people who belonged on each of these many levels were clearly seen as collectively forming a given *horizontal* "social class".

On the domestic as on the diplomatic front, then, the key word was *stability*. Having won independence from the Spanish Habsburgs in the late 16th century, Holland kept its relative tranquility and prosperity for most of the 17th century: if all the European powers had been as prudent or fortunate, the standard account of Modernity might have had some substance. Quite aside from the German tragedy, however, all the major European powers experienced a generation of turmoil and confusion; and after 1650 it was more than time to develop a new notion of the *polis*—of the principles governing relations among individuals and communities in the nation-state. Against this background, the loss of "cosmopolis" that John Donne keenly lamented was in due course made good. Current assumptions about the conditions of social order and stability provided a matrix for parallel ideas about nature, and the new "world picture" that carried conviction after 1700 treated nature and society as being twin, and equally rational, "orders."

After the catastrophic times from 1618 to 1655, a new and self-maintaining social order was gradually established. One thing helped the respectable oligarchy to take the lead in this reconstruction: this, we shall see, was the evolution of a new Cosmopolis, in which the divinely created Order of Nature and the humanly created Order of Society were once again seen as illuminating one another. Looking back, we may find the 18th-century demand for stable and predictable social relations too rigid, and see it as turning the ideal of stability into a Baconian "idol". (New ideas about Nature were in danger of going the same way.) With the social crisis of the 17th century in recent memory, however, preachers at that time were tempted to adopt the familiar rhetorical commonplace of "lest worst befall", caricatured in Hilaire Belloc's couplet that exhorts the child

> Always to keep hold of Nurse,
> For fear of meeting something worse.

1660–1720: Leibniz Discovers Ecumenism

The social reconstruction of late 17th-century Europe had posed two problems: that of restoring communication between nations which had for long been divided in theological views and religious loyalties, and that of rebuilding stable and coherent social relations among people to whose lives feudal relations were no longer relevant. Both these tasks had intellectual counterparts. For half a century, the breakdown in diplomatic and theological communication had been rationalized as a consequence of irresoluble religious antagonisms. From the 1650s on, honest serious-minded people from both sides of the barricades tried to hammer out mutually acceptable modes of discussion that would enable them to circumvent, if not overcome, their earlier doctrinal differences. After 1660, similarly, the development of new ideas of social structure placed the highest priority on social stability. This development, too, went hand-in-hand with the evolution of a stable vision of Nature.

Few historians of philosophy write of Leibniz's views on the need for a "principle of sufficient reason" in terms that show a proper feeling for the context of his work: only in the last few years have historians of science placed the ideas of Isaac Newton (even more, the contemporary reception of Newton's ideas) into the social or historical situation. In writing of Leibniz and Newton as much as Descartes, their custom is to "de-contextualize" their ideas and arguments, assuming that the relevant framework for studying them is a "timeless dialogue" among the great minds of the past. In both respects, there is as much to learn about the history of science and philosophy by "recontextualizing" the scientific and philosophical debates of the time (so relating them to the crucial historical developments of those years) as we learned about the virtues of the Euclidean model of theory, or about the reasons for the rejection of practical philosophy in favor of a program of philosophical "theory" and "certainty."

Once again, indications of such contextual relevance are not hard to find, if we only look for them. Writing as he did, at the low point in the Thirty Years' War, Descartes had good reason to understand the damage that the intellectual divisions in Christianity had done to humanity, and he dreamed of an ideal *method,* giving a knowledge that could transcend those divisions. Writing amidst the ruins left by the same war, Leibniz saw a deeper source of war and conflict in the multiplicity of languages and cultures, and dreamed of an ideal *language* that could be learned and understood by people of any country, culture, or religion. How, then, did he conceive of this dream? And is there any evidence that he meant it to address the urgent practical needs of his time?

From 1650 on, the task of reestablishing communication between countries on opposite sides in the worst of religious wars was an urgent political task, but it was never *only* that. The Jesuits and Calvinists, the Jansenists and Lutherans, Ferdinand in Vienna and Gustavus Adolphus in Stockholm, were involved in disastrous political confrontation; but each party believed that, at bottom, the dispute was one about basic doctrines in which their side possessed the Truth. By 1648, Europeans no longer had the spirit to go on fighting about doctrines; but the deeper dispute remained. Failing a new way of mediating it, it seemed, nothing could prevent the religious wars from starting up again, as soon as all those involved recovered their energy and enthusiasm.

Behind those political problems, however, there had been a deeper, intellectual issue. Descartes hoped that a rational method would provide a certainty that circumvented religious oppositions. Now, the need was to cash in on that promise, by getting people from the two religious camps to sit down together in a spirit of openness and develop an understanding of basic issues: agreeing on things about which there was little dispute, and isolating—even, dissolving away—those differences for which such a convergence of views was impracticable. In reading the philosophical response to the disasters of the early 17th century, the crucial figures were

Descartes and Donne: for the period after the Thirty Years' War, it is helpful to consider, rather, the life and career of Gottfried Wilhelm, Freiherr von Leibniz.

Leibniz was born in 1646, two years before the Peace of Westphalia. Growing up in Leipzig, where his father had been the professor of moral philosophy, he initially wrote on jurisprudence and philosophy of law, and started on a career in diplomacy, joining a mission to Paris in 1672. There, he found a group of mathematicians and scholars who fueled his existing enthusiasm for a logical analysis of thought (*ars combinatoria*) on which he had already written in 1666. From then on, Leibniz's life is divided between intellectual and practical affairs: indeed, he scarcely seems to distinguish them. Whatever problems come to his attention, he addresses them with analytic exactitude, and the vision of a universal language is his panacea for both political and theological ills. He was not alone in 17th-century Europe in this dream. The vision was shared by philosophers and scientists in many countries, not least the founders of the Royal Society of London; but we associate it specially with the name of Leibniz, and for good reason.

The case of Leibniz gives us some clues to the underlying things at stake for many of those who dreamed this same dream. As a boy, Leibniz tells us, he conceived of what he called a *characteristica universalis*—or "universal system of characters"—that would be able to "express all our thoughts". Such a system, he declared,

> will constitute a new language which can be written and spoken. This language will be very difficult to construct, but very easy to learn. It will be quickly accepted by everybody on account of its great utility and its surprising facility, and it will serve wonderfully in communication among various peoples.

Was Leibniz here anticipating the invention of an artificial language like Esperanto or Volapuk? There is more to it for him. True, one goal of his new language was to win speakers and hearers from all countries, and so overcome international misunderstanding; but it was not meant just to serve as a universal Creole or Pidgin. Instead, it would gain adherents by capturing the processes of rational thought and perception, and providing a way of comparing and exchanging experiences in terms undistorted by existing linguistic conventions. With this aim, Leibniz's language made use of a mathematical symbolism which (in his view) expressed *thoughts*

> as definitely and exactly as arithmetic expresses *numbers* or geometrical analysis expresses *lines*.

A universal language based on such a symbolism, Leibniz concluded, would not only have perspicuous meanings, so that people from different countries could *talk* together with shared understanding. It would also embody and codify all the valid modes of argument, so that people with different intellectual backgrounds could *reason* together without fear of confusion or error. His language was, thus, not only a practical method of promoting international understanding: it would also be "the greatest instrument of reason." And, throughout the rest of his long active career, Leibniz kept working at his project for this universal language, in which shared meanings and common rationality were guaranteed from the start. His research took him in a dozen directions. It led him to think up the infinitesimal calculus, to study the ideograms of Chinese, and to explore the divinatory techniques of the *I Ching*.

If we ask why Leibniz pursued this project so assiduously, and why, in the 1670s and '80s, the project of developing an ideal language was the topic of the hour for others as well, these questions once again deserve historical answers. Leibniz did not work at mathematics or metaphysics merely for their own interest: for him, they were also a means to more practical ends. His German origins and his experience as a diplomat lent encouragement to his lifelong mission as a theological "ecumenist." For 17th-century readers, mathematics and theology were not as distinct and separate as they tend to be today. When all the countries of Europe had a problem accommodating people of different religions, and the political and intellectual conditions of toleration were central to all of John Locke's work, the issue was even more urgent for Leibniz. Across Germany, the previous generation saw prosperous cities destroyed: some 35 percent of the country's population was slaughtered to the greater glory of a Calvinist, Lutheran, or Catholic God. How could a man with Leibniz's background and diplomatic contacts avoid asking how one might prevent a recurrence of this catastrophe? In fact, he hoped to create the practical conditions for renewing rational dialogue between the two theological camps, and gave much thought to the criteria relevant in such a debate. Against the backdrop of the ruined Germany of the 1670s, there was a special *actualité* to the dream of a *characteristica universalis,* to "serve wonderfully in communication among various peoples".

For some thirty years, Leibniz kept up a steady flow of letters to colleagues on both sides of the theological gulf. He set himself the goal of bringing together representatives of the opposed camps, in a meeting at which they could work their way toward a common understanding of the central and indispensable ideas of Christianity, and set aside issues over which a diversity of opinions must be accepted. He even tried to enlist the

French Catholic historian, Bishop Bossuet, in the noble work of theological reconciliation. But, as things turned out, Bossuet would not correspond with Leibniz on quite the same equal basis, or with quite the same shared expectations: he was less interested in participating in discussions that threatened to dilute sound Catholic doctrine than he was in discovering on what terms the heretic, Gottfried Wilhelm Leibniz, might save his soul by converting to Catholicism. The critical exchange of letters thus aborted, and Leibniz lost his last hope of organizing an effective ecumenical congress.

If Leibniz had persuaded the rival theologians to sit down together, what would they have discussed? The task he saw was to locate shared elements in all the rival bodies of doctrine, and use them to define the minimum system of beliefs that theologians from all Churches might recognize as grounded on "sufficient reason." He was not ready to admit that God might have placed humanity in an irreducibly mysterious world; and he was quick to condemn any suggestion that the world might be less than completely intelligible to careful reasoning by clear-headed humans. At times, indeed, he appealed to his "principle of sufficient reason" in a near-positivist way, to sift serious hypotheses from those that were meaningless. (Treating *space* as separate from *matter* led into nonsense, in his view, because it entailed that, at the Creation, God had to decide whether to create the Universe just where he did, or two hundred paces to the left. The very idea of such a "decision" was a sheer linguistic confusion, with no basis in experience: it was something a rationally well formed language had no terms to express, and so it could not be *said.*) The project for a *characteristica universalis* was never meant only as an "instrument of Reason" for use among philosophers with abstract philosophical purposes. Aside from its possible utility in diplomatic negotiations and other international exchanges, it would also help to heal the wounds in the body of Christian Europe. What *odium theologicum* had severed during the first half of the 17th century, a "universal language" might bind together again in the second half.

It was a noble dream, but a dream nonetheless. As we can now see, it rested upon two unrealizable assumptions: first, that the characters in such a perfect language could "express our thoughts" without any need for conventional agreements on their meanings; secondly that, by substituting this artificial language for the natural languages of different countries, their people might avoid the breakdowns in communication that fueled the Religious Wars. Unfortunately, there was and is no way of doing what Leibniz hoped to do: viz., to *equate* the private "thoughts" of people from different cultures, nations, *Lebensformen,* or language communities in wholly non-arbitrary ways. Nor, absent some divinely assured "providential harmony", can we *guarantee in advance* that the same "thoughts" are spontaneously evoked in people from different cultures when placed in similar situations. The project of constructing a universal language is not difficult, as Leibniz concedes: it is downright impossible. It assumes that the modes of life and concepts of people in all cultures are similar enough to yield the same "ideal languages" as *their end products:* that is, it assumes at the outset just what the enterprise was initially supposed to guarantee as *its final outcome.* Without independent assurance that different peoples perceive and interpret their experiences in sufficiently similar ways—as Leibniz said, that they "have the same thoughts"—there is no agreement about the "meanings" of the terms in our artificial language: without such prior agreement, there is no subsequent guarantee of mutual intelligibility.

How did Leibniz's historical experience influence his philosophical agenda? To that question, different people again give different answers. We may isolate Leibniz's metaphysics from its historical context, and ask about its coherence and plausibility, so preserving the detachment on which the standard histories of philosophy rely. Alternatively, we can view Leibniz as a German intellectual who accepted his responsibility to do whatever he could do to remedy the situation of Europe in his time; and this means looking to see how his research program was matched to the urgent tasks of that time. With Leibniz (as it turns out) a detached, decontextualized reading is even harder to sustain than with Descartes. The very way he threw himself into political correspondence, pursued a career in several German courts, and set himself to develop his lines of communication with scholars in all the countries of Europe, confirms that he, even more than René Descartes, was concerned with the pressing political and social tasks imposed by the demands of post-war reconstruction.

In the late 17th century, the problem of language was the tip of an iceberg, and the dream of an exact language had more than an *intellectual* stake. Similar problems face Europe today, though they have less to do with religious toleration than they do with cultural and racial diversity. (What status can a Turkish *Gastarbeiter* achieve in West Germany? Can a common European citizenship be reconciled with the currency of a dozen languages and cultures?) In its way, the project of using new tools of "communication and reasoning among various peoples" to transcend such cultural misunderstanding and diversity is as *actuel* for Europeans today as it was for Leibniz in 1675. As they reach 1990, they need not give up their own *langue française* or *deutsche Sprache, Svensk,* or English for a *characteristica universalis* constructed on a purely mathematical model, at least in everyday life. In business as in air traffic control, Esperanto is dead: the only serious question is, "Will Japanese ever undermine the dominance of English?"

On other levels, e.g., in debates about television and computer links between different countries, Leibniz's project remains alive. What will be the international standard for the transmission of television signals? Will worldwide computer networks use operating systems designed by IBM or Xerox, Toshiba or Machines Bull? Leibniz rightly saw Chinese as a special challenge: ideograms pose notorious problems in the design of computer software. In practical terms (we may thus say) the people with best claim to be today's legitimate heirs to Leibniz's program are the information engineers. But the bright aims of Leibniz's dream still face the same obstacles. Television and computers project across national boundaries not just "universal ideas" and "error-free reasoning", but also cultural *conflict* and international *mis*understanding. In 1677, the thirty-year-old Leibniz wrote about his plan in grandiose terms:

> I dare say that this is the highest effort of the human mind; and, when the project is accomplished, it will simply be up to humans to be happy, since they will have an instrument that exalts the reason no less than the telescope perfects our vision.

We resonate to an enthusiast's ideals, but we note that their expression is confused. Now, as 300 years ago, no technical system or procedure can guarantee its own humane or rational application. It is one thing to *perfect* an instrument, but it is quite another to make sure that it is only *put to use* in ways that are just, virtuous and rational.

The three dreams of the Rationalists thus turn out to be aspects of a larger dream. The dreams of a rational method, a unified science, and an exact language, unite into a single project. All of them are designed to "purify" the operations of human reason, by decontextualizing them: i.e., by divorcing them from the details of particular historical and cultural situations. Like Leibniz's universal language, the Scientific Revolution was, accordingly, Janus-faced. The New Science was meant to be both "mathematical and experimental"; but it was left unclear how these two leading features of the new method (its mathematical structure, and its experiential basis) dovetailed. This unclarity began as an oversight, but it soon became deliberate. The victory of Rationalism was regarded as confirming

Pythagoras' insight that any theory of mathematical power and elegance will have practical application in human experience.

In the three hundred years after 1660, the natural sciences did not march along a royal road, defined by a rational method. They moved in a zigzag, alternating the rationalist methods of Newton's mathematics and the empiricist methods of Bacon's naturalism. The triumph of Newtonian physics was, thus, a vote for theoretical cosmology, not for practical dividends; and the *ideas* of Newtonian theory were shaped by a concern for intellectual coherence with a respectable picture of God's material creation, as obeying Divine laws. This view too ignored the message of 16th-century humanism. The growth of scientific ideas was separated from concern with practical fruits, and scientific refinement of "pure" ideas was treated as distinct from the technical exploitation of "applied" techniques. Many people found Francis Bacon's concern with "human goods" vulgar, or even sinful: it was enough for scientists to find the laws ruling natural phenomena, the better to glorify God, who first created Nature. Using our understanding of Nature to increase comfort, or to reduce pain, was secondary to the central spiritual goal of Science. Rejecting in both method and spirit Bacon's vision of a humanly fruitful science, Descartes and Newton set out to build mathematical structures, and looked to Science for theological, not technological, dividends.

To understand why the Rationalists' threefold dream proved a dream, indeed, we may recall some maxims that capture the central contrasts. No formalism can interpret itself; No system can validate itself; No theory can exemplify itself; No formal language can predetermine its own meanings; No science can forecast just what technology will prove of human value. In facing problems about the use of new knowledge for human good, we may ignore the ideal of intellectual exactitude, with its idolization of geometrical proof and certainty. Instead, we must try to recapture the practical modesty of the humanists, which let them live free of anxiety, despite uncertainty, ambiguity, and pluralism.

1660–1720: Newton and the New Cosmopolis

Restoring the dialogue among the nation-states of Europe was only a first step. The second was to build up a body of knowledge that would carry conviction with *savants* of different countries and religions, and support a shared world view: exploring the possibility of a universal language was a preliminary to establishing such a shared view of nature and humanity. Leibniz devoted his prodigious enthusiasm and energy to this task, too; but in the long run the greater contribution was made by a very different man, Leibniz's English rival, Isaac Newton.

Leibniz's rationalism was subject to the same limitations as that of Descartes. It is one thing to demonstrate we "know for certain" that our self awareness (*je pense* . . .) necessitates, or presupposes, our existence (. . . *donc je suis*); but Descartes was not happy to rest with that insight. He also hoped for a decipherment of physical nature that came as close to certainty as the nature of things allowed. With Euclid as his example, he looked for clear, distinct ideas of *matter, motion,* and other dynamical quantities, so as to extend the geometrical method to cover mechanics as well. (If he succeeded, might not physics simply prove to be "geometry in motion"?) But it was not enough for the axioms of a dynamical system to be "clear and distinct". In the *Discourse,* Descartes argues that, like a house designed by a single architect, a system of natural philosophy can be fully convincing only if it is produced by a single mind. For Newton in his *Mathematical Principles of Natural Philosophy,* by contrast, the "axioms or laws of motion" do not rest on the work of any single theorist: in his definitions of *force, motion,* and *mass,* he appeals to collectively known facts about the motion of pendulums or buckets of water, and about the fluctuations in the sidereal calendar. In all this, Newton relied on other people's work, and he inaugurated the practice of collaborative research that has now lasted some three hundred years.

With Leibniz, the difficulty was similar. Working out the principles of a "universal language" is all very well; but it is also necessary to ask what is said in that language that scholars in all countries can accept. Once again, Leibniz assumed that any legitimate theory can be confirmed or rejected on grounds of "rational conceivability." He himself found the ideas of *atoms,* and of a *vacuum,* rationally repugnant, as placing limits on God's power. Limiting the subdivision of matter to atoms of a given minimum size was, in his eyes, restricting the possibilities of Creation needlessly, arbitrarily, and irrationally. Similarly, any region of Space was for him the locus of a physical substance of some kind. Even if nothing were present but a gravitational field, Space was not (by his lights) empty.

By 1710, several hypotheses were available to explain the motion of the planets, heat, light, magnetism, bodily cohesion, and a dozen other physical phenomena. Newton's account, which treated the interplanetary space as effectively empty, gained support in England. But, in France, most thinkers felt that the objections to "totally empty space" had weight, and favored Descartes' theory of an interplanetary ether, with vortices carrying the planets around the sun. For his part, Leibniz took seriously only a system of natural philosophy that met his *a priori* objections. His ecumenical procedure was a useful way to unravel issues over which Catholic and Protestant theology had been at odds, but he also hoped to use it to decide what theory best explains the elliptical orbits of the planets, and the acceleration of falling bodies.

Despite these differences, however, all these theories were framed within limits set by a deeper set of conceptual assumptions, over which there was less disagreement. That underlying framework of assumptions is what we will look at next, since here the renewal of cosmopolis was at last a serious issue. Between 1660 and 1720, few thinkers were *only* interested in accounting for mechanical phenomena in the physical world. For most people, just as much intellectual underpinning was required for the new patterns of social practice, and associated ideas about the *polis*. As a result, enticing new analogies entered social and political thought: if, from now on, "stability" was the chief virtue of social organization, was it not possible to organize political ideas about *Society* along the same lines as scientific ideas about *Nature*? Could not the idea of social order, as much as that of order in nature, be modeled on the "systems" of mathematics and formal logic?

The idea that society is a formal "system" of agents or institutions has exerted a major influence on the modern world. It was hinted at by Hugo Grotius (as we saw) in 1625, even before Descartes published; but its detailed content, and underlying assumptions, only took on definitive shape later in the 17th century. At this point, the Cartesian division of matter from mind, causes from reasons, and nature from humanity, was endorsed and continued by Isaac Newton, and ceased to be of concern to natural philosophers alone. From then on, it played a major role in social and political thought as well.

———————————

At the base of Descartes' epistemology lay the distinction between the *rational freedom* of moral or intellectual decision in the human world of thought and action, and the *causal necessity* of mechanical processes in the natural world of physical phenomena. This distinction cut so deep that, in Descartes' eyes, it justified separating the two "substances" of mind and matter; and his notorious "Mind-Body dichotomy" brought in its train a series of related dichotomies. An argument that began by cutting rationality off from causality thus ended by separating the world of (rational) human experience from the world of (mechanical) natural phenomena.

After 1660, there developed an overall framework of ideas about humanity and nature, rational mind and causal matter, that gained the standing of "common sense": for the next 100, 150, or 200 years, the main timbers of this framework of ideas and beliefs were rarely called in question. They were spoken of as "allowed by all men" or "standing to reason", and they were seen as needing no further justification than that. Whatever shortcomings they may have today, from 1700 on they were taken to "go without saying"; and, in practice, they often went unsaid. Between them, they defined a system of ideas that we may refer to as the Modern world view, or the "framework of Modernity." We may begin by listing the chief elements (or "timbers") that went into this framework. Then, we may ask about their intellectual status: notably, on what experiential or other basis they rested.

The chief girder in this framework of Modernity, to which all the other parts were connected, was the Cartesian dichotomy. The more the extent to which natural phenomena were explained in mechanical terms, as produced by cosmic clockwork, the more (by contrast) the affairs of humanity were allotted to a distinct sphere. The sharpness of this separation was new, and it is worth noticing how Descartes and Newton took it, and how their successors interpreted it. While it divides the modern framework both from Renaissance humanism and from the late 20th-century world view, it was seen around 1700 as having indispensable merits.

As such, it was taken to justify a dozen further dichotomies. To summarize: human actions and experiences were *mental* or spontaneous outcomes of reasoning; they were performed, willingly and creatively; and they were active and productive. Physical phenomena and natural processes, by contrast, involved brute matter and were *material:* they were mechanical, repetitive, predictable effects of causes; they merely happened; and matter in itself was passive and inert. Thus the contrast between reasons and causes turned into an outright divorce, and other dichotomies—mental *vs.* material, actions *vs.* phenomena, performances *vs.* happenings, thoughts *vs.* objects, voluntary *vs.* mechanical, active *vs.* passive, creative *vs.* repetitive—followed easily enough.

No one denied that human beings *act within* the natural world, or that collective human activities change the face of nature. But in 1700 the scale and significance of these interactions could still be minimized. Thought must influence the body's physiological processes at some point in the brain: maybe (Descartes suggested) in the pineal gland, which is centrally placed and has no other clear function. Fifty years on, such a conjecture was general doctrine: To Newton, it was evident that mental experience and activity take place within an Inner Theatre (or *sensorium commune*) to which the sensory nerves bring "ideas" from the peripheral receptors and from which, in turn, motor nerves carry the "commands" of the will back to the muscles. So (it seemed) the Mind, inhabiting the world of rationality and freedom but not wholly insulated from a world of causal automatism, affected the Body and the World "from outside". As for collective human action, since Nature was not yet viewed as an ecological network of biological systems in which the life of Humanity was just one more causal influence, human actions did not yet seem to affect the workings of nature significantly. Rather, nature was still a background or stage setting on which the human drama was being played out; and, since stage actors dismantle the scenery halfway through a play only in high comedy or as dramatic irony, so presumably this drama would run its course without changing the basic makeup of nature. This belief was bolstered by the short Biblical time scale in which the framework was conceived: with only a few thousand years available, there was little room for the collective activities of humanity to have major effects on the large-scale structure of nature.

The principal elements, or timbers, of the Modern Framework divide into two groups, reflecting this initial division of Nature from Humanity. We may formulate the dozen or so basic doctrines, and discuss them here in turn. On the Nature side of the division, we find half a dozen beliefs:

Nature is governed by fixed laws set up at the creation;
The basic structure of Nature was established only a few thousand years back;
The objects of physical nature are composed of inert matter;
So, physical objects and processes do not think;
At the creation, God combined natural objects into stable and hierarchical systems of "higher" and "lower" things;
Like "action" in society, "motion" in nature flows downward, from the "higher" creatures to the "lower" ones.

On the Humanity side, we find half-a-dozen similar beliefs:

The "human" thing about humanity is its capacity for rational thought or action;
Rationality and causality follow different rules;
Since thought and action do not take place causally, actions cannot be explained by any causal science of psychology;
Human beings can establish stable systems in society, like the physical systems in nature;
So, humans live mixed lives, part rational and part causal: as creatures of Reason, their lives are intellectual or spiritual, as creatures of Emotion, they are bodily or carnal;

Emotion typically frustrates and distorts the work of Reason; so the human reason is to be trusted and encouraged, while the emotions are to be distrusted and restrained.

Nature is governed by Fixed Laws set up at the Creation.   The changes and caprices of human thought and conduct set them apart from the causal phenomena of physics, so a way was open to treat nature as fixed in static, mechanical, repetitive, and unchanging patterns laid down by God at the Creation. In the late 20th century, the phrase "laws of nature" has lost its theological overtones, and means little more than "regularities." But, in 1700, the "laws of nature" were still a material expression of God's Will and Wisdom for the world: in revealing the laws by which nature operates, scientists saw themselves as doing God's work—even reading His mind.

Yet, this idea of a stable Nature governed by divine laws was novel. Early in the 17th century, educated Europeans viewed the lunar craters observed by Galileo, the occurrence of astronomical *novas,* and even the deterioration of the English climate, as signs of a decay in nature that presaged the End of the World. On the new view, all natural phenomena were natural effects of mechanical causes, and were not read as "omens"—let alone as warnings of Apocalypse. In natural philosophy as in other fields, the world picture changes rapidly. In 1590, skeptics still doubted whether humans can find universal regularities in nature; by 1640, nature was in irremediable decay: but, by 1700, the changeover to the "law-governed" picture of a stable cosmos was complete.

The structure of Nature was established a few thousand years ago.   This belief confirmed a traditional Christian view of *human* history, which had a temporal, dramatic element, as distinct from *natural* history, which was not "historical" in the modern sense. Natural history was the concern of "naturalists", whose work overlapped systematic biology and taxonomy more than it did historical sciences like evolutionary biology: only in 1859 did Charles Darwin finally open a door out of natural history into the history of nature. Within the Newtonian world view, the only "historical" events affecting Nature comprised the initial Creation, and a series of later cyclical processes. How long ago did the Creation occur? This was not generally agreed upon. If God had imposed unchanging repetitive patterns on natural processes, the present state of Nature could provide no conclusive evidence of its age. Many people, relying on literal-minded readings of the Bible, calculated that the present Dispensation had begun 5,600 years ago. Others doubted if scholars could ever throw light on its date—"No Vestige of a Beginning," as James Hutton was later to declare, "No Prospect of an End." Taking the Bible as a reliable record of human history, they still hesitated to look in it for exact dates of the Beginning and End of the World.

In any event, nothing in the new view forbade one to expand the time-scale of the past, in the light of fresh evidence. The Biblical chronology was set aside first in astronomy, next in geology and paleontology, last in historical zoology. It was two hundred years before scientists could juggle with millions, let alone thousands of millions of years, as they do now; but, by 1755, Kant could write about cosmic history in speculative Newtonian terms, without giving any sign that he was hemmed in by the demands of Scripture. When people inquired into the development of the natural order, however, they still treated the question in different terms from those applicable to human history. Nature presumably developed as a result of causal, material or mechanical processes. human history was a record of the practical aims, moral decisions and rational methods of human agents. The *rational* history of humanity and the *causal* history of nature thus remained, in crucial respects, distinct topics of inquiry until well into the 20th century.

The material substance of physical nature is essentially inert.   One particular belief was central to the new view. Material objects could not put themselves in motion, or initiate changes spontaneously. Motion and change were the products of rational agency, which was the monopoly of *conscious beings:* primarily God, but also human beings, in using the mental abilities that God gave them. God was thus the ultimate source of change both in the moral realm, through the rational actions of human beings, and in the material realm, through the motions that He had originally set going, and had sustained up to the present era.

For 17th-century natural philosophers, physical nature was made up of bare "extension" or brute "masses." Without the conscious, rational intervention of their Creator, material things would be merely passive. In physics, the motions exchanged between material objects on contact or collision were Divinely initiated; and, without any intervening agency, there could—despite the signs of electricity, gravitation, and magnetism—be no *action at a distance.* The question, "How does gravity operate?", was thus taken to mean, "What divinely instituted agency or mechanism transmits motion from an attracting to an attracted body?" About this, there were again two opinions. Leibniz and Descartes assumed that the Space between massive objects is filled with matter of a more tenuous kind: Newton saw "fields" as the evidence of God's continued action in Nature. Neither party, however, accepted "action at a distance" as a real possibility: as they agreed, "A Body cannot *act* where it *is* not."

Physical objects and processes cannot think or reason. From the assumed inertness of all material things there began a further dispute that has continued to our day. The basic question was, "Does Matter have a potential for Thought?"; or else, put in today's terms, "Can Machines think?" If all matter is inert, so that material systems interact in purely causal ways, *immaterial* agencies (whether mental or spiritual) are alone equipped to think. After 1700, the idea that matter in a sufficiently complex organization, as in a computer, could perform intellectual procedures was regarded as inconceivable. "Thinking is not mechanical, so no machine can think": the very phrase "thinking machine" became a contradiction in terms. A heretical minority (including John Locke) tried to keep the issue partly open, but the idea of thinking matter for a long time remained generally heterodox.

Even the idea of living machines met hostility. Since vital activity is goal-directed and functional in ways that were inconsistent with a narrowly mechanistic view of Nature, those writers who accounted for the operations of physiological systems mechanically were criticized as violently as those who did so for mental activity. Looking back, we may find the point ironical. Today, scientists reject "vitalist" or "mentalist" appeals to *immaterial* agencies to explain life and thought as hangovers from the Middle Ages. Yet, far from those two positions being medieval relics, they were forced on 17th- and 18th-century science for the first time, by the need to fill gaps left by the accepted definition of "matter" and "machines"; and, as such, they were purely modern novelties.

At the Creation, God combined natural objects into stable systems. The new picture of nature also embodied the *stability* that was so important in late 17th-century thought. The prime—and best analyzed—example of a Divinely created system was the solar system: there, the Sun "ruled" the planets by keeping them in their stable orbits. In his queries, Newton argued that all functional systems in the natural world (the physiological system of the body, as much as elementary mechanical systems) testify to the creative wisdom of God.

Higher and lower things are linked so that motion in nature, and action in society, flow from "higher" to "lower" creatures. The systems of Nature and Society also exemplified the role of *hierarchy* in 17th- and 18th-century thought. Passive and material bodies were lower in the natural hierarchy:

active and vital ones were higher. The basest material things had no power to move themselves, or to transmit motion, unless they obtained this power from other "higher" sources. This was true within the natural realm, where living and thinking beings influence the motions of material objects, and within the social realm, where differences of status apparently determine who has the authority to control the actions of whom. At this point, Newton, Descartes, and Leibniz again display significant disagreements. Descartes denies that God ever intervenes actively in the material world, and Leibniz later agrees with him, claiming that God acts at the present time, not through mechanical interventions in nature, but by acts of grace directed toward individual human beings. Newton held the opposite opinion. In his view, only the basic Particles of Matter are absolutely inert, and incapable of any spontaneous action: non-material agencies like electricity, magnetism, and gravitation are vehicles of Divine Action in Nature, by which brute matter is maintained in harmonious, functional systems. Either position was consistent with the presuppositions of the new cosmopolis: none of the protagonists doubted that the final source of activity in the world is God: the highest, most powerful, "self-moving" Agent in Nature.

On the other side of the Cartesian dichotomy lay the human world: there too, half-a-dozen assumptions which "went without saying" set the limits within which "modern" thinkers were free to speculate.

The essence of Humanity is the capacity for rational thought and action. Following Descartes, Newton took "experience" to mean the totality of sensory inputs that enter the Inner Theatre of the conscious mind, and the logical operations performed upon them during rational deliberation. All this occurs (Descartes implies) in an "unextended" realm of thought, locally associated with—but not causally dependent on—physiological mechanisms in the brain. The nature of this Mind/Brain interaction was enigmatic from the start: for those few scientists who still follow a Cartesian road, e.g. John Eccles, it remains no less enigmatic today. But, from the 17th century on, this was a price that the natural philosophers were ready to pay, to protect the elbowroom required by rational humans in the clockwork world of causal nature, if they were to be free to think and act for themselves.

There can be no science of psychology. This second presupposition followed closely on the first. From René Descartes in 1640, up to Immanuel

Kant in 1780, the subject matter of scientific inquiry is composed of material objects, physical processes, and causal mechanisms: all truly scientific concerns are on the natural side of the fence. Human thought, consciousness, and experience follow a more or less rational or logical course: they are not trapped into causal regularities, so there is nothing in them for "scientists" to study. About human thoughts and actions, the questions to ask are never of the form, "How do they [causally] *happen?*", but rather, "How well or badly are they [rationally] *performed?*" The mental experience of humanity is distinct from the mechanisms of material nature, and engages it only tangentially in, for example, the pineal gland. The generalizations required to explain human experience thus come, not from natural science, but from logic or ethics. Only in the 19th century did German post-Kantian scientists demolish the intellectual barrier between natural science and logic and ethics, as they sought to give rational accounts of the operations of the Mind, and explored neurology and psychophysiology as a source of causal explanations of the mechanisms of the Body.

Human beings also have collective power to establish "social systems." For 17th- and 18th-century thinkers, politics was not the science of social causality, but an exercise in collective logic. The work of social institutions, like the action of individual thinkers, does not just *happen*: it is planned and executed, either well or badly. How can human beings create social systems? The new framework left open all of the options familiar from antiquity: not least, that of treating natural systems like the planetary system as templates for social systems.

Humans are mixed beings—in part rational, in part causal.   Though rationality is the essence of humanity, it is not the sole fact about human experience. Daily experience shows that the working of the rational Mind can be distorted by the causal imperatives of the Body. The philosopher sits down to write, but is overcome by sleep; the attorney returns to Court, but his lunchtime cocktail clouds his judgment; the convalescent worries about the future, but his medical condition leaves him excessively pessimistic. Human life, even "mental" life, is subject in practice to physiological influences, which logic does not encompass. Alexander Pope's *Essay on Man* comments on the problems created by this "mixed nature" in a famous passage:

> Placed on this isthmus of a middle state,
> A being darkly wise, and rudely great: . . .

[Man] hangs between; in doubt to act, or rest,
In doubt to deem himself a god, or beast;
In doubt his mind or body to prefer,
Born but to die, and reasoning but to err;
Alike in ignorance, his reason such,
Whether he thinks too little, or too much:
Chaos of thought and passion all confused; . . .
Sole judge of truth, in endless error hurled:
The glory, jest, and riddle of the world!

Reason is mental (or spiritual), Emotion is bodily (or carnal).   The standard solution to Pope's puzzle is that proposed in Descartes' *Treatise of the Passions*. The experience of being "at the mercy of one's emotions" is that of having rationality overpowered by the causal powers of Body. We may leave aside the theological overtones of this doctrine: for reasons to be considered shortly, late 17th- and 18th-century thinkers found that the equation of the *emotions* with the *bodily* ("base" and "material") aspect of our humanity was powerful. Praise of reason and scorn for emotion were not only texts for 200 years of sermons: they were also the basis for a whole approach to moral education and social order.

The Emotions frustrate or distort Reason.   The irrational and damaging effects of the emotions were to be seen both in the lives of human individuals, in sickness or sleep, intoxication or anger, and in the collective lives of human beings, whose "good sense" might be overridden by emotions like enthusiasm and envy, so that the structure of the established social order broke down or was upset. In either case, the distrust of human feelings still familiar to many of us in the late 20th century won an established place among respectable people in both Europe and America, so reinforcing the Cartesian, or *calculative* idea of "rationality."

Not all of these dozen-odd assumptions were fully interdependent, or rigidly entailed by the underlying separation of Humanity from Nature; so, from 1700 on, not all the "better sort of people" endorsed them all with the same conviction. Still, they formed a tidy self-contained package; and people for whom some of them "stood to reason" or "went without saying" could easily accept the others as self-evident or beyond question. At the time, the basis of these beliefs in reason or experience was never closely examined, and it is worth taking a look at it here. Certainly, it did not reflect their "track record" as scientific hypotheses. No one who accepted Bacon's views about how new ideas about nature gain a basis in experience could regard them as *empirical*: they were far too general and unqualified, sweeping and doctrinal, for this description. Nor could anyone who shared Newton's ambition, to build a comprehensive system of natural philosophy on a mathematical basis, claim them as established by mathematical analysis: rather, they had to be accepted before the mathematics even began.

For this reason, it is best to describe them not as "assumptions" but as "presuppositions." An 18th-century Newtonian might refer to them as *axioms* of the Newtonian world view; yet this description is misleading. Such a doctrine as "Matter is inert" plays no direct part in mathematical explanations of gravitation. One can ask whether the force of gravitation decreases, say, as the inverse square or the inverse cube of the distance from the attracting body, only *after* the passivity of matter is securely assumed: if an inverse-square law can be squared with this doctrine, so too can an inverse cube law.

Nothing truly "logical" or "necessary" was at issue in this situation. If the timbers in the framework of Modernity had to be "presupposed" for the purposes of scientific argument, their correctness or incorrectness would surely affect the results of that argument—"inverse square, *si*: inverse cube, *no*!" But that is not the case. Their generality saved them from critical dependence on mere facts. As Joseph Priestley was able to show in 1777, in his *Disquisitions Relating to Matter and Spirit,* accepting or rejecting Inert Matter makes no difference to the soundness of Newton's explanations of planetary motion or anything else. If an inverse-square law matches the known form of the planetary orbits better than an inverse-cube law, that is just a fact.

Rather than seeing the elements of the modern framework as *axioms* from which scientific or philosophical consequences are inferred, we do better to treat them as an *intellectual scaffolding,* within which, from 1687 on, Newton and the other exact scientists constructed modern physics. The image of a *scaffolding* has particular advantages for our own narrative. It serves to remind us that, scientifically, the modern framework was suggestive, not directive. It defined possible lines of direction for future scientific work: it did not impose them by *fiat*. After 1800, the resulting world picture repeatedly changed shape in ways different from those foreseen in its original form, and the results of the lines of study it suggested cast doubt on one or another of its members. As a result, modern science outgrew its framework, with scandalous results, and respectable opinion struggled (in ways we shall look at shortly) to maintain the scaffolding intact, while removing its individual timbers one by one. The scaffolding of Modernity was, thus, a set of provisional and speculative half-truths. Despite the optimism of the rationalist philosophers, it was so short of logical proof (or even factual support) that its claims to "self-evidence" will lead us, in retrospect, to ask what else was implicitly at stake, *below the surface.*

Certainly, any suggestion that all these doctrines were "scientific" or "mathematical" does not bear close examination. If that had been so, they would have had to be defended far more diffidently and tentatively. Again, and again, doctrines that had not been proven by mathematical or experimental standards—that had not been demonstrated as geometrical theorems, and had little factual support—were presented as conclusions that "stood to reason" and "went without saying." How could that be? What sort of commitment to "rationality" did this attitude represent? Something more was going on here than philosophers of science have so far managed to digest. It is therefore time for us to turn back to the historical record, and see what else this "something more" involved.

1720–1780: The Subtext of Modernity

After 1660, the reconstruction of Europe went ahead on both the social and intellectual fronts. By the late 1680s, the future pattern of the new *Europe des patries* was largely clear; few people foresaw a renewal of the Religious Wars; while Isaac Newton's comprehensive new system of dynamical theory and planetary astronomy (which appeared in 1687 on the eve of King James II's flight to France) opened a way to restore the union of physics and cosmology that had been in prejudice since the time of Copernicus. Meanwhile, the larger body of general presuppositions about nature and humanity that we have here called the Scaffolding of Modernity won widespread acceptance among educated people in England and France.

At this point, the problem is to account for the popularity of these ideas. If the texts on which the appeal of the new world picture rested were the mathematical and scientific works of the natural philosophers, that was certainly not the whole story. The confidence with which most people adopted this framework went far beyond the mathematical and experimental grounding that Cartesian or Newtonian physics had earned at the beginning of the 18th century. If we dig below the surface, the reception given to this picture of nature from 1700 on (like that given to the Quest for Certainty in the 1650s) rested on other, parallel *subtexts,* whose

meaning had little to do with deducing mathematical theorems or explaining natural phenomena.

Certainly, the acceptance of Newtonianism among orthodox English
thinkers in the early 1700s did not depend on reading its primary texts. In
1687, only a handful of European mathematicians followed Newton's
Principia with any understanding: from the content of Leibniz's attacks,
even he seems to have read only a couple of dozen pages with any care.
(Finding ammunition to challenge Newton's theology of Creation in the
opening pages of the book, he did not trouble to check the calculations or
observations that form the bulk of Newton's argument.) Nor do the extra
Queries added to successive editions of Newton's *Opticks,* from 1704 to
1717, give any more than general reasons for taking his picture of nature
seriously, as an account of the structure with which God created Nature.
Unlike Descartes, Newton makes no claim to *certainty*—geometrical or
cryptanalytical—for his story. As he said in one of his final Queries:

> All these things being consider'd, it *seems probable to me,* that God
> in the beginning form'd matter in solid, massy, hard, impenetrable,
> movable particles, of such sizes and figures, and with such other
> properties, and in such proportion to space, as most conduced to
> the end for which he form'd them;. [etc.]

As a matter of 18th-century "common sense", Newton's ideas provided the
fabric of an oral tradition that carried conviction among *bien pensants*
readers and preachers in England for more than two hundred years; and,
thanks to Voltaire, this enthusiasm for Newtonianism was soon shared by
readers in the other major nations of Europe. What were the source and
point of this commitment? Evidently, they were something other than
those at issue in the purely scientific debates of the time.

The hidden agenda of the Newtonian Framework is not evident in the
surface meaning of the texts: it is at most implicit, below the surface, in the
way his ideas were commonly understood. For lack of any plain account
of what was at stake in the new world picture for people who were not
themselves mathematicians, we must go behind the texts and see what
other, less direct kinds of evidence can be found. For this purpose, three
questions are specially worth asking. We are concerned, first of all, with
the *receptiveness* of late 17th- and early 18th-century English readers to
Newtonian ideas, so that we can ask:

> *Were all readers in England, say, open to these ideas to the same*
> *extent, whatever their class, religion, or other background? Or were*
> *there genuine differences in this respect between people coming*
> *from different backgrounds?*

We can next go on to compare the receptiveness of people in different countries to the new world picture, asking:

> *How tenaciously was the new world view held by people in, say, Germany or Scotland, as compared with England and France? Were people in some countries more, or less, ready to challenge its presuppositions than those in others?*

Finally, since the hidden agenda with which the texts were read cannot be discovered in their manifest content alone, we may ask, also:

> *What echoes and overtones do these primary texts carry? Are there any special occasions when their writers take the trouble to spell out the doctrines that were usually "left unsaid"?*

If we speak of the new framework as finding a wide audience, what was the nature of this audience? Did the ideas have universal interest? Or did they carry weight only with subgroups of the potential audience? The self-appointed spokesmen for the view imply that its doctrines were universally agreed upon ("allowed by all men"), but that was always something of an exaggeration. Looking more closely, we find its ideas welcomed enthusiastically in some quarters, ignored in others, and in others again severely criticized. In England, the new picture became a commonplace among the progressive-minded Anglican clergy and an educated oligarchy whose influence was dominant after the bloodless *coup d'état* of 1688; and, when it gained similar currency in France and other countries, its supporters once again came from the educated oligarchy.

In centralized Nation-States, with well developed social classes and institutions, the Modern Framework soon appeared not just respectable, but even "official". The keenest advocates of the new view were the very people who organized the public schools, and had ready access to printing and publishing, and their views were well represented in books from that period. How far the framework carried the same weight among the rest of the population is another matter. Setting aside the illiterate groups studied by scholars like Carlo Ginzburg, a substantial class of literate, thoughtful people in 17th-century England was excluded from political power and public influence on account of class background, religious nonconformity, or distance from the capital. The Newtonian framework was popular with respectable writers and preachers in London and Paris; but for our purposes it is more relevant to ask, "How did it play in towns like Birmingham and Clermont Ferrand?"

Even before the Commonwealth, many of the English "lower orders" (notably, skilled craftsmen) escaped from the illiteracy common in the peasantry of Continental Europe. The literate underclass in England developed a nonconformist theology and social organization parallel to the traditional culture, education, and Church hierarchy of the English upper class. When censorship of the printing press was suspended for some years under Cromwell, this nonconformist culture was the focus of a visible and vigorous debate about theology, society, and politics; and the habits of thought generated in this debate survived the Restoration, though mostly in the provinces, and partly underground.

At the back of its mind, respectable English society always kept the traumatic shadow of Charles I's execution, and it was happy to treat the Commonwealth sects as a closed chapter of English history. As a result, some historians doubt whether the memory of the Commonwealth long survived, even in the Nonconformist provinces, once Anglican orthodoxy was back in place. By now, it is clearer that it lingered on, if only as a secondary tradition, behind the dominant culture. Commonwealth debates, notably about the ideas of Winstanley and the Levellers, are echoed in the political rhetoric of Australia, and have left an enduring mark on the country's social attitudes. The literate convict-settlers were conscious rebels, either from industrial England, or from harshly colonized Ireland: not for nothing, Australians chose for themselves the Cromwellian nickname of "Diggers."

From 1660 on, then, the culture of Nonconformity was an open and direct threat to the newly restored oligarchy, as peasant superstitions about witchcraft never were. This threat was recognized: after the Restoration, Anglican preachers were conscious of being not merely a minority, but a hated and despised minority. The basis of this popular dislike was political as much as doctrinal. Along with censorship, the Commonwealth struck down the power of Anglican Bishops, compulsory Church attendance on Sunday, and the Established Church's right to levy general tithes: those who did not benefit from their reimposition after 1660 saw it as an arbitrary and needless burden. The resulting conflict between Nonconformists and Anglicans carried further the old saga of "the Two Nations": as they faced their sullen congregations in the 1670s, Anglican preachers must have felt like Polish Communist Party officials addressing union workers during the suppression of Solidarity.

The difference between the dominant culture of the Anglican "Ins" and the secondary culture of the Nonconformist "Outs" strongly affected their attitudes toward the new framework of ideas. The crucial doctrine of the inertness of matter is a good case study—"Matter is in itself inert: it cannot set itself in motion, and it can generate physical effects, only if set in motion by a higher agency". This was an essential element in the Newtonian framework, and it survived in the public mind until the mid-20th century, when it was finally shaken by the success of quantum mechanics. Newton took this particular doctrine over from Descartes, and it was challenged in England as early as the 1650s, well before the publication of Newton's *Principia*. Commonwealth sectarians read any proposal to deprive *physical* mass (i.e. Matter) of a spontaneous capacity for action or motion, as going hand in hand with proposals to deprive the *human* mass (i.e. the "lower orders") of the population of an autonomous capacity for action, and so for social independence. What strikes us as a matter of basic physics was, in their eyes, all of a piece with attempts to reimpose the inequitable order of society from which they had escaped in the 1640s.

After 1660, conversely, English intellectuals stopped questioning the inertness of matter, for fear of being tarred with the same brush as the Commonwealth regicides. Traces of the earlier view hung on only in those who kept a sympathy for the Commonwealth reformers. In writing to his pupil Princess Caroline, for instance, Leibniz disparaged not only Newton's theological ideas, but also some arguments advanced by Locke, before he died in 1704:

1. Natural religion itself, seems to decay (in England) very much. Many will have human souls to be material: others make God himself a corporeal being.
2. Mr. Locke, and his followers, are uncertain at least, whether the soul be not material, and naturally perishable.

In his reply, Samuel Clarke defends Newton, but he has little to add about Locke. Still, the *tone* of his words is worth noting:

That Mr. Locke doubted whether the soul was immaterial or no, may justly be suspected from some parts of his writings: but herein he has been followed only by some materialists, enemies to the mathematical principles of philosophy; and who approve little or nothing in Mr. Locke's writings, but his errors.

In 1715 Locke was too noted a figure to be disowned, but his reputation still lay in the shadow of his earlier, more radical years. Clarke did not repudiate him, but he did not accept him as a good Newtonian, either. He merely held him at arm's length, hinting that he had kept bad company. (The phrase "some materialists" is probably a slap at John Toland, who continued to maintain a Cromwellian freedom of thought in the face of the new orthodoxies.)

Certainly, Locke never saw "Mind/Matter dualism" as an axiom, or as indubitable: his intellectual and political views were formed before the new framework achieved respectability, and he speculated without fear about matters that later writers were to find ticklish and delicate. Above all, he never took the inertness of matter for granted: instead, he was ready to consider the possibility of "thinking matter"—i.e., material systems that can perform rational procedures—quite seriously. By the time of the Leibniz-Clarke correspondence, he had been ten years dead. Men of respectability and power at the Hanoverian Court forgave him a lot, but they never wholly forgot the rumors of "unsoundness" that clung to his memory. Given the opening for a sniffy comment, Clarke could not resist the chance to slip in a posthumous knife.

The idea that Matter could form "living" or "thinking" systems was heterodox throughout the 18th century: those who troubled to defend it were nonconformist by temperament. In the 1720s, their spokesman was Julien de la Mettrie, a scandalous writer whose works were read at the time as deliberately outrageous paradoxes. La Mettrie had never been a re-spected member of the French academic élite. After studying with Boer-haave in Holland, he published two striking books, *L'Homme Machine* and *L'Homme Plante,* in which he ridiculed the dogmatic distinctions in terms of which 17th-century scientists classified the subjects of nature. In par-ticular, he rejected Descartes' equation of Matter with Extension as putting needless restrictions on the richness of Nature. Aside from that, he said, we could accept the vital and mental activities of organisms as natural outcomes of their material structures. He then went on to visit Maupertuis, the French director of Frederick the Great's Berlin Academy. There he died from food poisoning, it was said, after eating tainted pheasant pâté. When news of his death reached Paris, right-minded French scholars gave a collective sigh of relief.

No less striking is the case of Joseph Priestley, who, in his *Disquisitions* (1777) had argued that Newton's explanations in no way depend on the doctrine of inert matter. Priestley was a quintessential educated provincial Nonconformist: as a Unitarian, his standing in the intellectual or clerical establishment of England was no more respected than was La Mettrie's in France. He was a self-marginalized intellectual: a Socinian, not an Anglican, who studied at the Dissenters' Academy at Daventry, not at Oxford or Cambridge; and he worked with Josiah Wedgewood's Lunar Society in

Birmingham, not with the Royal Society in London. In a word, he was no *gentleman.*

Priestley blotted his copybook irrevocably after 1789. He applauded the success of the French Revolution, gave a banquet to celebrate it, and was publicly reviled for condoning the crimes of Revolutionary regicides. (There was widespread sympathy in England for persecuted Huguenots, but the events that followed the Revolution awoke bitter memories of Charles I's death, and evoked general horror.) Priestley saw his house burned down by the mob, gave up his pulpit, and emigrated to America, where he spent his last years in Northumberland, Pennsylvania. Did his case for active matter convince impartial readers in England? It did not. Perhaps there were no "impartial" readers: perhaps the deeper matters at stake (whatever they were) seemed too grave to be put at risk.

———————

After 1700, then, the framework of Modernity did not carry equal conviction, in England and France, with people of *all kinds and classes.* If we compare the ways in which it was received in different *places and countries,* we shall also find some peoples quicker to challenge it than others. When it came to questioning the self-evidence of the new world view, or disputing its right to "go without saying", the centralized nation-states proved the least hospitable environment for such discussions. The ideas of the Diggers were transported to Australia, along with their convict descendants; and it is no coincidence that a Frenchman like Julien de la Mettrie died in Berlin, and an Englishman like Joseph Priestley in America. In 18th-century England or France, nonconforming scientists were not compelled to emigrate, but it certainly helped to do so. Even those who stayed found their independence of mind easier to protect in the provinces: in Birmingham, not London; in Montpellier, not Paris. And when it came to proposing new disciplines, whose claims contradicted the presuppositions of the whole Modern Framework, it was far better to work elsewhere.

As to some other planks in the scaffolding of Modernity: around 1700, this framework left no room to speculate about any deep-seated historical changes in the order of nature. God had apparently created the world a few thousand years earlier, and it had presumably had the same structure throughout this time; so it was unreasonable to look for any significant geological changes in so limited a time. When speculatively minded 18th-century travellers in the *Massif Central* of France remarked that the mountains had silhouettes like those of active volcanoes today, and asked if they might be the remains of extinct volcanoes, most French readers were incredulous. (If the Mont Dore had erupted during the millennia since the Creation, this would surely have been noted and remembered!) Issues in the history of Nature were thus embraced with difficulty, and could readily be addressed only away from the centers of scientific orthodoxy.

In the late 18th century, the most influential theories in historical geology were thus those of James Hutton in Scotland and Abraham Gottlob Werner in Germany. Respectable English opinion held speculations about the Earth's origins at arm's length well on into the 19th century. In 1815, when the Geological Society of London defined its agenda, it disavowed theories of the Earth's development, in favor of fieldwork designed to establish a stratigraphy of its present crust. Indeed, until the late 19th century, in both England and France, issues in historical geology provoked theological dispute, and even a serious defense of historical geology might be labelled as a proof of "the veracity of Moses as an historian".

The argument about the legitimacy of a scientific history of Nature was only aggravated, not initiated, by the appearance of Darwin's *Origin of Species,* in 1859. As a student at the University of Edinburgh in 1819, Darwin had been exposed at first hand to the controversy about William Lawrence's *Lectures on Physiology, Zoology and the Natural History of Man,* which was denied copyright protection on the ground that a "materialist" view of human physiology was blasphemous; and this memory stayed with him for the rest of his life. There he learned to keep his head down and do his work alone. A family friend of the Darwins was afflicted by aphasia: he was unable to understand in words the message that it was "time for dinner", though he could recognize it visually, if shown a watch or a clock. In his private reflections, Darwin explored the possibility that such a cognitive deficit was a result of brain injury following, for example, a stroke, but he knew better than to put his speculations into print, and confined them to his personal *Notebooks,* from which they were published only in the 1970s. Even in his work on organic evolution and the biological ancestry of the human species, he evaded public debate: at his country house in Kent, he cultivated his reputation as a solitary eccentric, and left it to T. H. Huxley (his "Bulldog") to carry the banner for his theories in public.

Another field dismissed from the new world view was *psychology;* and, once again, it was no accident that psychological issues were first discussed with real seriousness in Germany and Scotland. Scotland had lost its national autonomy *de facto* in the 1600s, when King James VI of Scotland succeeded Queen Elizabeth I and moved his base to London, and *de iure* in 1707, on passage of the Act of Union that established Great Britain.

Germany, too, was a patchwork of larger and smaller units without a tradition of cohesion and centralization, until the 19th-century dominance of Prussia and the politics of Bismarck launched it, late in the day, on the road to nationhood. By escaping political centralization, both Germany and Scotland also escaped the cultural pressures that national centralization created; and this ensured greater freedom, for scientists and public alike, to pursue speculations of a kind frowned on elsewhere as being "offensive" to respectable opinion. In England, the hostility aroused by Lawrence's enthusiasm for "atheistical" French physiology was more threatening still to would-be psychologists: even after English physiology had won its spurs in the 19th century, psychology was still accepted only as a by-product of, for example, neurophysiology or clinical neurology.

As for the "human sciences": many English people are suspicious of them to this day. Anthropology was fortunate: it began as an offshoot of Colonial administration. Sociology was under a cloud in England until at least 1960. Only *economics* flourished, beginning in Adam Smith's Scotland as an aspect of moral philosophy, and achieving mathematical exactitude in Cambridge without losing its philosophical roots. Alfred Marshall was a philosopher at first, John Maynard Keynes was a student of G. E. Moore, while Anglo-American economic theory stayed firmly on the "reason" side of Cartesianism. Economics did not explore the *causal* tangle of motives or feelings behind real human choices, exploring instead the *rational* choices of "ideal" producers or consumers, investors or policymakers. For the purpose of economics, "causal" factors were set aside, in favor of ever more precisely "rational" calculations. In this way, modern proprieties were protected in the life of the intellect, as well as in respectable English society.

To turn to the documentary evidence: one source throws particular light on the "subtext" of the new world view. We cited previously the 1714–1715 correspondence between Leibniz and Clarke, who was acting as a "front man" for Newton. The target of Leibniz' opening letter, we saw, is Newton's inability to prove mathematically that the solar system must be *stable*. As the correspondence goes on, the debate broadens out and more of the presuppositions of the new world view enter the exchange. If we look behind the content of these letters to the rhetorical devices used in them, we shall see something more of the interests at stake in this confrontation between natural philosophy and theology.

At first, the letters appear to focus on *a priori* arguments about physics:

"Can there be such a thing as a vacuum?", "Do material particles have a smallest possible size?", "Could not the universe have come into existence 200 yards to the left?", "Can bodies attract each other across millions of miles of space, without the help of any intervening agency?" But all these issues have nonscientific overtones, and are interspersed with appeals and exhortations whose deeper significance is too easily overlooked. Even the argument about the stability of the solar system turns out to carry a deeper message. As Leibniz puts it:

> When God works miracles, he does not do it in order to supply the wants of nature, but those of grace. Whoever thinks otherwise, must needs have a very mean notion of the wisdom and power of God.

Newton should be ashamed to publish a theory of planetary dynamics so lacking in edifying implications—"Surely God would know better than to create an unstable planetary system?" The argument continues, not just about the regularities that actually govern natural phenomena, but about whether this picture of nature displays God's Rationality with sufficient clarity to support a "rational" theology.

In their replies, Clarke and Newton never challenge Leibniz, when he directly appeals to the presuppositions of the new world view:

> That there are some in England, as well as in other countries, who deny or very much corrupt even natural religion itself, is very true, and much to be lamented.

Whenever this happens, they prefer to back off, concede the general point in question, and vary their statement of Newton's position, so that it is no longer vulnerable to Leibniz's objections. Of course, a body cannot *act* where it *is* not; but Newton's theory of gravitation was never meant to entail that it can. Of course, God's Decision where in Space to Create the Cosmos was not "irrational"; but humans may not be able to discover the reasons for which He chose as He did. Nor do they question that natural philosophy should provide an edifying vision of God's Plan for Nature. Newton was always happy to see his ideas "work with considering men for belief in a Deity"; but, in the *Principia,* he had merely been aiming to show the presence of mathematical relations among the phenomena of dynamics and astronomy. This was at most a first step along the way to a comprehensive vision of God's Natural Creation, not the whole journey; but he was confident that the final picture would support the theological interpretation of Creation that preoccupied Leibniz.

The rhetorical appeals in the letters on both sides display several points of agreement: behind their words lie shared images and analogies. If Nature were as the philosophers believed, we could take a whole string of other theses for granted. God would never set up the order of Nature less rationally and prudently than a wise King would organize the State: nor would God care for Nature with any less concern than a Husband and Father has for his Wife and Family. If we read the correspondence with an eye to these analogies, a latent picture will become visible, with the gradual vividness of an instant photograph.

Once again, the leading themes implicit in the correspondence are "stability" and "hierarchy". Everything in the natural order testifies (or can be *made* to testify) to God's dominion over Nature. That dominion extends through the entire fabric of the world, natural or human, and is apparent on every level of experience. What God is to Nature, the King is to the State. It is fitting that a Modern Nation should model its State organization on the structures God displays in the world of astronomy: the *Roi Soleil,* or Solar King, wields authority over successive circles of subjects, all of whom know their places, and keep their proper orbits. What God is to Nature and the King is to the State, a Husband is to his Wife, and Father to his Family: the paternalism reestablished in respectable circles after 1660 is thus given a justifying place in the order of Nature. In all these ways, the order of Nature and the order of Society turn out to be governed by a similar set of laws.

One footnote is worth adding. The hidden agendas of cultures, as of individuals, are often seen as much in their symbols as in their deeds. An image of Family and State as modeled on the solar system dominated the imagination of respectable Europeans and Americans for generations: one symbolic monument is to be found in the graveyard at Stockbridge, Massachusetts. Speaking about the death of his cousin, Edie Sedgwick, John P. Marquand, Jr., asks:

> Have you ever seen the old graveyard up there in Stockbridge? In one corner is the family's burial place; it's called the Sedgwick Pie. The Pie is rather handsome. In the center Judge Theodore Sedgwick, the first of the Stockbridge Sedgwicks and a great-great-great-grandfather of Edie's and mine, is buried under his tombstone, a high-rising obelisk, and his wife Pamela is beside him. . . . [All around them] are more modest stones, but in layers, back and round in a circle. The descendants of Judge Sedgwick, from generation unto generation, are all buried with their heads facing out and their feet pointing in toward their ancestor. The legend is that on Judgment Day when they arise and face the Judge, they will have to see no one but Sedgwicks.

The form of the family burying ground—a planetary system, in which the patriarchal Judge is the *père soleil*—testifies to the social power of the traditional astronomical image.

In studying the sub-texts of the Newtonian world view, therefore, all our three kinds of evidence are circumstantial; but this circumstantial evidence, though having quite different sources and implications, all points in the same direction. If any doubt remained that more is at stake in this world view than there is in a 20th-century scientific theory, a perceptive reading of the Leibniz–Clarke letters dispels it.

We are here concerned, not with "science" as the modern positivists understand it, but with a *cosmopolis* that gives a comprehensive account of the world, so as to bind things together in "politico-theological", as much as in scientific or explanatory, terms. Those who reconstructed European society and culture after the Thirty Years' War took as guiding principles *stability* in and among the different sovereign nation-states, and *hierarchy* within the social structures of each individual state. For those who carried this task forward, it was important to believe that the principles of stability and hierarchy were found in all of the Divine plan, down from the astronomical cosmos to the individual family. Behind the inertness of matter, they saw in Nature, as in Society, that the actions of "lower" things depended on, and were subordinate to, oversight and command by "higher" creatures, and ultimately by the Creator. The more confident one was about "subordination and authority" in Nature, the less anxious one need accordingly be about social inequalities. Likewise with the "irrationality" of Emotion: if subjects ordered their lives indiscreetly, this gave rise to social disturbances of kinds that might be diverting to read about in the novels of Daniel Defoe, but were highly disagreeable to deal with in real life.

The comprehensive system of ideas about nature and humanity that formed the scaffolding of Modernity was thus a social and political, as well as a scientific device: it was seen as conferring Divine legitimacy on the political order of the sovereign nation-state. In this respect, the world view of modern science—*as it actually came into existence*—won public support around 1700 for the legitimacy it apparently gave to the political system of nation-states as much as for its power to explain the motions of planets, or the rise and fall of the tides.

Conversely, the Nonconformists, who called into question the presuppositions of the framework, were not attacked for intellectual temerity: they were exposed to scorn and contumely on other grounds. Either, like

Julien La Mettrie, they were suspected of disreputable habits; or they were attacked as political subversives, like Tom Paine, John Toland, and above all Joseph Priestley, whose unforgivable offense was to argue that there was good in the French Revolution. (What else could one expect of a man who denied that matter is inert, and claimed that mere "atoms" may be centers of autonomous power?) What was challenged was never the adequacy of the scientific explanations the Nonconformists gave: rather, what was condemned was their character, their supposed lack of religious piety, or their supposed lack of general respect for established society. Once again, what from our perspective two hundred years later seems in its language to be a scientific dispute, proves to have been part of a broader debate, the practical consequences of which were concerned with political and social, quite as much as with scientific or intellectual, issues.

The Second Step Back from Rationalism

We have come a long way from *La Grande Encyclopédie,* and from the received view of Modernity. Instead of "modern" philosophy and science being abstract, context-free inquiries, which might have been embarked on by reflective *ésprits* from any country and historical period, we have seen here that they took idiosyncratic forms, for reasons that are deeply embedded in their historical situation. Far from the rise of philosophy in the 17th century being unconnected with events like the Thirty Years' War (as historians of the subject often imply) such an account leaves crucial aspects of the process unexplained.

Our revised account leads us to divide the years from 1570 to 1720 into four generations, in each of which European life has a distinct tone. Until 1610, there is a widespread but not universal confidence in the ability of humans to run their lives by their own lights, and tolerate a diversity of beliefs: aside from Michel de Montaigne, both Francis Bacon and William Shakespeare manifest this confidence up to the last phases of their work. Shakespeare explores the possibilities of human character robustly, with no sense that his hands are tied by a concern for what is orthodox and respectable: his tone changes only in *The Winter's Tale,* the *Tempest,* and other late plays. As for Bacon, he is born in 1561, some thirty-five years before Descartes, and his attitudes to life and thought are largely formed before the end of the century: his writings show none of that "closing in of boundaries" that is prevalent from the 1610s to the 1640s. On the contrary, Bacon is one of the first social philosophers who is open to the prospect of a long-term future for human beings, subject only to their

willingness to take command of their own techniques and destinies: for
Bacon as for Montaigne, Experience puts the limits on Theory and Doctrine, not the other way about.

After 1610, a tone of confidence is replaced by one of catastrophe.
Theologically committed Europeans believe not in specific doctrines over
which no consensus exists, but in *belief itself.* Doctrine and experience are
at loggerheads. A poet like John Donne—whose first-hand experience of
life and love was coupled to familiarity with the interminable debate about
Counter-Reformation theology—captures this deadlock between experience and theory in a single line:

"Batter my heart, three person'd God"—

which runs spirituality into headlong collision with all the theological
problems of the Trinity. Compounding the paradox, he calls on the Angels
to "blow their trumpets . . . at the round earth's imagined corners." There
could hardly be a more striking contrast with Shakespeare, who had been
born less than ten years earlier than Donne.

A commitment to doctrines that no one could "prove" to the general
satisfaction, or square with their personal experience, generated as its
by-product a perfectionism that was to become one of the hallmarks of
Modernity. Descartes pursued a rational method for resolving scientific
puzzles, but turned his back on Bacon's modest empirical methods, and
saw no serious hope in anything less than a quest for outright certainty. In
the long run, as he understood, every theory must come to terms with
experience; but he had no doubt that the intelligibility and certainty of
"clear and distinct" mathematical concepts had a higher priority than the
empirical support of intellectually disconnected facts. The new research
program of the 17th-century natural philosophers was presented as being
both "mathematical" and "experimental." But it was, first and foremost, a
pursuit of mathematical certainty: the search for experiential support and
illustrations was secondary.

Hence, the schizophrenia we found in the arguments of Descartes,
between Descartes the cryptanalyst and Descartes the foundationalist: he
could not bridge the gap between mathematically lucid but abstract
theories of nature, and detailed decipherments of concrete *phenomena* in
experience. Perfectionism bred the same schizophrenia elsewhere. The
Abbaye de Port Royal, outside Paris, was home (or a home away from
home) to a community of Jansenists comprising some of the most distinguished writers and intellectuals of mid-17th-century France: these playwrights and philosophers found it hard to reconcile the spiritual
perfection they aimed at, while in the Abbey, with their more mundane

achievements. So long as he lived as a member of the community, Jean Racine felt bound to condemn his own talents as a playwright; while the mathematician and devotional writer, Blaise Pascal, found his intellectual talents equally ambiguous. Half the time he could exercise them to good effect, and with undoubted personal satisfaction: the other half, he agonized that these same talents were leading him astray, by distracting his attention from his relationship to God.

After 1650, there was a transitional period of forty years, in which the doctrinal conflicts of the previous century were set aside, and effort devoted to reconstruction. Diplomatically, the European nation-states agreed to disagree: at home, conformity mattered more than conviction. Matters of doctrine lost their centrality, and a tone of cynicism entered the debate: "I am always of the opinion with the learned if they speak first," as William Congreve quips. This cynicism can hardly be a surprise, in a time when Ministers of the Established Church preached to congregations who were there to hear them only because they were required to attend by law. There was still some room for doubt about the question, whether the "struggle for stability" was really won, or whether the Restoration of the *status quo ante* would prove only temporary, either politically or doctrinally; but, for the time being, cynical compromise was a small price to pay for the blessings of *détente*.

Only at the very end of the century do lingering uncertainties give way to reassurance, or even complacency. Newton had at last answered the astronomical questions left over by Copernicus, and had revealed an order in nature that apparently justified a commitment to stability and hierarchy found equally in Louis XIV's absolute monarchy in France, and William III's constitutional monarchy in England. Meanwhile, matters of orthodoxy fade into the background. It is not that people have by now revived Shakespeare's robustness of characterization, or Montaigne's omnivorous curiosity about human experience. It is rather that the old battles over matters of doctrine no longer appear worth all that effort. According to Alexander Pope, "practice" is all that counts:

> For forms of government let fools contest;
> Whate'er is best administered is best;
> For modes of faith let graceless zealots fight;
> His can't be wrong whose life is in the right.

(It was a long time since anyone had got away with calling the zealots "graceless".)

Little of our revised account, as summarized here, was recognized or understood by historians of science or philosophy before the 1960s: what

little they recognized they dismissed as irrelevant. Committed to a rationalist view of science, they saw all empirical data as "supporting", "failing
to support", or "lending partial support to" new hypotheses, as measured
by numerical and probabilistic indices. Only the explanatory success of
new ideas—quantitative, for preference—was relevant to their rational
appraisal. Even in the 1970s, their only concession was to allow that we can
study conceptual and theoretical evolution with an eye to changes in the
explanatory content of Science. Our position here is more radical. When
we ask, "What was at stake for people who accepted the Newtonian world
view in 1720?", the considerations that weighed with them went beyond
anything that 20th-century philosophers would call "explanatory." In
particular, the cosmopolitical function of the world view counted for as
much as its explanatory function, and probably more; and we can give an
accurate account of its acceptance only if we "recontextualize" it, and so
remove all limits on the factors that may be accepted as "relevant".
Circumstantial the historical evidence may be, but it places the welcome
for Newtonianism—like the Quest for Certainty—squarely in the social
and political framework of its time.

Until the 1970s, the history and philosophy of science were written by
people with a rationalist outlook, who were interested above all in the
intellectual aspects of natural science. When non-scientists read ethical or
political implications into the results of science, that was (for them) a
historical accident that threw no light on the meaning of the results. At this
time, T. S. Kuhn's book, *The Structure of Scientific Revolutions,* struck many
people as daring, simply because it implied that people at different times
may properly frame scientific explanations around quite different patterns
of explanation. Yet, when it came to judging whether to accept or reject
novel scientific ideas, even Kuhn did not allow social and political interpretations to enter the equation. Only in the 1980s have scholars gone far
beyond changes in the internal content of the sciences, and asked how the
external context influences their choice of problems and patterns of
explanation.

Attention to the broader practical context of speculations is as old as
Plato's *Republic,* and the dream that a "cosmopolis" unites the orders of
nature and society has been part of our tradition for at least that long. Yet
for fifty years, from the 1920s on, a rationalist view of science was so deeply
entrenched in Academia that references to the "social function" of science
were liable to be attacked as left-wing heresies. Only now is it publicly
acknowledged that scientific ideas have hidden as well as explicit agendas,
and that, even after all the explanatory work is done in theory, we need to
look at the secondary interests that new ideas serve in practice. Following

the changing face of science from 1750 to 1920, we must consider not just the theoretical content of physics from Isaac Newton to Albert Einstein, or of biology from John Ray up to T. H. Morgan, but also the role of Newtonianism as a "cosmopolitical" justification of the "modern social order". At this point, two features call for attention: the insistence that the necessary organizing principle of both nature and society is stability and the tension between reason and the emotions in individual and collective conduct.

From 1700 on, social relations within the nation-state were defined in *horizontal* terms of superordination and subordination, based on class affiliation: the "lower orders" as a whole were seen as subordinate and inferior to the "better sort" as a whole. Each class had its place in the horizontal system that constituted a nation-state, and at the summit of the structure was the King. Social place was typically defined by the status of the men involved, and was applied to their wives and children by association. As a by-product of the nation-state, class distinction became, as never before, the crucial organizing principle of all society. In France especially, the key force in society was the monarch's "solar" power to control (and illuminate) the state's activities. The Sovereign supervised the Court and the royal agencies, and influenced the actions of the nobles and gentry directly: those of the lower orders or "masses" followed suit indirectly and at a remove. The sub- or superordination of classes was horizontal in theory, but, in the social exercise of power, it was in practice orbital. Social stability depended on all the parties in society "knowing their place" relative to the others, and knowing what reciprocal modes of behavior were appropriate and rational.

Here, the planetary model of society was explicitly *cosmopolitical.* Without such a justification, the imposition of hierarchy on "the lower orders" by "the better sort" of people would be arbitrary and self-serving. To the extent that this hierarchy mirrored the structure of nature, its authority was self-explanatory, self-justifying, and seemingly rational. The philosophical belief that nature obeys mathematical "laws" which will ensure its stability for so long as it pleases God to maintain it, was a socially revolutionary idea: both *cosmos* and *polis* (it appeared) were self-contained, and their joint "rationality" guaranteed their stability. As recently as the 1650s, people worried that the World was grinding to its End: by 1720, their grandchildren were confident that a rational and omniscient Creator had made a world that ran perfectly.

This idolization of social stability had practical implications. Any family's position in society was defined by that of its male members, so gender-discrimination (or sexism) became constitutive of the new state. This worked in several ways. A young man might endanger his standing by a "bad" marriage; but a young woman "bettered herself" by marrying above her social origins. It is no accident that the novel took shape and became popular at this stage in history. When Henry More made ethics a matter for philosophical theories, he left to literary writers an interest in substantive moral issues. After 1660, the field was open for Defoe and Richardson to explore the adventures or misadventures of characters (for example, Moll Flanders) who showed the changes and chances that coexisted with the new social constraints. From Defoe and Richardson right up to Thackeray and Edith Wharton, the tragicomedy of social climbing was to keep the storytellers busy.

Meanwhile, Britain and the other European states consolidated their colonies overseas, in Ireland and America, Asia, Australia, and Africa. The horizontal mode of organization that covered the relations of classes and genders was extended to those of races. Patterns of discrimination invented at home were reapplied to conquered peoples: racism became an expression of the God-given subordination of the colonized "inferiors" to their colonizing "betters." In themselves, of course, racial, sex, and class discrimination were not novel practices. Conquered populations had been enslaved, inheritance had been confined to the male line, populations had been trapped in the roles of hewers of wood and drawers of water often before. But the new *cosmopolitical* framework gave such discriminatory patterns a new respectability, implying that they were essential parts of God's Plan for nature and humanity.

The other socially crucial feature of the new world view was the hard-line contrast between reason and the emotions. This was not just a theoretical doctrine, with intellectual relevance alone: rather, from the late-17th to the mid-20th century, it shaped life in Europe on both the social and personal level. Like other elements in the scaffolding of Modernity, this contrast frequently "went unsaid", being embedded in the everyday social life of the nation-state. Calculation was enthroned as the distinctive virtue of the human reason; and the life of the emotions was repudiated, as distracting one from the demands of clear-headed deliberation. In this social sense, "emotion" became a code word for sex: to those who valued a stable class system, sexual attraction was a main source of social disruption. A generation ago from now, many young men—at any rate, "healthy" young men—were kept ignorant of the fact that young women—at any rate, "nice" young women—can actually enjoy sex; while nice young women, too, were discouraged from taking active pleasure in sexual relations, as "unladylike." What began as a theoretical distinction in Descartes, between the intellectual power of human "reason" and the physiological "causes" of the emotions, turned into a practical contrast between (good) rationality and (bad) sentiment or impulsiveness.

These taboos were again *class-based*. The healthy young gentlemen and nice young ladies who were encouraged to renounce "emotionalism" came from families that belonged (or aspired to belong) to the educated oligarchy: the same was less true with children from the "lower orders". Further, this was a novel attitude to sexuality: it became compulsory for the "respectable" classes only in the 17th century. Montaigne's *Essais* display little sign of it: on the contrary, they treat sex as spontaneous, mutually pleasurable, and equal between the sexes. The tide of Puritan anxiety about sexuality rose precipitously in the mid-1600s. Thus, the inhibitions from which Freud sought to liberate people at the end of the 19th century were not immemorial, or age-old: they sprang rather from the fears that came into existence *de novo,* when the class-based state was devised as a solution to the early-17th-century's problems. Matters remained like this, for as long as the Modern Cosmopolis held its power: from Daniel Defoe to *Lady Chatterley's Lover*. By the time it ended, the class basis of this sexual prejudice was almost humorous: prosecuting Penguin Books on grounds of obscenity, for their unexpurgated edition of *Lady Chatterley,* Mr. Mervyn Griffith-Jones, Q.C., asked a witness, "Is this a book you would wish to see put into the hands of your maidservant?", and right across Britain his question evoked derisive laughter. If he saw D. H. Lawrence's book as subversive, it was not for its ideas about *sex*. Maidservants, like the lower class generally, were presumably more libidinous than the middle class. If the novel was a source of danger, that was because the illicit sexual relations that it depicted cut across class boundaries. What if everyone's housemaids imitated Lord Chatterleys' gamekeeper? How, then, could servants be kept in their place?

The social implications of the new cosmopolis share one feature: they foreshadow a notion that has recently played a part in political and social rhetoric—that of "traditional values." Throughout the Middle Ages and Renaissance, clerics and educated laymen understood that problems in social ethics (or "values") are not resolved by appeal to any single and universal "tradition". In serious situations, multiple considerations and coexisting traditions need to be weighed against one another. Until the 17th century turned ethics into a branch of theoretical philosophy, "case ethics" was as intellectually challenging as constitutional interpretation in the judicial practice of the United States. It did not aim to provide a unique resolution of every moral problem: rather, it triangulated its way across unexplored ethical territory, using all the available resources of moral thought and social tradition.

About the status of ethics in historic Christianity, we may thus say, "Traditionally, there was either *no* tradition, or a *plurality* of traditions: not one single tradition, but a number of parallel traditions, narrower or more liberal, but all of them acceptable." Whatever hard-line Counter-Reformation preachers taught, the more severe-minded Augustinians never had all the good tunes. Nor did Medieval or Renaissance theologians see a plurality of traditions as something to be deplored, far less eliminated. Historically, the Western Church was a transnational institution, and it dealt realistically with people from Scotland to Sicily, from Poland to Portugal. Moral issues had pluralism built in from the start; the wisest resolution came from steering an equitable course between the demands that arose in practice, in specific cases.

Only after the invention of ethical theory, when *dogma* acquired an imperative sense, were people finally convinced that moral questions have unique, simple, and authoritative answers. In the years before the Reformation, moral and general theology were open for discussion in the Provinces of the Church, on a collegial basis: the Papal Curia issued its rulings on general moral issues, with Papal authority, only after 1700. This drive toward centralized authority was a tactic to strengthen the Church's defenses against the Protestant heresies, as later *Pio Nono* was to try and strengthen the Church against the corrupting consequences of the French Revolution.

From its start around 1700, then, the idea of "traditional values" was an instrument of conservative rhetoric. In medieval Christianity, people lived happily with an Aristotelian idea of "prudence", in which it was not just needless but foolish to impose a single code of moral rules—a code that ignored the crucial difference between abstract problems in a theory like geometry, and concrete problems of moral practice. The scaffolding of Modernity was used to rationalize respectable moral and social doctrines that had hitherto been merely the "rigorist" extreme of an acceptable spectrum: in this way, the educated oligarchy used its social power to reinforce its position in a self-serving way. This being so, it is perhaps less surprising that a freethinker like Julien La Mettrie, a nonconformist like Joseph Priestley, and an original like Charles Darwin, felt compelled to kick against the pricks.

Notice what our second retreat from rationalism does, and does not, entail. On the one hand, it shows that the success of science has rested, historically speaking, on political as well as explanatory considerations. We offer no theoretical interpretation of this fact: neither suggesting that the

Newtonian view was, say, the theology of nationhood, nor that it was the ideology of the bourgeois state, nor yet the "intellectual superstructure" of capitalism. Instead, we present it as one element in a syndrome whose significance can be seen only by resorting to ethnographic or other empirical methods. Without even circumstantial evidence, we would have had no reason to link the success of the Newtonian framework to the social imperatives of the centralized 18th-century nation-state. Our revised account may or may not stand up to further factual examination, but at least it is based on circumstantial observations and plausible interpretations.

From the 1920s to the 1950s, philosophers treated Science as an abstract enterprise, whose progress could be defined and appraised without reference to the historical situation in which that progress was made. By the 1960s, they were open to the idea that standards of progress in Science are variables, subject to "paradigm shifts" and other changes of direction and emphasis. In our inquiries, we see a need to go yet further. In earlier centuries, scientific work was done as part of "forms of life" or "life worlds" very different from those within which it now goes on. Newton and his colleagues, for instance, were not much concerned with the technological applications of science: they were interested, rather, in the theological implications of new scientific ideas; while many of their readers were concerned with their implications for cosmopolitical issues, having to do with political obligation and social structure.

All the relevant considerations may not have been exactly stated here. But at least we have taken the step of reopening the empirical question: viz., "What was *at stake* for scientists, and readers of science, in this or that particular period?" Instead of bringing our current standards of judgment to bear on the ideas of earlier generations, we do better to put ourselves into the heads of people living in a given historical situation, and try and recognize what gave scientific ideas the charms that won them a place in the "common sense" of the time.

CHAPTER FOUR

The Far Side of Modernity

The High Tide of Sovereign Nationhood

*T*he years from the 1690s to 1914 saw the high tide of sovereign "nationhood" in Europe. For two centuries and more, few people seriously questioned that the nation-state was the central political unit, in either theory or practice. These years were also the high tide of the view of nature we called the framework of Modernity. Above all in England and France, only hardy souls who were content to remain intellectually and socially out-of-step with their contemporaries challenged either the Cartesian separation of human reason from the natural machine, or the stable, hierarchical Cosmopolis which the Newtonians built on that foundation. After 1914, however, those scientific ideas and social practices were again widely questioned. For the first time, the absolute sovereignty of the individual nation was seen to be dysfunctional and anachronistic; and, at the same time, science was discrediting the last timbers in the scaffolding of Modernity.

The new emphasis on the unity, stability, and integrity of the nation, as a focus of organization for "modern" state and society, was always a philosophical ideal more than it was a description of political actuality. In theory the ideal was embodied in the social and political organization of France and Britain, but this embodiment was never perfect: Holland came closer to the ideal, as a small country created in 1579, with very little historical baggage and an unusually homogenous culture. (Since it was dependent on international trade, the balance between the merchants and the aristocracy helped make it a more just society, free of the grosser inequities that needed legitimation in France and England.)

In some countries, the population was so mixed that the sense of "nationhood" was slow to develop. In Ulster, the mixture of Protestant Scots and Catholic Irish is still, notoriously, as immiscible as oil and water.

In Macedonia, even now, neighboring towns may have populations with any of half-a-dozen cultures and languages. (The French do not call mixed chopped vegetables a *macédoine* for nothing.) France, Britain, and Holland approached the ideal of the nation-state more quickly, and more closely, than Italy and Germany which, for historical and geographical reasons, were fragmented until the mid-19th century. Some 200 years earlier, Leibniz dreamed of a culturally unified Germany—*Teuschtum*—but it achieved political unification only after the liberal uprisings of 1848. In Italy, similarly, the local power of the traditional city states and provinces (not least, those under the political control of the Papacy) was overcome only by Mazzini, Garibaldi, and Cavour.

The unity of the nation was thus the basis of political legitimacy in theory, and the support of state unity in practice. Between 1650 and 1950 few political philosophers challenged this basic assumption, or questioned that "nationhood" is the natural basis of State formation: their central question was, "How do nation-states acquire and retain legitimacy, and by what means are they entitled to enforce the political obedience of their subjects?" The prior question—"To what extent does the nation-state have only limited value as the focus of political organization or social loyalty?"—remained unaddressed.

Cosmopolitically, the process of social construction took different routes in different European countries, and the significance of the new world picture was interpreted in correspondingly different ways in, for example, Germany, Britain, and France. Growing up in a Germany traumatized by the Thirty Years' War, for instance, Leibniz insisted more strictly than the Newtonians on the need for the foundations of philosophy to be both mathematically and metaphysically "provable": Newton's readiness to explore undemonstrable hypotheses, such as gravitation, seemed to him deplorable and dangerous. A generation later, with Leibniz and Newton, Louis XIV and William III, all out of the way, the founders of the French Enlightenment took up the modern cosmopolis again in a different spirit from its creators. In England, this cosmopolis was the possession of the *bien pensants* Anglicans involved in the constitutional diplomacy that passed the British monarchy first to the House of Orange, and later to the House of Hanover, which has occupied it ever since. One virtue of the new cosmopolis, for them, was just the way it made constitutional monarchy appear a "rational" pattern of state organization, and therefore appropriate to a modern nation. In England, godly, right-minded, respectable members of the Establishment adopted it. They saw nothing radical or atheistic in it: rather, it carried a message of comfort—that the British political system was in harmony with the Divine System of Nature.

The situation in France was different. Louis XIV's great-grandson and successor, Louis XV, may be styled *le Bien-Aimé,* but he was still an absolutist autocrat. In the France of the 1750s, constitutional monarchy was perceived as a radical and subversive idea: Catholic royalists found an admiration for English ideas and politics just as outrageous as Joseph Priestley's acceptance of the French Revolution seemed in England after 1789. The notorious Voltaire was the first to popularize Newton's ideas in France, after a visit to London: Diderot, d'Alembert, and Holbach began publishing the main instrument of the Enlightenment, the famous multi-volume *Encyclopédie,* in 1751. At the time, this vast series was seen as the product of dissidents: even its smaller 20th-century successor, *Le Petit Larousse,* still calls it *une machine de guerre.*

Facing an alliance of Bourbon autocrats and the Gallican Church, the Encyclopedists were less concerned than Newton about the theological respectability of the new cosmopolis. In giving the established French political system an intellectual shakeup, they did not mind shocking the religious authorities, too. The audacious Paul Henri, Baron d'Holbach, transformed Newton's account of Nature: instead of remaining the prop of a vaguely respectable theism, Newtonianism now became the conscious vehicle of atheism and materialism. Holbach, that is, secularized the Newtonian philosophy and made it into a weapon against Catholic be-lievers in the Divine Right of the Bourbon Monarchy.

This possibility had always been implicit in the new physics. Some of Descartes' early supporters, we saw, were drawn to the Deist view, that God actively created the Universe, but then turned His back, leaving it to operate automatically by laws built in at the outset. For Holbach, even the Creator-God of Deism was a needless hypothesis, which could quietly be thrown overboard without loss. Yet, despite this crucial difference, Hol-bach's *Système de la Nature* recognizably rewrites, in secular terms, the natural philosophy which was used forty years earlier, by Clarke and the Newtonians, to legitimate the Hanoverian establishment. Holbach's view of Nature was still *systematic:* he found Newton's theology uncongenial, but he embraced with enthusiasm the rational order that the Newtonians had brought to the understanding of nature and society. Its theological frills stripped away, this System stood on its own feet, and showed the harmony between the causal Order of physical nature and the rational Order of a *constitutional* Society.

Each generation of philosophers interpreted the broader meaning of science in its own way, to meet the demands of its own situation. The Rationalist project of Descartes and his admirers, Henry More and the Cambridge Platonists, was one thing; the Newtonian project, to unite mechanics and astronomy in the new Cosmology, was another thing; the Enlightenment project of Voltaire, Rousseau, and the Encyclopedists was something else again. The political implications of Newtonian rationalism were conservative: they lacked the radical bite of the Enlightenment. The Enlightenment philosophers did not *reject* the modern cosmopolis, which had been the scientific basis for social reconstruction after the Religious Wars. They accepted the system in its entirety, but used it to fight *from within* the restrictive tendencies inherent in the nation-state. Under all the circumstances, this move was politically less urgent, and carried less conviction, in England than in France, where it helped to set a pattern for the tension between the Philosopher and the Establishment, the Priest and the Schoolmaster, that has shaped the French cultural scene ever since.

The phrase, "the Enlightenment project", then, is sometimes used in ways that telescope ideas in Britain, France, and Germany over three or four generations. Descartes' project was slanted to make it acceptable to liberal Counter Reformation Catholics: Leibniz's project was more impartial between the Christian denominations, yet still programmatic. Newton took the "mathematical and experimental" philosophy of nature beyond that level, developing a system of cosmology and matter theory which (*pace* Leibniz) was the foundation of a long-hoped-for World View. In England, this worked in favor of respectable conservatism and against the embers of Commonwealth radicalism: in France, where the Bourbons still clung to *pouvoir personel,* the same Cosmopolis was emancipatory. Beginning with a plan to translate Chambers' *Cyclopedia,* making English ideas available to the French reading public, the *Encyclopédie* turned into a series of radical manifestos, which the political authorities tried hard (in the long run, in vain) to suppress.

In contrast with respectable English Newtonianism, the ideas of the Encyclopedists thus became a first step toward dismantling the modern scaffolding. Without questioning the "national" basis of the state, they challenged the autocracy of the French State. Without undermining the original Cartesian separation of action and passion, reason and emotion, Jean-Jacques Rousseau likewise raised the question, "How can reason be educated to handle the life of the emotions?" Yet, despite this novelty, Rousseau did not threaten the foundations of rationalism. Rousseau's admirer Immanuel Kant, for example, strongly insisted on setting reason, which bears the burden of moral reflection, against "inclination" and the emotions, which at best confuse, and at worst block our moral capacity. Only Kant's successors found in his work the starting point for a serious science of psychology, and worked their way back to a position that set aside the Cartesian separation of reason from emotion.

Questions about the social order, then, refer to human societies in a given "natural scheme of things": here, our task is to focus less on the development of social and political ideas between 1700 and 1980, than on the changes in the underlying picture of the natural order by which those political or social changes were cosmopolitically rationalized. From 1750 on, the picture was at all stages open to revision; and, from Newton to Holbach, Kant, and Herder, and on to Darwin, Marx, and Freud, every basic change in accepted ideas about nature carried implications for accepted ideas about society as well.

In 1727, the venerable Isaac Newton finally died, in his mid-80s. At that time, most people (above all, in England) took on trust nearly all the timbers in the scaffolding of Modernity. For the time being, it seemed, "self evidence" immunized these doctrines against criticism. If any of them was openly questioned, people crossed their hearts and swore that it "stood to reason"; and it took a whole generation after Newton before influential writers argued for scientific hypotheses incompatible with those presuppositions.

By the late 20th century, the position of both the scientific élite and the general public has so changed that *not one* of those doctrines is still a part of educated common sense, in any but an attenuated form. Today, we need no longer assume either that nature is generally stable, or that matter is purely inert, or that mental activities must be entirely conscious and rational. Nor do we any longer equate the "objectivity" of scientific work with "non-involvement" in the processes being studied. Least of all, do we see the distinction between "reasons" and "causes" as necessitating the separation of Humanity from Nature.

Living in a time when our understanding of ecology prevents us from ignoring the engagement of humans in the causal processes of nature, we know how damaging this last assumption can be: once we undo that knot, the rest of the fabric quickly unravels. The ecological reinsertion of human beings into the world of natural processes is, however, quite a recent feature of thought. From 1720 well into the 20th century, most philosophers and natural scientists continued to defend, in one way or another, their investment in keeping Humanity apart from Nature—"in a world by itself."

The dismantling of the modern scaffolding, thus, cut across the grain of accepted ideas. Each challenge to it initially faced hostility, and even scorn.

Growing experiential testimony forced the supporters of the respectable account to conduct a rearguard retreat. But, as they conceded defeat on one count, they reassembled the surviving timbers of the scaffolding into a stable new configuration. So, the modern world view preserved its original stability a little longer. Looking back, some writers have interpreted these hard-fought disputes as the marks of an enduring conflict between science and superstition. This reading of the facts is anachronistic. Before the Reformation, Christianity had little investment in doctrines which natural science had any reason to dispute. What scientific innovation went on, for example, at the hands of Albert the Great or Nicolas of Cusa, was exposed to few theological constraints. (In the mid-1400s, Nicolas played with ideas about possible worlds which proved lethal to Giordano Bruno in 1600.) The alleged incompatibility of science and theology was thus a conflict *within* Modernity, which arose as the growth of experience gave scientists occasion to question beliefs used by Counter-Reformation Catholics and Protestants alike *after* 1650, in their edifying sermons on the wisdom of God's creation.

Similarly, the Catholic hierarchy and their Protestant opponents were under pressure, and reacted defensively, *after* the Reformation. From then on, recurrent controversies over such topics as the age of the Earth, the origin of species, or the material nature of physiological processes, pitted a system of dogmatic theory against the skeptical testimony of human experience, and challenged the position of people whose position was less a belief in any particular doctrine than a belief in belief itself. One early victim from 16th-century Spain was the Unitarian physician and theologian, Michael Servetus, who had escaped trial by the Catholic Inquisition in France and taken refuge in Geneva, only to be burned at the stake there in 1553, at Calvin's urging. Still, one thing must be noted. The theories at issue in the attacks on such men as Servetus, Bruno, and Galileo did not involve long-standing matters of medieval theology: they all turned on the novel assumptions about the order of nature that made up the scaffolding of the modern world picture. Far from perpetuating "medieval" intolerance, the condemnation of Galileo, Bruno, or Servetus represented cruelty of a specifically "modern" kind.

It is time to look in more detail at the ways in which the "modern" scaffolding came under criticism, and was bit by bit demolished. How, then, did people come to recognize how little empirical basis the new physics yet rested on? When did they discover how little their scientific goals justified such arbitrary restrictions on the scope of speculation? Some timbers in the scaffolding proved more defensible than others; and their differing cosmopolitical importance made it more urgent to defend some of them than others. The dismantling of the less critical timbers had already begun by the 1750s, but (we shall see) the entire task would not be completed until well into the 20th century.

1750–1914: Dismantling the Scaffolding

The first doctrine to be questioned was the denial that Nature has a History, and the reliance on developing a Biblical time-scale for Nature. That doctrine was most popular in Britain. The scholar who added up the years in the Old Testament before the birth of Jesus, and reached a date for Creation of 4,004 B.C., was an Anglican Archbishop: more traditional scholars took seriously Augustine's warning, from the last days of the Roman Empire, against trusting such numerological calculations. While many Anglicans assumed that God made the world with its chief features in their present form only a few thousand years ago—which left no room for any long-term historical development of Nature—by the 1750s this restriction was being widely ignored. In 1755, Immanuel Kant published his book on *Universal Natural History and Theory of the Heavens,* in which he used the Newtonian ideas of motion and gravitation to show how the whole astronomical universe might have developed from a first random distribution of material particles. This (he thought) fulfilled Newton's mission, rather than undermining it, even though his account took it for granted that the Cosmos must have existed for far longer than previous Newtonians had assumed.

The 18th century also saw new work in historical geology and in the humanities. The Edinburgh of David Hume and James Hutton, like Vico and Giannone's Naples or the Königsberg of Kant, Herder, and Hamann, lay at the margin of 18th-century Europe. Away from active centers of politics and religion, undisturbed by the pressures of nationalism, an Immanuel Kant could go his own way at home more easily than in Rome, London, or Berlin. While James Hutton was at work in geology, Adam Smith made ethics a jumping off point for economics, Johann Gottfried Herder raised new questions about the historical development of human ideas, and so opened a door into the history of culture; while his colleague, Johann Georg Hamann, made equally original excursions into the theory of language.

The collision between historical geology and the Bible came to its head in England. In his book, *Les Époques de la Nature,* the 18th-century French naturalist, Géorges Buffon, had long ago read *Genesis* in less restrictive terms: there was, to him, no problem in taking the "days of Creation" as geological eras. But, as in America today, religious fundamentalists in Victorian England set their horses at impossibly high fences: as a result, the groundwork for the controversy over Darwin's theory of the evolution of species had already been prepared by geologists in the 1840s and 1850s. After a bruising debate, only a few irreconcilables continued to fight on that front; and, by now, little is learned about the history of nature from reading the Bible, except for those who see the cosmological "big bang" as evidence of Divine Creation.

The extension in the natural time scale from thousands to millions, and even thousands of millions of years, went only partway to putting human and natural history on a par; and there is still a residual dispute among philosophers over the question of how far this can really be done. Hegel opposed doing so: for him, natural processes were still repetitive, and only human actions creative. By contrast, Marx was a forerunner of the "monists". Reading Darwin, he saw that one can no longer treat all natural processes as equally mechanical, and deny creativity to nature: for him, the evolution of nature is a precursor to the history of humanity. The relative status of human history and natural history still turned, for late-19th-century philosophers, on the relationship of (causal) processes to (rational) actions; and there, for students of hermeneutics or action-theory at least, it remains.

Other cosmopolitical doctrines were defended more obstinately, and took longer to dislodge. One was specially hard to undermine: the belief in "inert matter" which had created intractable problems in explaining vital and mental activities. Reading Bertrand Russell's *Autobiography,* we can see that educated people in Britain still took this on trust in the 1880s. So, in the late 19th century, Russell enters philosophy by the same road as Descartes. Struck by the "passivity" of natural processes, considered in mechanistic terms, he can find no room in Nature for the experiences he sums up in the word "consciousness", and feels bound to treat Mind as a coequal with, but distinct from Matter. His program of philosophical analysis did not identify those categories—as Descartes had done—as separate "substances"; but it committed him to stating the issues of epistemology in dualistic terms. As the old wisecrack has it,

"What is Matter? Never Mind! What is Mind? No Matter!"

The scientific ground for the belief in "inert" or "passive" Matter had in fact been undercut long before Russell. La Mettrie had criticized the assumption in the 1720s; and, in 1777, Joseph Priestley showed that it makes no difference to the explanatory power of the Newtonian theories, whether you treat his material particles as intrinsically inert, or else as centers of physical action. In some respects, treating material objects as "active" made their properties easier to account for: Priestley quotes the Jesuit philosopher, Roger John Boscovich, who showed that one can view the "impenetrability" of a body—always a key feature for physics and philosophy—as the effect of a "strong force of repulsion" operating at its surface. Boscovich was embarrassed by Priestley's support: he did not want a notorious materialist as an ally. But, once the dust kicked up by Priestley had settled, his ideas were ignored, and the general belief in the axiom of inertia was left unshaken.

The early-20th-century revival of epistemology, in the work of Mach and Russell, and later of Viennese and Anglo-American philosophers in the 1920s and 1930s, started off once again from questions that took the inertia of matter for granted. For purposes of theoretical physics, this presupposition was undercut by the rise of quantum physics after 1900, and notably by Schrödinger's wave mechanics and Heisenberg's quantum mechanics in 1927. To John Dewey's credit, his sense of the weaknesses in Descartes' program allowed him to see at once how destructively the new system of physics affected the program of modern philosophy. His 1929 Gifford Lectures not only criticized the Quest for Certainty as a central goal of modern philosophy; but also showed how Heisenberg had emancipated us from the constraints imposed in the 17th century, when people began to view nature as a giant *machine,* and so created the Cartesian divisions between matter and mind, causality and rationality, nature and humanity.

———————

One final timber in the Modern Framework was for a long time quite intractable: this separation of rationality from causality, and humanity from nature. In the 1980s, it has been a commonplace that we need to reintegrate humanity (and the rational conduct of agents) with nature (and the causal interactions of objects), and find places for them within an *ecological* account of the larger world—whether "human" or "natural". Right up to our own days, however, many people were unwilling to give up this separation of Human Nature from Material Nature; and, by this stage in our inquiry, the reasons are clear enough.

From 1750 to 1914, as the generations passed, philosophers, exact scientists, novelists and poets alike found ways of regaining the cultural ground that had been lost as a side effect of the Thirty Years' War. But it was a hard business, and all this ground had to be won back, inch by inch. The surgery imposed on European thought by the 17th-century zealots and perfectionists was so drastic that convalescence was unavoidably slow. The apotheosis of logic and formal rationality struck deep roots, and for a long time had made the status of "feelings" or "emotions" problematic. Both humanists and scientists—on the one side, novelists; on the other, physiologists and psychologists—faced thorny tangles in their attempts to record and explain our emotional experience.

On the humanist side, the story of this regained ground is a chapter in the history of the novel. For Daniel Defoe in the 1720s, character and episode are still largely matters of circumstance: in this, he writes like a casuist, and continues the tradition of medieval and Renaissance moral theology. Fifty years later—though the author's intentions are satirical—the heroes (or villains) of Laclos' *Les Liaisons Dangereuses* still act on the rational calculations of Cartesian Mind. Jane Austen's plots rest on honest feelings, and more or less well developed self-appraisal; but Anthony Trollope and Charles Dickens show the possibility of characters who are too "driven" to master the arts of self-understanding. So, a road opened up that led to "psychological" novelists, like Fyodor Dostoevsky, Henry James, and Virginia Woolf.

To say this is not to make the Novel an inescapably "romantic" genre. As a 19th-century position, romanticism never broke with rationalism: rather, it was rationalism's mirror-image. Descartes exalted a capacity for formal rationality and logical calculation as the supremely "mental" thing in human nature, *at the expense of* emotional experience, which is a regrettable by-product of our bodily natures. From Wordsworth or Goethe on, romantic poets and novelists tilted the other way: human life that is ruled by calculative reason alone is scarcely worth living, and nobility attaches to a readiness to surrender to the experience of deep emotions. This is not a position that *transcends* 17th-century dualism: rather, it accepts dualism, but votes for the opposite side of every dichotomy.

In science, the development of physiology in the early- and mid-19th century broadened the scope of scientific inquiry not just in substance, but also in method. Reading the history of science after 1700, we might infer that it changed because scientists extended the *range* of their subjects, continually reapplying a common "scientific method" to new phenomena. The truth is more interesting. As scientists moved out into historical geology, chemistry, or systematic biology, and later into physiology and neurology, electromagnetism and relativity, evolution and ecology, they did not employ a single repertory of "methods", or forms of explanation. As they attacked each new field of study, the first thing they had to find out was *how* to study it. Historical geology is *historical,* so its problems can neither be stated in the same terms, nor solved by the same methods, as

Newton's problems in mechanics. Reconstructing the history of the Earth demanded *historiographical* reflection, also.

Similarly, in the 19th century, when French physicians turned to the ideas of physics and chemistry to create the new science of physiology, they did not simply weigh and measure living organisms, as though they were no different from orbiting planets or inanimate rocks. Instead, their concern with the relevance of physiology to the understanding of health and sickness obliged them to develop new types of explanation, focussed on terms like "function" and "dysfunction"—i.e., good and bad modes of bodily operation—which are irrelevant to physical objects and systems. (Planets do not have "good" or "bad" orbits: they simply move as they move.) As Claude Bernard put it, "experimental medicine"—as he called his new science—may be indebted to physics and chemistry, but it is to "physics and chemistry carried out *in the special field of life*"; and this qualification is crucial. How are we to tell if someone's heart is in good shape? How can we ease cardiac insufficiency? The "good" and the "bad" are built into the foundation of such issues. It is still possible for a molecular biochemist to use *value-free* methods; but medical research, like clinical medicine, has essentially to do with what Aristotle called "the good and the bad for human beings."

By the mid-19th century, then, the natural sciences were no longer, *in practice,* coldly factual products of "value-free" reason, as they might have remained if they had continued to restrict their fields of study to objects and systems that were in fact inert, inanimate, and unthinking. Having taken this crucial step away from the mechanistic theories of 17th-century physics, 19th-century scientists went further. The further steps, from bodily functions to the sensory functions of the eye and ear, and on to the so-called "higher" mental functions, were a simple progression. Immanuel Kant had seen insurmountable obstacles to a Science of Psychology: that, in his eyes, meant treating "mentality" as another mathematically predictable causal phenomenon, governed by laws as rigid as those of planetary motion. But his successors in Germany moved into psychology from physiology rather than from physics, and so circumvented his objections. Questions in sensory physiology, about the functioning or malfunctioning of the eyes and the visual system, can be regarded as physiological ones, like questions about any bodily organs; but, since the organs in question are *sensory* ones, the functions in question are "mental" and can be viewed, as well, from the other side of the Cartesian divide. From the 1860s on, then, Hermann Helmholtz and his colleagues restated the issues of mind and body in terms designed to escape from that Cartesian dualism. They called the resulting system "monism"; but, until the late 19th century, their focus was on "cognitive", not "affective" functions.

As a result, the emotions did not become topics for scientific study either quickly or easily. For much of the century, indeed, psychiatrists saw madness as rooted, primarily, in cognitive confusion or brain injury. That is the background against which Sigmund Freud began his odyssey: as a student of Meynert working on the neurology of aphasia—the loss of a capacity to understand or to produce speech—he was always a monist. When he turned to medicine, he was faced by cases of hysteria, obsession, and compulsive behavior, yet he initially took it for granted that those conditions too were, in some way, caused by neurological defect, and so were, in a sense, effects of "bad nerves." It was an ironical but crucial change. The philosophical problems of mind and body were not instantly decided in favor of monism; but now the emotions were squarely on the agenda of science and medicine. Nor could they be treated any longer as "subjective" or "fanciful": they represented "real" features of human life and experience, and had to be studied as such.

As Freud soon rediscovered, throughout the Modern Era the word *emotions* had been a screen word, to allude to (without actually naming) the disreputable topic of sexuality. By now, Montaigne's candor had long been out of fashion: in referring to an orgasm, an 18th-century author would use a euphemism like "the height of passion". Of all strong human feelings, sexual emotion appeared the gravest threat to the hierarchical Nation-State. Novelists from Defoe to Thackeray and on knew that "love", and "falling in love" are no respecters of class distinction. A scientist who loved his Goethe, and who, like Goethe, saw no strict division between science and the humanities, Freud took pleasure in emphasizing the power of repressed sexuality in the life of "respectable" social climbers.

———————

By 1914, then, all the material was ready to hand to justify dismantling the last timbers of the intellectual scaffolding that had, since the late 17th century, established the parameters of acceptable thought. A few people were also beginning to have a proper feeling for the depth of the impending changes. Recalling pre-World War I days from 1924, Virginia Woolf declared, with a charming exaggeration, "In or about December 1910, human nature changed." She was alluding to the effect of the major post-impressionist exhibition organized in London in that month by two fellow Bloomsbury figures, Roger Fry and Desmond MacCarthy. For England just before 1914, that exhibition, along with Diaghilev's *Ballets Russes de Monte Carlo,* was taken to mean that the tyranny of Victorian ideas was over. In 1914, too, the political and cultural structures of Central Europe were losing political and social credibility, in the ways splendidly presented in Robert Musil's novel, *The Man Without Qualities*. This was notably so in the Vienna of Mach and Wittgenstein, Schoenberg and Klimt, Freud and Musil. The Habsburgs chose to make their city the guardian of the Counter-Reformation: the Viennese were therefore responsive to any criticism of its values, and many of the intellectual and artistic battles of the period began in Vienna, before they went on to affect the other cultural centers of Europe.

The evidence of those battles is plain to see. Across the spectrum from physics to psychology, no branch of the natural sciences any longer relied on support from the 17th-century faith in the rationality of Nature: all of them could stand on their own, with methods of explanation based on their own first-hand experience. From 1890 to 1910, the physicists J. J. Thomson, Albert Einstein, and Max Planck broke the links between current physical theory and earlier Newtonian orthodoxy. The new physics so created—particles smaller than the lightest atom, space and time that lack sharp-edged distinctness, matter and energy that seemed interchangeable—undercut the last pretense that Euclidian geometry and Newtonian mechanics are certain, final, and indispensable to the rational understanding of Nature.

Meanwhile, Darwin's theory was underpinned by the work of William Bateson, who revived and extended Gregor Mendel's ideas about genetics; while Malinowski, Lévy-Bruhl and other colleagues revived the study of humanity, extending and enriching the work of 19th-century historians by their studies of comparative religion and cultural anthropology. Finally, the very axle of the Modern World View, around which all else rotated—the separation of reason from emotion, thinking from feeling, with the associated devaluation of *eros*—was open to damaging assault by Freud and the psychoanalysts, who called in question the Cartesian equation of "mentality" and "conscious calculation", and of "reasonableness" with "formal rationality". For the first time, a general reader could feel that Hume's insistence on the indispensability of feelings as springs of human action was more than a source of witty paradox, as when he declared,

"The Reason is, *and ought to be,* a slave of the passions."

By 1910, culture and society in Western Europe were on the verge of returning to the world of political moderation and human tolerance which was the dream of Henri de Navarre and Michel de Montaigne. Given this material, the 1910s and 1920s might have seen a definitive demolition of the modern scaffolding. Natural scientists were free to pursue all their subjects by independent methods. Anthropologists could celebrate the diversity of different cultures. For their part, politicians had the chance to encourage a decent modesty about claims to sovereignty by the nation state, as Norman Angell urged in *The Great Illusion,* and so to create the transnational "League of Nations" that might have prevented the spasms of intra-European violence that began in 1914. In Western Europe, then, humanity was ready for a cultural and social emancipation, and might have experienced it in the next few years, *if other things had been equal.*

1920–1960: Re-renaissance Deferred

All other things were not equal. Instead of Europe returning to the values of the Renaissance, the roof fell in. No League of Nations existed, nor could other institutions, transnational or subnational, restrain the ambitions or curb the actions of Europe's self-willed sovereign nations. It was fifty more years before people in Europe and North America were truly open to a revival of Renaissance attitudes. Meanwhile, four years of reckless slaughter by sovereign nation-states were followed first by an inequitable peace, rationalized in terms of self-righteous half-truths, then by financial collapse and economic depression; and all of this led to a five-year renewal of warfare, which engulfed the globe from Norway to New Zealand, London to Tokyo. Thereafter, those who had survived the collapse of the inherited system of sovereign states, and the subsequent economic catastrophe, spent the fifteen years after 1945 hoping just to reestablish the *status quo ante.* Even in the 1950s, it was too soon for most people to contemplate any radical changes of mind.

Shortly after November 1918, it is true—with the vindication of Einstein's theories over Newton's by observations of the solar eclipse of 1920—the frailty of the last remaining timbers of the scaffolding was at last evident. The defeat of the Central Powers in the First World War finally imperilled the diplomatic settlement achieved in the Peace of Westphalia in 1648. In Germany, and even more strikingly in Austria-Hungary, two major dynastic régimes of Europe crumbled, and saw their dependent territories dispersed. These changes now seem a faint echo of the 17th-century cataclysm, but they were enough to compel a reappraisal of the "absolutely sovereign" nation-state. Norman Angell's critique, put into practice by Woodrow Wilson, led to an acceptance of the need for transnational institutions: first, the League of Nations, and thirty years later the United Nations, the World Bank, and a dozen functional and technical intergovernmental agencies. The years 1920 to 1960 were a time of transition, during which a generation grew up for whom the respectable opinion of the years from 1700 to 1914 lost its traditional cosmopolitical support, without finding any clear alternative.

From 1910 to 1960, then, a return to the values of the Renaissance (a "re-Renaissance", so to say) was deferred. This is so not just on the political and social level, but in most fields of art and science as well. Rather than pursue the possibilities opened up by the demolition of the 17th-century framework—exploiting the richness of anthropology and history, reintegrating thought and feeling, and restoring humanity to its proper place within (not apart from) the order of nature--intellectuals and artists of Europe again turned their backs on these tasks. Just as the ground was readier than at any time since 1610 for a renewed toleration of diversity, ambiguity and uncertainty—the hallmarks of Renaissance culture and rhetoric—political collapse and military conflict pointed the other way. Richness of feeling and content were suspect: formal rigor and exactitude were again the Order of the Day.

By the standards of our narrative, then, those who led the intellectual and cultural response to the disaster of the First World War chose not to move in a humanistic direction but rather to return to formalism. In a dozen areas, late-19th-century artists and thinkers had explored those areas that the first generations of "moderns" most undervalued: history and psychology, notably the psychology of the emotions. For forty years after 1920, the tide went into reverse. In music, Gustav Mahler's chromatism was condemned as romantic excess, overripeness verging on corruption like the texture of a persimmon, while Anton Bruckner's symphonic grandeur was seen as a dead end: the intellectual rigor of "twelve-tone" music, exemplified by Arnold Schoenberg, Anton Webern, and Alban Berg, was assumed to mark the road to the musical future. Painters and other visual artists subjected "representation" to the same scornful fire as romanticism in music: the works of Piet Mondriaan and the constructivists, for instance, displayed the same intellectual cool as twelve-tone composition in music. True, in Germany, George Grosz and the expressionists were exploring further the road into the emotions opened up before 1914 by (for instance) Oskar Kokoschka and Egon Schiele; but the greater part of the European *avant garde* chose to revive the rationalist dream of a clean slate and a return to abstract fundamentals.

The same move away from the historical, concrete, or psychological, toward the formal, abstract, or logical, is evident in natural science in the 1920s and '30s. The leading mathematicians of the time concentrated not on applied problems (let alone, computers) but on problems in "pure" analysis, differential geometry, and other eminently non-applied fields.

Physicists applauded the fact that the concepts of general relativity and quantum mechanics eluded attempts at grasping them intuitively, aside from their mathematical definitions. In biology, J. H. Woodger tried to recast genetic theory in an axiomatic system, but the results of his work proved that formal logic limits the theoretical imagination as much as facilitating it: if working geneticists had taken it more seriously, it would have delayed—not accelerated—a biochemical attack on the genetic code. Even the behavioral scientists attempted to construct axiomatic theories, or homeostatic systems, which might give psychology and sociology the abstract power of Euclid's geometry or Russell and Whitehead's logic. In retrospect, they would have done better—like their predecessors, Wilhelm Wundt and Max Weber, before 1914—to set aside dreams of a universal recipe for theory construction, and focus instead on the varied demands of their specific problems.

One key example of this general return to formalism is the revival of positivism by the Vienna Circle philosophers in the 1920s. Descartes' methods (as we saw) always had a double focus, in part cryptanalytical—to decipher the "language" in which the Book of Nature was "written"—and in part foundationalist, to give both science and epistemology a "provably certain" basis. The Vienna Circle, too, embodied two different strands. Members like Hans Reichenbach and Rudolph Carnap, both of whom were more German than Austrian, set out to reformulate the issues of natural science and philosophy in abstract, universal terms. Others, like Otto Neurath, who was a minister in Austria's postwar Socialist government, had a more pragmatic bent. The Vienna Circle's chief preoccupation, with reviving "exactitude" and building a "unified science" around a core from mathematical logic, was thus diluted by a practical concern with issues of social and political reform. Still, the nostalgia for the certainties of 17th-century philosophy that motivated this alliance of positivism with formal logic, notably within the "unified science" movement, is hard to overlook—"Where Euclid was, there Russell shall be!"

The effects of this nostalgia were not all happy. As the sciences progressively extended their scope, between 1720 and 1920, one thing working scientists did was to rediscover the wisdom of Aristotle's warning about "matching methods to problems": as a result, they edged away from the Platonist demand for a single, universal "method", that of physics by preference. In the 1920s and 1930s, philosophers of science in Vienna returned to the earlier, monopolistic position. Of all the natural sciences, theoretical physics had most in common with formal logic and pure mathematics, so (it seemed) one only needed suitable redefinitions of its basic concepts in order to build formal bridges linking physics to the system of *Principia Mathematica.* Biology too might be brought into the resulting "unified" science, if only biophysics and organic chemistry were placed at its core. That left only the "soft-centered" fields that Descartes had excluded all along—cultural anthropology, sociology, etc.—outside the rigorously reconstructed house of "science".

The most revealing illustration of the direction of European culture between the Wars, apart from the Vienna Circle, is found in *architecture.* The pioneer critics of "modernism" today, those who call most forcefully for a "post-modern" style, are to be found among architects. Given the ambiguities in the term *modern,* their calls may appear irrelevant to the Modernity that has been our subject here. But they have something of broader significance to say, if we sharpen up our analysis of the varied *styles* of modernism. Some see the "modernist" movement in architectural design as starting in the 1890s, with Charles Rennie Mackintosh in Glasgow, Otto Wagner and Josef Hoffmann in Vienna: as such, it overlaps what we call *art nouveau.* Yet, even before 1914, the biologically inspired forms of *art nouveau* were already being superseded in the buildings of Hoffmann and Adolf Loos and in the furniture of the Wiener Werkstätte. Before 1920, then, much of modern architecture and interior design relied more on stylistic novelty than on radically new design principles: where the *art nouveau* designers and architects took their decorative details from plant forms, Hoffmann and his school looked to geometry.

For his part, Adolf Loos rejected all reliance on decoration that wholly lacked a function, though he never opposed matching buildings to their uses or places. In his view, any design should *show us what the building is for:* however "modern" it might otherwise be, a chalet by Loos could never be mistaken for a home in the city, let alone an office block or art museum. After the First World War, architecture took a fresh direction, turning away from the lush and decorative, the historical and emotional; the resulting revolt against ornament and local color (or color of any kind) is one leading mark of what became the central movement in "modernist" architecture, which culminated in the buildings and writings of Mies van der Rohe.

As a theorist of modern architectural design, Mies is a figure of the inter-War years: as a practitioner, it was he who gave his own theories their most spectacular applications. Mies abhorred local color. Instead, he looked for *universal* principles of design, equally appropriate to all geographical locations. This was not just a technical choice. His wish for "universality" was the explicit expression of a Platonist point of view, which he claimed to have derived from reading St. Augustine. These principles defined the central structure of a building, not in functional, but in structural (geometrical) terms, so he did not share Loos's belief that the form of a building must display its use: on the contrary, he was happy to transform a design first intended for a corporate headquarters into a museum of modern art. In this respect, Mies' ideas were not just universal but abstract, like the universal abstract ideas at the base of Descartes' philosophy. His program for architecture produced buildings whose technical mark was mathematical clarity and precision, but which could be used for a dozen different purposes, and were equally at home (or out of place) in any city or country. An apartment block by Mies may thus be used to illustrate a text on Cartesian or "coordinate" geometry, in which spatial locations are referred back to a given "origin of coordinates" (O), and to the given "axes of reference" (Ox, Oy and Oz).

In Mies' principles, we see the man who dominated architectural design in Europe and North America right up to the 1950s rejecting the diversity of history and geography, and the specific needs of particular human activities, in favor of universal, timeless principles. This is the step that Descartes and the 17th-century rationalists took, when they ignored the varied practices and the ambiguous, uncertain opinions that were endemic to 16th-century humanism, in favor of pursuing *theories and proofs* that could command consensus. Between the two World Wars, other fine arts went the same way, wiping the slate clean and making a fresh start, as witness the paintings of Josef Albers; and, in due course, the renewed dream of a "clean slate" became a central theme of culture *entre deux guerres*. To that extent, the movement we now know as "modernism" in the arts echoed the founding themes of 17th-century Modernity as surely as did the philosophical program for a formally structured unified science: so understood, the "modernism" of architecture and fine arts in the 1920s shared more with the "modernity" of rationalist philosophy and physics than we might otherwise suppose.

Given these unforeseen similarities, the further question arises: "How far did the political and cultural situation in Europe in the 1920s and '30s compare with that in the heyday of 17th-century rationalism?" If we considered only intellectual styles, artistic genres, and the like, these resemblances might appear thin, superficial, and even accidental. But, if we go deeper, stronger links are apparent. Whether in science or philosophy, ethics or the fine arts, the focal issues in both periods won attention, not just for reasons of intrinsic elegance and formal cogency— "decontextually"—but because the actual situation compelled Europeans to take seriously the seeming need to begin again "from scratch" on both practical and theoretical levels.

By 1920, one could reasonably conclude that Europe was facing the problems of national and international organization all over again. After the First World War, the established political order of nation-states and monarchies was in crisis, just when the Newtonian foundation of current cosmology was meeting its most damaging challenge. The effect of this joint crisis was nowhere more obvious than at the core of the Habsburg domains. None of the pre-1914 Powers collapsed more completely as a result of the War than did the Austro-Hungarian Dual Monarchy; nor did any other city see its *raison d'être* more suddenly destroyed than Vienna. As Austria lost its Imperial identity, and had to construct a Republican identity from scratch, the contemporaneous defeat of Newton's natural philosophy—the basis of the Modern Cosmopolis—by Einstein's relativity physics, called for equally "constructive" efforts in science and the arts. It is no wonder, then, that in Vienna, of all places, the cultural ambitions of the 17th century were revived with special enthusiasm.

Those of us who grew up in England in the 1930s learned to accept both the myth of Modernity and the need for a fresh start, at the very time when the politics and culture of Europe and North America were most riddled with uncertainties. In our generation, as in those of Donne and Descartes, all received ideas about nature and society came in question at the same time. In the 1930s as in the 1630s, the traditional system of European states was in dispute: the dismemberment of the Habsburg Empire redrew the entire map of Central and Eastern Europe, while the economic ruin of Germany opened it up to the demagoguery of Adolf Hitler. In the 1930s as in the 1630s, too, the received cosmology was seemingly discredited: the scientific work of Albert Einstein and Werner Heisenberg undermined all the earlier certainties, even the public intelligibility, of physics. As a result, the 17th-century crisis of belief was replicated, not just in form, but in substance as well.

During the First World War, skeptical humanism had little chance. Begun in a spirit of dogmatic nationalism, the conflict ended in a flurry of idealistic slogans—"a War to end War" or "to make the World safe for Democracy". (During the Second World War, Allied rhetoric was not much more profound.) Later on, the nationalistic rhetoric of the two World Wars was replaced by the ideological rhetoric of the crusade against Communism: this shifted the ground of the argument, but did not otherwise modify it. (Hostility between Papists and Heretics had been sedulously kept alive, long after the Thirty Years' War: so too, now, with the Free World *vs.* the Reds, and International Socialism *vs.* Capitalist Imperialism.) Between the Wars, serious-minded European intellectuals faced the same task as had faced Leibniz after 1670: to find a neutral basis of communication between former enemies, devise a rational method for comparing ideas from different nations, and build transnational institutions that could prevent a renewal of international war.

Unfortunately, the attitudes and institutions available at the time were once again inadequate to this task. After 1930, when the business slump in the industrialized countries triggered economic disaster across the world, the middle ground shrank, and people's attention was focussed more and more on the two extremes. As so often, poets were the first to sense the way the wind was blowing: William Butler Yeats' prophetic vision of anarchy in *The Second Coming* ("the centre cannot hold"), which we compared to John Donne's *Anatomy of the World,* was written in 1921. With economic collapse, as the values of nationhood were corrupted into the unbridled brutality of a racist nationalism in Germany, Yeats himself was drawn toward the home-grown Irish version of Fascism; while other intellectuals in Britain, France, and elsewhere, in despair at the inability of their own national governments to deal constructively with the crisis in domestic and international affairs, felt obliged to consider seriously the policies and practices of the Soviet Union, as the one multinational power that openly presented itself at the time as concerned to deal with issues on an internationalist—or even "post-national"—level.

It has been easy enough in the 1970s and 1980s for the lucky inhabitants of the United States of America to look back at the history of the Popular Front in the 1930s, and see as madness the readiness of the democratic Left in Europe to join hands with the Communists. Those who lived on the spot through those years remember them very differently: as they knew at first hand, there was then no clear alternative. The Soviet show trials and purges of the 1930s were repulsive enough, but little was yet generally known about the even worse savageries in the Ukraine; and, besides, who else would stand up to Hitler and Mussolini? Many eminent members of the respectable oligarchy in Britain were equally ready to overlook and forgive the viciousness of Hitler's Nazi gangs, to the point of treating his Ambassador to London, Ribbentrop, as a welcome addition to the country-house life of an English weekend. Under the circumstances, it was not just weak-minded to see the defense of the fledgling Spanish Republic as an honorable cause.

By the late 1930s, the political and cultural situation in Western Europe was little better than in the 1630s: the "middle of the road" was nearly as empty as it had been after the murder of Henri IV. On the left, a few solid characters like Ernest Bevin in Britain found the régimes in both Germany and Russia equally unacceptable; in the dwindling center, the *Manchester Guardian* was not wholly dissatisfied at being officially banned in both countries; but, on the right, Winston Churchill had only a small band of allies, and was mostly seen as an eccentrically obstinate figure in an inappropriately Cromwellian mold. After September, 1939, with the renewed outbreak of war in Europe, first in Poland, in Belgium and France, Finland and Norway, and eventually worldwide, only Sweden and Switzerland among the European nations remained sedulously outside the conflict; while many conservative politicians in Europe continued to wonder if they were not in the wrong war at the wrong time, against the wrong enemy. As in the 1620s and '30s, however, it was hard for anyone to set the claims of nationhood aside, and look beyond the military tasks of the moment to a world that would be free to put the immediate crisis behind it and think ahead to institutions that could indeed help to prevent a further recurrence of "national" wars. Only after December 1941, when the Japanese attack at Pearl Harbor had pushed the United States into a pool it never freely chose to jump into, were the long-term prospects of an Allied victory clear enough for such questions to be raised.

The parallel between the 1630s and the 1930s requires one gloss. As developed in the 1920s and 1930s, the myth of modernity and the dream of a fresh start did not replicate the 17th-century rationalist research program perfectly; nor did they reaffirm without change the model of formal exactitude that underlay 17th-century natural philosophy. Rather, the ideas of strict "rationality" modeled on formal logic, and of a universal "method" for developing new ideas in any field of natural science, were adopted in the 1920s and 1930s with *even greater* enthusiasm, and in an *even more extreme* form, than had been the case in the mid-17th century. After Descartes, the notions of "exactitude" and "rigor" were themselves refined and sharpened. In the late 19th century, David Hilbert showed what a truly "pure" mathematical system must be like: as a result, the system of formal logic and arithmetic built up by Frege and Russell was in the end even "purer" than Euclidian geometry, which had served as René Descartes' model. The Vienna Circle program was, thus, even more formal, exact, and rigorous than those of Descartes or Leibniz. Freed from all irrelevant representation, content, and emotion, the mid-20th-century *avant garde* trumped the 17th-century rationalists in spades.

By 1914, then, the intellectual and artistic ground was ready for a revival of Renaissance humanism: for a reintegration of humanity with nature, a restoration of respect for Eros and the emotions, for effective transnational institutions, a relaxation of the traditional antagonism of classes, races and genders, an acceptance of pluralism in the sciences, and a final renunciation of philosophical foundationalism and the Quest for Certainty. The ground was ready, but the time was still not ripe: a revolution was in the making for which its beneficiaries were not ready. Rather than pursue the possibilities opened by demolishing the "modern" world view, people had to learn the hard way. Thirty years of slaughter in the name of religion preceded the setting up of the modern system of nation-states: thirty years of slaughter in the name of nationhood were needed before Europeans and Americans were ready to acknowledge its shortcomings.

1965–1975: Humanism Reinvented

The Second World War, then, represented the culmination of social and historical processes that began in the 1650s, with the creation of the Modern era—the "modern" world, the "modern" state, and "modern" thought. As such, it was the last time when the people of Europe could endorse, and act out, the ideals and ambitions of Modernity in a quite *unselfconscious* manner. Writers like Oswald Spengler had argued in the 1920s that Europe's world dominance was ending; but the claim that Modernity is already "over and done with" was to come only after 1945. From 1940 on, Winston Churchill's oratory kept the spirit of nationhood vigorously alive in Britain, while its preeminent sovereignty bled away: in response, its people staged a final reenactment of their self-image, as invented in Shakespeare's *Henry V*. "There'll always be an England," they sang, but ignored the subtext, "England will never be the same again."

Before the painful recovery after 1945 went very far, it was clear that the *Europe des patries* (or of sovereign nations) would survive longer in the nostalgia of a Charles de Gaulle or a Margaret Thatcher than it would in the reality of late 20th-century economics and politics. The question was no longer whether Europe and the world would create "transnational" institutions at all: the only practical questions were, how soon those institutions would be set up, what forms they would take, and which functions they would take over from the omnicompetent sovereign nation state.

The intellectual and cultural situation in Europe and North America was just as deeply transformed, between the 1920s and the 1970s, as it was from the 1590s to the 1640s, but *in reverse*. By 1650, the humanist tolerance of uncertainty, ambiguity and diversity of opinion gave way to Puritan intolerance, rationalist insistence on universal and exact theory, and an emphasis on certainty in all things. Dressed up as "respectable opinion", the resulting cosmopolis kept its authority until well into the 20th century. By 1910 it was weakening, but its grip outlasted another thirty years of warfare among the nations of Europe, and people were ready to suspend the Quest for Certainty, acknowledge the demolition of the modern cosmopolis, and

return belatedly to the humane and liberal standpoint of the late Renaissance, only when the Second World War was well behind them.

No one who lived through the 1960s and early 1970s in New York or
California, Britain or West Germany, could doubt the scale of the social and
cultural changes they then saw. Many people of fifty or more hated all
aspects of it. Some of them misunderstood what was happening, and
blamed the younger generation as "out of hand" and "losing their values":
hence, the famous *generation gap*. But that question-begging phrase hid
the real issue. Cultural change always takes generational differences as a
vehicle: the distinctive thing about this one was the profundity of the
changes involved. The highly visible counter-culture of the 1960s was not
essentially a youth culture: the intellectual, psychological, and artistic
material for the new movement had been there for fifty years, waiting for
a generation to see the point and seize the day. Others have put the changes
in the two decades down to the Vietnam War, but that too at most is just
part of the story. The war was an *occasion* for these changes, but it had little
to do with their *content*.

By the 1950s, there were already the best of reasons, intellectual and
practical, for restoring the unities dichotomized in the 17th century:
humanity *vs.* nature, mental activity *vs.* its material correlates, human
rationality *vs.* emotional springs of action, and so on. The spasms of a
moribund world-view stopped those reasons from being effective until
after 1960, so the first generation to respond comprised Americans and
Europeans born in the 1940s and early 1950s. That was in part because they
had strong personal stakes in the then-current political situation. Facing
the risk of going (or seeing their contemporaries go) to kill their fellow-
humans in Vietnam, without a plausible color of self-defense, shocked
them into rethinking the claims of the nation, and above all its claim to
unqualified sovereignty. Rachel Carson had shown them that nature and
humanity are ecologically interdependent, Freud's successors had
brought them a better grasp of their emotional lives, and now disquieting
images on the television news called the moral wisdom of their rulers in
doubt. In this situation, one must be incorrigibly obtuse or morally
insensible to *fail* to see the point. This point did not relate particularly to
Vietnam: rather, what was apparent was the superannuation of the modern
world view that was accepted as the intellectual warrant for "nationhood"
in or around 1700.

To complete this ironical undoing of the counter-Renaissance, the
three-hundred-year drama of Modernity was framed by a new emblematic
assassination. Looking back at John Kennedy a quarter-century after his
death, we recognize that, for his contemporaries, he was larger than life.

In his inaugural address, he called America and the world to a new task, to think about humanity with the idealism and imagination on which the politicians of the 1980s have ostentatiously turned their backs. Since he invoked a "new generation" as the agents of this new work, the young of his time saw themselves as that generation. He himself, however, never shared their doubts about patriotism and nationalism: he launched the policy in Vietnam for which Lyndon Johnson was later blamed. With an Irish Catholic background, too, it was harder for John Kennedy than for some of his younger contemporaries to "hang loose" and work his way to a new vision of love, marriage, and family. His reputation as "a ladies' man" does not fully echo Henry of Navarre's reputation as *le vert galant*. Rather than displaying a feeling for gender equality, his extra-curricular activities had a more traditional character.

At both ends of Modernity, the accuracy of popular memory is one thing: its significance is another. After May 1610, people saw Henry's murder as the disaster that removed a last obstacle to the final, most catastrophic outburst of the Religious Wars. Had he lived, in fact, Henry might not have prevented (or even *tried to* prevent) the Thirty Years' War; yet this does not destroy the emblematic meaning of his policies, or of his death. The same is true in the case of John Kennedy. At the end of the day, our reservations about Kennedy the man leave untouched his wider status, as an *emblem*. He captured the imagination of America, and also of the world. Even if the perception is unrealistic, people in many lands still see him as one who (if he had lived) had the strength of character, intellectual power, and golden tongue needed to carry the world through into the new "post-national" age. To this day, pinned on the wall of, say, a Mexican farmhouse, one is likely to find two icons: the photographs of President John Kennedy and of Pope John XXIII. They embody that *aggiornamento*—that opening of the windows onto a new day—of which people in all countries still feel a need.

In thinking back to the transformations of the 1960s and 1970s, then, we must distinguish their timing from their content. As to their timing, the Vietnam War was a powerful stimulus to a generation whose parents were quiescent during the "scoundrel times" of Joseph McCarthy's 1950s; but, as to their content, the revolution of the late 1960s was a revolution *waiting to happen*. Once it began in earnest, all of the issues that had been forged together in the 17th-century scaffolding of Modernity were reconsidered in rapid succession. It may look as though issues of ecology and psychotherapy, biomedical science and voter registration, Mies van der Rohe's architecture and inequalities between the sexes, do not have any intrinsic connections; but, once the system of presuppositions and prejudices embodied in the traditional cosmopolis was taken apart, all of these things came into question, many of them irreversibly.

At the base of the Modern Cosmopolis lay the Cartesian opposition between the (supposed) "mechanical causality" of natural phenomena and the (supposed) "logical rationality" of human action. Treating the vital and mental activities of human beings as distinct from the physical and chemical phenomena of nature had put needless obstacles in the way of any effective physiology and psychology, and these obstacles had been circumvented only in the late-19th and early-20th century. Still, much of what had been successfully achieved on the level of theory had not yet been carried through into actual practice.

Even after Hiroshima, politicians and industrialists at first acted as though the activities of human beings need only be considered in rational, economic terms, and had a negligible influence on the causal economy of the natural world in which we exist. As late as 1960, the word "ecosystem" had not yet won a place in the political vocabulary of industrial nations. John Muir and Aldo Leopold had crusaded for the environment, and for the threatened populations of endangered species. But Rachel Carson's book *Silent Spring* first spoke, in 1962, to the entire public audience—that is, to an audience that was now ready to hear its message. From that time on, the political change was so rapid and profound that, within 20 years, no developed nation could feel self-respect unless its government had a "department of the environment" or an "environmental protection agency." This choice of name might often be self-serving or hypocritical, given the actual activities of the departments concerned, but as usual hypocrisy responds to the perceived demands of respectability. From 1970 on, politicians had at least to feign concern with the damage done to the natural world by industrial and other human activities.

Another basic element in the modern scaffolding was the idea that "mentality" should be logical and principled, calculative and unemotional. At its core, the ethos of the modern world, from Descartes to Freud, was rooted in expectations of *self-command.* In Europe and North America, notably in countries with a Puritan culture, individual human beings were expected to execute their life projects without letting themselves be "carried away" by their feelings, or turning for help to priests or doctors or anyone else. The Confessional was still available to Catholics; but there was a widespread sense through the whole Modern Age that putting oneself under spiritual guidance was a mark of weakness, consulting a psychiatrist a confession of failure. For the generation of the 1960s, that undervaluation of the emotions was at an end. Self-doubt was no longer inadmissible. At last you were free to confess to confused intentions or ambiguous feelings; nor were you asked to do your emotional homework singlehanded. For a new generation, "getting in touch with your feelings" was of such importance that seeking outside professional help became the sensible, obvious choice. Being in therapy was no longer a mark of weakness: now, it became the mark of true seriousness.

The turn to abstract, rationalist formalism in natural science and the arts, which had such power in the 1920s and 1930s, meanwhile lost its plausibility and charm. In music, the "twelve-tone" system of Webern and Schoenberg was no longer the exclusive way ahead to the musical future: one was again permitted to enjoy, admire, and even emulate the music of Gustav Mahler: new roads opened in America for composers like Philip Glass, Steve Reich, and John Adams. In parallel, there was a significant attack on the longstanding contrast of "serious" with "popular" music. The scaffolding of Modernity embodied a class based vision of modern society, so disillusion with injustice and inequality spilled over into music and the arts. Beginning with the Civil Rights movement and singers like Woody Guthrie in America, and the Beatles in Europe, popular ballads and protest songs ceased to be merely an artistic form and became a political force. Those who sang "We shall Overcome" in the 1960s meant what it said, as in South Africa today; while the governments of the Soviet Union and its East European colonies saw balladeers as a real political threat.

Abstract formalism has been no more durable in the visual arts than atonalism in music. For all the solid merits of a Josef Albers, no one after 1965 could argue that his was the only way ahead. The gestures of a Warhol or a Rauschenberg now seem in some respects exaggerated; but they dynamited a way back to half-a-dozen *genres* and styles that are far less abstract and less coolly calculated than those of the inter-War formalists and constructivists. Finally, the young architects were rebelling against the influence of Mies, which left indistinguishable buildings across the globe. With a fanfare typical of their profession, and a display of rhetoric against the Platonism of Mies, these younger architects led their fellow artists into a "post modern" World.

Parallel changes went on, more quietly, in the natural sciences. In the 1950s, many scientists and philosophers of science still conceded the imperial claim of physical theory to impose its explanatory patterns on all branches of science. (James Watson, whose work on the structure of DNA helped to launch molecular biology, could still regard evolution as a footnote to biochemistry; while Carl Hempel, as a late Vienna-Circle philosopher, denied that Darwin's evolution theory was scientific at all.) The growing power of ecology and medical science made it harder to deny to biology, however, a place of honor alongside and even equal to that of physical theory. Instead of being varied parts of a single, comprehensive, "unified science", the sciences now represented, rather, a confederation of enterprises, with methods and patterns of explanation to meet their own distinct problems. "Science" was no longer taken as a *singular* noun: instead, the phrase "natural sciences" is *plural,* and the Platonist image of a single, formal type of knowledge is replaced by a picture of enterprises that are always in flux, and whose methods of inquiry are adapted—as Aristotle taught—to "the nature of the case."

Even in mathematics, a new feeling for the concrete and particular entered the profession. Before the Second World War, there was some prejudice against "applied" work: from 1965 on, mathematicians were no longer ashamed to admit a preoccupation with mundane computer theory. Even in physics, abstract cosmic fields or research like general relativity began to lose their intellectual preeminence: it now became respectable to admit that questions about superconductivity, for example, are not just of practical weight but of theoretical importance. In biology likewise, immediately after 1945, the problems of medicine were seen as peripheral or incidental to theoretical biology: from the 1960s on, it was clearer that sickness and health provide the best places in which to study the nature of biological functioning, and the portmanteau phrase, "biomedical sciences" (rarely heard before 1960) achieved a new academic currency.

The changes in the 1960s and 1970s had far-reaching effects, too, on the style and content of political debate. Before Kennedy's time, politicians thought of their issues as resting on matters of technique. They took for granted the *goals* of national politics, and argued about the best *means* of fulfilling them. In those days, attention was focused on the "search for a better mousetrap", and the air shuttle between Boston and Washington flew politicians and technical advisers to and fro, from the District of Columbia to the Massachusetts Institute of Technology and back. After 1965, this changed: aside from the Vietnam debates, the 1960s saw a move away from a politics of national goals—which aimed at *consensus*—toward a politics aimed at redressing traditional injustices, driven by a *confrontation* of sectional interests. In the 18th and 19th centuries, the upper ("respectable") classes had assumed that the varied and numerous lower ("unfortunate") classes "knew their places", and could, if necessary, be kept in those places by social pressure of some kind.

Now, all these classes began to speak up for themselves, in distinct but concerted tones. In theory, the interests of the NAACP, La Raza, the Grey Panthers, and the Gay and Lesbian Alliance, were anything but identical: in practice, they united in opposition to those structural rigidities that "respectable" people had viewed as inevitable preconditions for a stable social order. There followed a sequence of assaults on the inequalities entrenched in European society around 1700, and legitimated by the new cosmopolis. Institutionalized racism, a flagrant injustice left long unaddressed, was the first to become a target of the civil rights movement. This was followed by others. Throughout the 1970s, all the inequalities built into modern society came under attack in turn: women, the elderly, the handicapped, lesbians and gays, all spoke up, one group after the other. Those who never questioned the rights and wrongs of modern nationhood found it a terrible shock. Jesus said, "The poor ye have always with you"—i.e., deserving objects of charity are always near at hand. Now, many believers in "traditional values" understood Him to mean, rather, that it is the business of the poor to stay poor, of blacks to stay deferent, of women to stay home, of the handicapped to stay in the back room, and of homosexuals to stay in the closet.

If the traditionalists' shock was intelligible, what came next was a realization of their deepest fears. They had always suspected that the class basis of society could be preserved only by expelling sex from the realm of respectability. Now, factors of several kinds—among others, attacks on gender-discrimination, and the new openness to the emotions—conspired to call the traditional sexual taboos in doubt. A generation that took its emotional homework seriously turned its attention to "personal relationships" (the accepted euphemism) and looked for styles of life that embodied more equitable social roles for women and men, within as well as beyond their sexual relations. The ensuing critique of sexuality, inside and outside the family, led to widespread rejection of the sacramental view of marriage that was emphasized (even invented) at the Counter-Reformation, and to a revival of customary common law relations that had been widely practiced before the Reformation. Those members of the educated oligarchy who for so long advocated traditional respectable values saw their children living together as couples without blessing of Church or State, and could not find effective ways to state their objections to the practice in ways that wholly met the next generation's moral defense of those new modes of life.

Last of all, from 1960, the misuse of "superpower" by the American and Russian governments deepened the doubts about claims to absolute sovereignty. The idea of nations as self-justifying centers of power had played a central part in European politics since the Peace of Westphalia, but now it discredited itself. What the destruction of Melos had been to Classical Athens, the atrocities at My Lai were to the United States: a disgrace that forced on America a self-examination whose pain only deepened and ramified for the next 15 to 20 years. Guilty of atrocities in Afghanistan, the

Soviet government also found its moral authority evaporating, even in its loyal client-states. As a result, the limits of national autonomy and the inevitability of transnational interdependence finally succeeded in impressing the rulers of the superpowers, and began to reshape the language of international debate.

The Twin Trajectories of Modernity

Our narrative has come full circle. The culture and society of 17th-century Europe were transformed by changes that set aside the tolerance of late Renaissance humanism for more rigorous theories and demanding practices: these changes culminated in the new cosmopolis built around the formal structure of mathematical physics. After 1750, that change was undone, bit by bit. The history of science and philosophy from 1650 to 1950 was not simply a triumphal procession of geniuses building on the work of their predecessors: rather, it had both light and shade, both an up and a down side. As the experience of humanity was collected and digested, the fundamental picture of nature went through major changes, the presuppositions of the new cosmopolis were discredited, and by the mid-20th century the demolition was complete. At that point, thought and practice were free to return to the vision of the Renaissance.

Over these three centuries, the two aspects of Modernity—doctrinal and experiential, metaphysical and scientific—traced out quite different trajectories. The formal doctrines that underpinned human thought and practice from 1700 on followed a trajectory with the shape of an Omega, i.e."Ω". After 300 years we are back close to our starting point. Natural scientists no longer separate the "observer" from the "world observed", as they did in the heyday of classical physics; sovereign nation-states find their independence circumscribed; and Descartes' *foundational* ambitions are discredited, taking philosophy back to the skepticism of Montaigne. In neither intellectual nor practical respects are things still systemic or self-contained. Meanwhile, in experiential terms, the situation is very different. None of the restrictions that "respectable opinion" placed on our ideas about nature carries scientific weight today, and the growing empirical reach of science makes it unnecessary to limit speculation to the areas licensed by the Modern framework. Current theories of Nature have a hundred thousand roots in experience, of which Newton could only dream: from the 17th century on, the progress of natural philosophy has been cumulative and continuous, and Descartes' *cryptanalytical* hopes have proved more than justified.

Doctrinally, then, the trajectory of Modernity has closed back on itself, into an Omega; but experientially it has headed broadly upward. As people in Europe and North America have learned from the experience of modernity, and have attacked the inequalities built into the "modern" scaffolding, they have developed a discriminating care for human interests. In the 1770s and 1780s, the revolutions in America and France successively challenged social self-awareness; and, ever since, the emancipation of the classes which the New Cosmopolis labelled as the "lower orders"—those human groups whose needs and interests were long disregarded without compunction—has been a consistent theme of political debate. Despite setbacks and counter-revolutions, there has since 1776 been a growing perception that such inequities cannot be justified by appeals to "the Nature of Things" or "the Will of God" or any other mere doctrine.

The same has been true in the natural sciences. In outgrowing the scaffolding of Modernity, it has finally become the "experiential" quest that Bacon foretold in the late 16th century. La Mettrie and Priestley, Hutton and Darwin, Marx and Freud had to take seriously the objections of "respectable opinion"; but, now that the last timbers of that scaffolding—the separation of humanity from nature, and the distrust of emotion—have lost their intellectual credibility, no obstacle remains to studying nature however our experience requires. Of a dozen recent examples, the most striking is perhaps that of the conservative Surgeon General of the United States, forced to choose between his scientific understanding and his ideology, sponsoring a campaign for sex education and for wider use of condoms.

Since the 1960s, then, both philosophy and science are back in the intellectual postures of the last generation *before* Descartes. In natural science, the imperial dominion of physics over all other fields has come to an end: ecologists and anthropologists can now look astronomers and physicists straight in the eye. In philosophy, Descartes' formalist wish—to refute the skepticism of the Renaissance humanists, by substituting the abstract demands of logical certainty for their concrete reliance on human experience—is now seen to have led the enterprise of philosophy into a dead end. Scientifically and philosophically, that is, we are freed from the exclusively theoretical agenda of rationalism, and can take up again the practical issues sidelined by Descartes' *coup d'état* some 300 years ago.

Not only has our narrative brought us back closer to the humanists than was foreseeable: it has also given us the means to answer our own initial questions about "Modernity". At the outset, we raised issues of three kinds. There are historical issues about the standard account of the origins of Modernity, in particular the transition from 16th-century humanism to

17th-century rationalism; there are historiographical ones, about the reasons to see Modernity as starting after 1600, so treating it as a 17th-century
novelty; and there are philosophical ones, about the very idea of Modernity; e.g., whether the ambitions of the modern age are relevant today, or
whether our intellectual and practical affairs will now have to move in
radically novel ("post-modern") directions.

As to the *historical* issues: the deeper our inquiries have gone, the
further they have taken us from the standard account of Modernity: as a
result, we have replaced it by a revised account, which avoids the false
assumptions that underlay the former story. On the received view, the
origin of the "modern" era had five key features—the prosperity of
17th-century Europe; the weakening of Church controls over intellectual
life; the development of secular, vernacular culture; the political centrality
of the nation; above all, the adoption of "rational" methods in science and
philosophy. Modern thought thus supposedly began with the physics of
Galileo Galilei, the epistemology of René Descartes, and the political
science of Thomas Hobbes, while modern social and political practice
began with the rise of the class-structured, sovereign nation-states.

All these indications of a 17th-century Modernity turned out to be false
or misleading. The 17th century was a time not of prosperity but of
economic crisis; ecclesiastical pressures on science and scholarship intensified rather than diminished, while the scope of rational thought did
not expand but shrank. Nor was lay culture a 17th-century novelty: it grew
steadily from the late 15th century, and had already won success by the
work of 16th-century humanists. The received view thus played down the
contributions of the Renaissance to Modernity. Lacking rational methods,
16th-century thinkers (on this view) played fresh variations on medieval
themes. Erasmus and Rabelais, Montaigne and Shakespeare were seen as
the last, if not least of the late medieval thinkers, whose recovery of texts
from classical antiquity emancipated them from medieval conservatism;
but they never took the definitive step forward into the "modern" world
of logic and rationality. Historians of philosophy and science were in this
way committed to myths about the progressive character of 17th-century
life and thought which (as they ought to have known in their heart of
hearts) falsified the historical record.

If the received view carried such conviction in the 1920s and 1930s, it
did so only because, at that time, the basic validity of the rationalist position
was taken for granted. In picking as the founders of Modernity thinkers
like Galileo and Descartes, and rulers like Cromwell and Louis XIV,
historians endorsed the absolute claims of 17th-century rationalism and
elevated it to the level of Established Truth. Far from being categorical

and unconditional, independent of circumstances and decontextual-izable, its validity proves on a closer look to be hypothetical and circum-stantial. It had carried conviction in the 17th century as a by-product of a special occasion: the political and economic breakdown in the political order of early modern Europe, and a concurrent breakdown in the accepted order of nature. By contrast, the stability, hierarchy, and coher-ence of the nation-state gave political assurance to people who saw the social organization of Europe disintegrate over the 150 years after the Reformation; while the ideas of Newton's *Principia* appealed to those who had been lacking a consistent cosmology since Copernicus had under-mined Ptolemy's views a century before. These achievements were com-plementary outcomes of the "struggle for stability" in Europe, twin responses to a comprehensive crisis that would (as it seemed) be over-come, only if people cleaned the slate, started from scratch, and con-structed a more rational Cosmopolis, to replace the one lost around 1600.

As to the *historiographical* issues: in judging how our views of the 17th century are influenced by the historical mirrors we use to view it, we asked, "Why did people in the 1920s and 1930s accept so distorted an account of the last 300 years? What was at stake in the 1920s that led them to admire a time of economic stagnation, religious intolerance, and ideological slaughter, and devalue our legacy from the previous century, of greater prosperity and maturer humanism?" By now, the material for an answer is to hand. Our historical and historiographical questions—i.e., "What *really happened* in the 16th and 17th centuries?", and "How are we taught to *think about* those centuries?"—may seem quite distinct, but their answers prove to be closely connected.

Historiographically, we needed to explain the renewed investment in rationalism in the 1920s and 1930s; and we can answer that question once again by looking at the conditions of the time—a breakdown of confidence in the political order of Europe and a concurrent crisis in accepted ideas about Nature. What the Peace of Westphalia did to create the political pattern of Modernity in 1648, the First World War destroyed. From 1920 on, it was hard to deny the need for a new political and diplomatic order, which no longer focussed exclusively on the unfettered sovereignty of nation-states: after the butchery in the trenches of the First World War, the class-based structure of modern society aroused cynicism as much as loyalty. Cosmologically, too, the constructive work of the 1600s fell apart after 1900: Einstein's relativity and Planck's quantum theory were the death of classical Newtonian physics. Answering Alexander Pope's epitaph for Newton,

Nature and Nature's Laws lay hid in night:
God said, *Let Newton be!* and all was light,

Sir John Squire remarked that, with the advent of Einstein, the Devil had restored the *status quo*. Like all good jokes, this comment held a kernel of truth. The rationalism of the inter-War years simply replaced Newton by Einstein, cast Russell in the role that Descartes gave to Euclid, and substituted the dream of a logically unified science for the cosmopolis of Modernity.

The crisis in European affairs precipitated by "the War to End War" thus generated the same twin responses as that of the late 17th century: in both political and scientific respects, it seemed, "stability" could be restored only if people were again ready to start from scratch and build up new ideas and institutions—even a new cosmopolis—to replace those that were lost. Second time around, however, this recipe was more desperate. For Descartes, geometry was not "pure" (i.e. *formal*) mathematics alone, but a science of spatial relations, dealing with Space *as encountered in experience;* so he could appeal to Euclid's axioms as the "foundations" of a physics intended to make comprehensive sense of all material nature. When philosophers put Russell and Whitehead's logic to the same service in the 1920s, however, David Hilbert had long since shown that pure mathematics can be viewed as a body of formal operations that does not refer to our experience of nature; so it was a little bizarre for them to treat the axioms of *Principia Mathematica* as the "foundations" of an *empirical* natural science.

Politically, dismantling the Austro-Hungarian Empire, which for all its faults was truly multicultural and multinational, only had the effect of fragmenting Eastern Europe into a congeries of states, each of which claimed the sovereignty that the modern world viewed as the reward of nationhood. Rather than maintain the federal structure of the Habsburg domains within a decentralized democratic order, the political brokers of Versailles divided up the territory in a way that gave sovereignty to Masaryk's Czechs and other squeaky wheels, establishing "nation states" that were unitary in theory, but almost as heterogeneous in practice as the Habsburg lands had been. This multiplication of sovereignties, like the League of Nations, proved a temporary solution of lasting problems: of all the successor states, the one that best tried to confront the problems of the multinational state—Yugoslavia—still experiences tensions from trying to maintain state unity in theory, while also allowing a great diversity of provincial religions, languages, and customs in practice.

The last, *philosophical* questions about "post-modernity" are less straightforward. The dispute between the critics and the defenders of Modernity is hard to resolve, because the very phenomena are so complex. Yet, if we keep in mind the dual trajectory of Modernity—the strand of experience continuing ahead, and the strand of doctrine closing back in an Omega—we may arrive at tentative answers. Both critics and defenders of Modernity have some sound points to make, but on closer examination they are directed at very different issues.

Critics like Jean François Lyotard see us as heading inescapably in a new, post-modern direction. For Lyotard, the epistemological mark of our post-modernity is the loss of authoritative underpinning conceptual structures to serve as the "foundation" of rational knowledge, such as Descartes looked for in Euclid. To the extent that the aim of Modernity involved organizing knowledge into "systems" (logical systems in the natural sciences, institutional systems in sociology, or cultural systems in anthropology) this is a real change. For Descartes, Euclid's geometry was an ideal rational system, and it has no plausible successor: nor is there a plausible successor, either, to Russell and Whitehead's *Principia Mathematica,* which philosophers in the 1920s and 1930s appealed to as the ultimately self-validating system of knowledge.

Still, the intellectual program of Modernity is not for that reason a *failure.* We no longer ground all our knowledge in universal, timeless systems today, only because the rationalist dream was always illusory. Descartes never faced classical skepticism *on its own ground:* instead, he pointed to subjects in which, within practical limits, formal logic can provide a kind of coherence to which Montaigne had done something less than full justice; but the implication that these examples were the model for all intellectual disciplines remains an unfulfilled dream. Nor does the fact that no such model is available today imply the "death" of Rationality: rather, it marks our awakening from a transient, ambiguous daydream. Undermined by d'Alembert, Holbach, Priestley and Kant, the scaffolding of Modernity is now demolished; and Modernity has at last *come of age.* If such critics as Lyotard see the absence of a foundational system as substituting "absurdity" for "rationality", this objection shows only that their attack on Cartesianism shares Descartes' prejudice in favor of "systems". If, instead, we re-analyze "rationality" in *non*-systemic terms, there need be nothing "absurd" in that.

To turn from the critics to the defenders of Modernity: the scourge of the Parisian "post-moderns" is Jürgen Habermas of Frankfurt-am-Main.

Habermas uses the name "modernization" for the emancipatory movement that began with the French Revolution, and was given a rationalization in Kant's universalistic theory of Ethics. Thanks to an ironic ambiguity, his "modernity" equates with our "escape from modernity"—the dismantling of the hierarchical stability imposed on both scientific theory and social practice in the hundred years up to the French Revolution. Habermas, then, sees the distinctive mark of modernity, not in a reliance on rationalist theory, but in a commitment to egalitarian practice. Kant began his critique of the then-current world view in the *Allgemeine Naturgeschichte* (1755) by arguing that Nature has a history no less than Humanity. Under the influence of Rousseau, his moral theory added the further claim, that a well-ordered community admits of no inequalities, but treats all rational agents as autonomous, coequal citizens in a Commonwealth of Ends. To this, Habermas adds a series of consequential questions, about the factors that may tend to distort both the perception of social relations, and our understanding of the language of political discourse.

Philosophical critics and defenders of Modernity are, thus, directly at cross purposes. Many of the reasons that contemporary French writers give for *denying* the continued validity of "modernity" refer to the same features of the 20th-century scene that Habermas points to in *asserting* it. They take opposite sides on issues about modernity not for reasons of substance, but because—as seen from their respective points of view—the word "modern" means different things. French writers take "modern" in a Cartesian sense. For them, formal rationality has no alternative but absurdity; so, for lack of a formal grounding, the 20th-century situation leaves no room for constructive responses, only for *de*constructive ones. In Habermas, the word "modern" points rather to the moral critique of Rousseau and Kant, so, in his eyes, there is still plenty of life left in the *con*structive program of Modernity.

Between those who see Modernity as done for, and those to whom it is still vital and valid, the middle ground belongs to two sets of writers. There are artists, architects, and critics for whom terms like "modern", "postmodern" and "modernism" have quite another historical focus—e.g., the *fin de siècle* years when the arts were transformed by Hoffmann and Loos, the *art nouveau* movement and the *Sezession,* or those between the World Wars, with Mies van der Rohe, Josef Albers, and the constructivists. The others include social critics like Peter Drucker, who invented his term, "post-modern", to mark off the political and institutional limits of the sovereign nation-state. Neither group engages Habermas or the Parisians head-on. The artists and critics are interested in showing how early 20th-century painters, musicians, and architects moved beyond academicism to a new and lighter style of art and design. Meanwhile, Drucker exhorts people to challenge the sovereign claims of the nation, and so trigger a reappraisal of social and political institutions. His essays are aimed at practical problems, and his account is no more "absurd" than anything in Habermas: instead, he has wise things to say about the limited utility of "national" institutions, and the value of agencies that can operate on other levels—nonnational, subnational, or transnational.

As a philosophical debate, then, the discussion of the "modern" and "post-modern" ends in a stand off. Looking backward, critics of Modernity proclaim or regret (it is not clear which) the absence of any established foundations for contemporary thought. Their observation is accurate: the dream of *foundationalism*—i.e., the search for a permanent and unique set of authoritative principles for human knowledge—proves to be just a dream, which has its appeal in moments of intellectual crisis, but fades away when matters are viewed under a calmer and clearer light. Looking forward, its defenders insist on the moral importance of continuing the *emancipation* that began in the Enlightenment, and still goes on in South Africa and elsewhere: struggling against those human inequalities that offended Jean-Jacques Rousseau, and that stick in the craw of people of goodwill to this day. In the middle ground of the debate a spectrum of issues emerges, covering the field from physical theory to ecological practice, and from politics to architecture.

At the outset, Modernity struck us as simple, straightforward, and beneficent. Here, at the far side of Modernity, its history proves more complex than we thought. To begin with, we saw the story of Modernity as the onward march of human rationality, but this has turned out to hide ambiguities and confusions. Whether the 17th-century enthronement of "rationality" was a victory or a defeat for humanity depends on how we conceive of "rationality" itself: instead of the successes of the intellect having been unmixed blessings, they must be weighed against the losses that came from abandoning the 16th-century commitment to intellectual modesty, uncertainty, and toleration. In our final section, we may ask whether, in future, we can regain the humane wisdom of the Renaissance, without in turn losing the advantages we won during the three hundred years in which intellectual life was dominated by Cartesian philosophy and the exact sciences.

CHAPTER FIVE

The Way Ahead

The Myth of the Clean Slate

We can reconcile the twin legacies of the exact sciences and the humanities only by a change of direction; and, for that, we must first see clearly how the agenda of "modern thought" over-reached itself. By now, it will be clear that we need to balance the hope for certainty and clarity in theory with the impossibility of avoiding uncertainty and ambiguity in practice. But the received view of Modernity rested not only on the Quest for Certainty and the equation of Rationality with a respect for formal logic: it also took over the rationalists' belief that the modern, rational way of dealing with problems is to sweep away the inherited clutter from traditions, clean the slate, and start again from scratch.

Looking back over our whole inquiry, indeed, we see that the idea of "starting again with a clean slate" has been as recurrent a preoccupation of modern European thinkers as the quest for certainty itself. The belief that any new construction is truly *rational* only if it demolishes all that was there before and starts from scratch, has played a particular part in the intellectual and political history of France—the English have usually been more pragmatic; but no one who enters into the spirit of Modernity wholeheartedly can be immune to its influence. The most spectacular illustration of this is the French Revolution: on that occasion the dream of cleaning house and making a new beginning crossed the Channel, to arouse the enthusiasm of William Wordsworth and his generation—

> Bliss was it in that Dawn to be alive;
> But to be young was very Heaven!

A recent essay on the Revolution underlines the point:

> The revolution reached into everything. For example, it re-created time and space. . . . [T]he revolutionaries divided time into units that

they took to be rational and natural. There were ten days to a week, three weeks to a month, and twelve months to a year.

The adoption of the metric system represented a similar attempt to impose a rational and natural organization on space. According to a decree of 1795, the meter was to be "the unit of length equal to one ten-millionth part of the arc of the terrestrial meridian between the North Pole and the Equator." Of course, ordinary citizens could not make much of such a definition. They were slow to adopt the meter and the gram, the corresponding new unit of weight, and few of them favored the new week, which gave them one day of rest in ten instead of one in seven. But even where old habits remained, the revolutionaries stamped their ideas on contemporary consciousness by changing everything's name. . . .

Hitherto, treating *rationality* as "starting with a clean slate" had been a dream of intellectuals: with the French Revolution, it became a political method. While the Revolution retained its purity, Catholicism was officially repressed, in favor of a "religion of rationality": Notre Dame became the Temple of Reason. Rationalism invaded the world of politics, the program of rationalist philosophy was transformed into a revolutionary program, and assumptions that had operated hitherto on an intellectual level were transmogrified into maxims of political action.

The events that began in 1789 even gave the word *révolution* a new meaning:

> no one was ready for a revolution in 1789. The idea itself did not exist. If you look up "revolution" in standard dictionaries from the eighteenth century, you find definitions that derive from the verb to revolve, such as "the return of a planet or a star to the same point from which it parted."

This was true above all of France. In Britain, by contrast, the memory of the events of 1688, when the unimpeachably Protestant King William III displaced the Catholic James II, were already celebrated by Englishmen as a Glorious Revolution. (When Joseph Priestley and his friends gave their dinner in honor of the French Revolution, for example, they wore copies of the centennial medal issued for Nov. 4, 1788, bearing the inscriptions "Revolution Jubilee" and "Britons never will be slaves.") Even so, the 1688 revolution was never intended to refashion the political situation in Britain from the ground up. It was always thought of more as a restoration of the *status quo ante,* undoing the pro-Catholic policies of the later Stuarts, and reinstating the independence of English tradition, like the astronomical return of a planet to its previous orbit.

As a philosophical goal, the ideas of a clean slate and a fresh start had special power in their original context. By 1630, at the midpoint of the Thirty Years' War, the traditional consensus that had underlain the intellectual enterprises of Europe was apparently stripped away. There was no unanimity in ethics, in politics, in religion, or even in physics. Faced with this collapse, philosophers looked for an alternative starting point for human thought and practice: an alternative set of "grounds" or "data" that was available in the shared experience of reflective thinkers. If such a universal starting point was found, it might be a "scratch line" from which the scientists and philosophers of any age or culture would be able to make a start.

Different schools of modern philosophers had different ideas about where exactly this "scratch line" was to be found. For rationalists like René Descartes, the proper starting point lay in shared *basic concepts,* or "clear and distinct ideas": for empiricists like John Locke, it was shared *sensory evidence,* or "ideas of sense". But neither Descartes nor Locke had much doubt that the very diversity and contradictions of traditional, inherited, local ways of thought required philosophers to emancipate themselves from the constraints of those traditions. In the subsequent debate, empiricists did not insist as strongly as rationalists on the need to arrive at "certainty": many admitted that our methods of inquiry are essentially fallible, and cannot yield anything more than "probabilities." Even those who no longer aimed at certainty, however, were committed to the idea of a clean slate. Right up to the 1950s, philosophers of both empiricist and rationalist stripes assumed that an unchallengeable starting point *of some sort* was available, as the natural "scratch line" for beginning rational reflection in philosophy.

Seen from the present, the modern philosophers' key arguments showed signs of strain from the start: the exact location of the rational point of departure was less self-evident than they had at first supposed. When Descartes picked on the ideas of Euclidean geometry as "clear and distinct", he faced the question, "Can we be certain that Euclidean ideas are equally available to reflective thinkers in all epochs and cultures?" In reply, he argued that a Benevolent God had presumably implanted these ideas in all human beings alike; but he did not trouble to ask whether, as a fact of ethnography, people in every part of the world, or at all stages in history perceive, interpret, and describe spatial and spatial relations in ways that conform to the Euclidean pattern; or whether, in other places or other times, other ways of perceiving, interpreting or describing them may not find a place in human experience. John Locke, too, assumed that similar ideas of sense will, with repetition, generate similar ideas of reflection (or "concepts") in people from all milieux: he failed to ask, "Is repetition enough? Or is not the acquisition of concepts dependent on the repetition occurring within a specific cultural context?"

As we now know, both definitions of the philosophical "scratch line" were not merely arbitrary, but rested on factually false assumptions. Descartes assumed that God gives all humans the propensity to develop Euclidean ideas. Yet, even today, there exist cultures in which spatial relationships are handled in ways that diverge from the Euclidean ideal: the people involved even *perceive* spatial relations differently from the way they are perceived in modern industrial cultures, and are subject to other optical illusions. Equally, with Locke's supposedly shared ideas of sense: there is evidence that certain colors (e.g., black, white, and red) stand out in everyday color perception, and so are easily recognized as primary colors by people of many cultures. But in our *ideas of reflection*—talking or thinking of colors, naming or describing the colors of objects—cultural diversity recurs. The step from Locke's "ideas of sense" to his "ideas of reflection" (from sensory inputs to concepts) involves not just repeated exposure to the given stimuli, but also a shared enculturation and language. The diversity of color terminology among languages and cultures is less drastic than the ethnographers once supposed, but it is striking enough to undercut the empiricist choice of neutral "sense data" as a rational starting point for constructing an intelligible world. For reasons of ethnographic fact, as much as of analytical argument, neither proposal for a rational philosophy—starting from either shared concepts or shared sensations—still holds water today.

The burden of proof has shifted; the dream of finding a scratch line, to serve as a starting point for any "rational" philosophy, is unfulfillable. *There is no scratch.* The belief that, by cutting ourselves off from the inherited ideas of our cultures, we can "clean the slate" and make a fresh start, is as illusory as the hope for a comprehensive system of theory that is capable of giving us timeless certainty and coherence. The quest for certainty, the dream of a clean slate, and the equation of rationality with formal logic, all played their interdependent parts in the program of 17th-century philosophical theory. Descartes saw the logical necessity of geometry as an exemplar of certainty, and so equated the rationality of a science with its readiness to form a logical system. In turn, since systematicity was essential to rationality, his theory had no room for given ideas or practices to *change continuously* into other different ideas or practices. Once one questioned the claims of any given social or intellectual system, the only thing left to do was to raze it, and construct another, different system in its place.

The account of "rationality" underlying the philosophical program of

Modernity thus rested on three pillars—certainty, systematicity, and the clean slate, and when after 300 years John Dewey and Richard Rorty read the burial service over this program, their obsequy had wider significance. The idea that handling problems rationally means making a totally fresh start had been a mistake all along. All we can be called upon to do is to take a start *from where we are, at the time we are there:* i.e., to make discriminating and critical use of the ideas available to us in our current local situation, and the evidence of our experience, as this is "read" in terms of those ideas. There is no way of cutting ourselves free of our conceptual inheritance: all we are required to do is use our experience critically and discriminatingly, *refining and improving* our inherited ideas, and determining more exactly the limits to their scope.

More specifically, the last thirty years' work in the history of science, cultural anthropology, and elsewhere shows that, however impeccably we meet those demands, we are no closer to a self-justifying starting point. No neutral "scratch line" exists from which to jump to a self-sustaining, tradition-free intellectual system. All of the cultural situations from which we pursue our practical and intellectual inquiries are historically conditioned: this being so, the only thing we can do is to make the best of starting with what we have got, here and now.

This thought is one that Americans, in particular, find disappointing. The dream of a clean slate was always attractive to people who believed that, by leaving behind the tyranny and corruption of traditional European society and coming to a new Continent, they had earned a chance to start again from scratch. But, whatever the political gains of the Pilgrims in the 17th century, and the Founding Fathers at the end of the 18th century, neither the first Colonists nor the Revolutionaries defined their options in any terms but those that crossed the Atlantic with them from Europe. When the inhabitants of the Thirteen Colonies cast off the tow line from the Mother Country, many new-made Americans were aiming to restore the traditional order in society, so as to enjoy the immemorial liberties of Englishmen, which the Hanoverian Kings had put in peril.

Despite their interest in the political theories of Hobbes and Locke, then, the goals and methods of the American Revolutionaries were more pragmatic than those of their successors in France a dozen years later. The aim of the American Revolutionary War, like the Glorious Revolution of 1688, was more a restoration of the *status quo ante* than it was—as the French Revolution was to become—a reconstruction of society from the ground up. Where Calvin and Luther had stripped away the corruptions defacing the institutions and practices of Christianity, hoping to reform them from within, the Founding Fathers of the United States hoped to strip away the corruptions defacing the British Monarchy and devise a Republic that embodied traditional English virtues in purified form.

Even the French revolutionaries did not, in the event, start entirely from scratch. Many of their "rational" reforms struck no deep roots in the hearts of the French people: from 1805 on, for example, it was easy for Napoleon to restore the traditional calendar. In public administration, also, many "standard operating procedures" survived the Revolution with little change: here, too, the radical intentions of the leaders of the Revolution had eventually to compromise with the need to maintain public services and other social functions.

Humanizing Modernity

After the horrors of 1914–1918, we saw that Europeans again felt a need to clean the slate, make a fresh start, and carry through their own Quest for Certainty. In doing so, they developed a retrospective account of the 17th-century origin of Modernity that gave support to their cause. But, by thrusting the 16th-century humanists into the shade, this account of Modernity was misleading, and impoverished our view of the Modern Age. We are not compelled to *choose between* 16th-century humanism and 17th-century exact science: rather, we need to hang on to the positive achievements of them both.

As matters now stand, our need to reappropriate the reasonable and tolerant (but neglected) legacy of humanism is more urgent than our need to preserve the systematic and perfectionist (though well-established) legacy of the exact sciences; but, in the last resort, we cannot dispense with either. We are indebted to Descartes and Newton for fine examples of well-formulated theory, but humanity also needs people with a sense of how theory touches practice at points, and in ways, that we feel on our pulses. The current task, accordingly, is to find ways of moving on from the received view of Modernity—which set the exact sciences and the humanities apart—to a reformed version, which redeems philosophy and science, by reconnecting them to the humanist half of Modernity. In that task, the techniques of 17th-century rationalism will not be enough: from this point on, all the claims of theory—like those of nationhood—must prove their value by demonstrating their roots in human practice and experience.

As things stand, we can neither cling to Modernity in its historic form, nor reject it totally—least of all despise it. The task is, rather, to reform, and even reclaim, our inherited modernity, by *humanizing* it. These words are not empty exhortation. They have a specific sense, which can be illustrated in this final chapter: first in relation to the natural sciences, then to define a new agenda for philosophy, finally as they apply to the practice of politics, as we move beyond the absolute nation-state. By this standard, much of what is good in modern thought and practice has in fact already gone some way toward *redeeming itself*. In particular, the natural sciences, as they exist in the closing years of the 20th century, have come a long way from the mechanistic physics—or "natural philosophy"—that took shape in the 75 years after Descartes' manifesto in the *Discourse on Method*. Far from being formal systems based on abstract theoretical ideas alone, with a "certainty" borrowed from geometry, today's sciences are deeply grounded in experience; while, increasingly, their practical use is subject to criticism, in terms of their human impact.

Since the Second World War, the intellectual preoccupations of the sciences have undergone a shift. In the 1960s and '70s, for instance, new ideas about the chemistry of very complex molecules gave biologists a fresh handle on central problems in genetics, physiology and medicine. At first, some onlookers saw "molecular biology" as one more victory for mechanistic materialism, and read its wider implications as irredeemably reductionist and antihumane. The mature reaction to this change is more hopeful, recalling that biochemical processes are rooted in the local ecology of particular "microhabitats" within the body. The Platonist drive toward universal theory can, thus, reach a balance with an Aristotelean attention to the times and places, circumstances and occasions of biological events, and with the ways in which their sheer variety creates practical problems for biology.

More strikingly, the line dividing the moral and technical aspects of medicine has become thinner and thinner during the last twenty or thirty years, as technologists have developed new ways of extending patients' lives, to a point at which the mere prolongation of body function is no longer clearly worthwhile. In the present phase of medicine, all attempts to freeze the distinction between "facts" and "values" are overwhelmed by the practical demands of new problems and situations. From now on, indeed, the very definition of a "medical" problem must be given in terms that cover both its technical and its moral features: not merely the fact that the oxygen in a patient's arterial blood is at a life threatening level, but also the fact that the patient has, say, expressed a clear wish not to be resuscitated by burdensome technical means, if they add to the chance of continued biological life only marginally, and to the quality of life not at all.

What is true of biology since 1945 is true of contemporary physics, as well. When the atom bombs were dropped on Hiroshima and Nagasaki, many observers concluded that nuclear physics, too, was irredeemably destructive and antihuman. Yet these events led, in reaction, to a change in the consciousness of physicists themselves, from abstract purity and "value free" detachment toward greater concern with the political and social effects of scientific innovation. The immediate consequence of this change was the founding of *The Bulletin of the Atomic Scientists,* which still gives a monthly transnational, nongovernmental commentary on the politics of nuclear weapons and related topics.

The depth of this change should not be underestimated. So long as the Manhattan Project was little more than a theoretical exercise, the scientists at Los Alamos could speak about the soldiers, politicians, and bureaucrats who supervised their work as "sons of bitches"; and, up to the moment the first bomb was actually exploded, they saw themselves as a different breed. The change came only with the first test explosion at Alamogordo. Robert Oppenheimer's colleague, Bainbridge, reacted by reportedly declaring, "We're all S.O.B.s now!" From then on, there was a groundswell of rational sentiment among the atomic scientists, in favor of entering as direct participants into the political debates about the use of nuclear weapons and nuclear power.

A similar "humanization" can also be found in technology. The last forty years have transformed public attitudes to engineering projects. As late as the 1950s, the agencies that execute large-scale engineering projects, such as the U.S. Army Corps of Engineers, were moved above all by technical considerations, and happily built any dam that promised to assist agriculture or transportation, on the basis of technical feasibility alone. By the late 1980s, no such agency could still ignore questions of "environmental impact". Instead, they were legally required to spell out, in advance, the benefits and harms liable to flow from their projects; and the harms they were obliged to analyze and evaluate covered harms to non-human, as well as to human beings. Earlier, the possibility of using natural resources like waterfalls in the service of human good was a compelling argument by itself. By now, people understand that "nature" is not just a source of neutral resources, to be exploited for our benefit: quite as much, it is *our terrestrial home.* In political and social debate, therefore, questions about "ecology"—the Greek roots of this word mean "the science of household management"—have irreversibly moved to the center of the practical stage.

Between them, these changes in the focus of science and technology have shifted attention from the exactitude of theoretical physics and the world view of High Modernity (which saw nature and humanity as distinct and separate) toward a humanized Modernity, which reintegrates nature and humanity, and puts the local, circumstantial arguments of ecology on a scientific footing with the universal arguments of electromagnetism and other physical theories. No one today questions Newton's brilliance in demonstrating that the content of the central theories of physics (i.e., dynamics) could, as Descartes proposed 50 years earlier, be presented as a logical system on the model of Euclid's geometry. It never followed from this, however, as the advocates of "Unified Science" dreamed, that the totality of science—comprising the discoveries of physics, biology, and all other sciences—itself forms a similar, but more comprehensive system. On the contrary, the ability of scientists to move into fresh fields, and develop techniques for handling aspects of experience that were not previously in their reach, rests on their capacity to renegotiate (so to say) the relations between different branches of scientific theory, so as to meet the novel demands of each new field.

So long as natural science developed within the Modern scaffolding, and respected a hardline distinction between the "rationality" of human thought and the "causality" of natural mechanisms, people in other fields modelled their ideas on the axiomatic pattern of Newton's mechanics. Now that this scaffolding is dismantled, however, scientists no longer separate nature from humanity, and the contrast between theoretical ("pure") science and practical ("applied") technology has lost its earlier sharpness. Scientists are now able to reconcile the exactitude of Isaac Newton's theories with the humanism of Francis Bacon's forecasts. As they redirect science, technology, and medicine toward humanly relevant goals, they are humanizing their view of Modernity, too.

Intellectually, the unreconstructed Modernity whose rise and decline we have chronicled here had three foundations: certainty, formal rationality, and the desire to start with a clean slate. So understood, scientific theories and nation states alike were fully rational only if they formed stable "systems": in one case logical systems *à la* Euclid, in the other institutional systems with determinate relations. With the reconstruction of Europe after 1648, the rigidity of the structures that developed in response to those demands had real merits: they met the demand for "stability" that was a prime preoccupation of Europeans at that time. As we approach the third millennium, our needs are different, and the ways of meeting them must be correspondingly rethought. Now, our concern can no longer be to guarantee the *stability and uniformity* of Science or the State alone: instead, it must be to provide the elbowroom we need in order to protect *diversity and adaptability.*

Nostalgia for the Modern Cosmopolis exposes us to the frailty of the image of Nature on which it rests: of a stable physical system of bodies moving in fixed orbits around a single, central source of power—the Sun and the planets as a model for the Sun King and his subjects. This model served constructive ends in the 17th century, but the rigidity it imposed on rational practice in a world of independent and separate agents is no longer appropriate in the late 20th century, which is a time of increasing interdependence, cultural diversity and historical change. Intellectual and social patterns that had the virtue of being *stable and predictable* in earlier times turn out, in our time, to have the vice of being *stereotyped and unadaptable*. By continuing to impose on thought and action all the demands of unreconstructed Modernity—rigor, exactitude, and system— we risk making our ideas and institutions not just stable but sclerotic, and being unable to modify them in reasonable ways to meet the fresh demands of novel situations.

The issues at stake in humanizing Modernity were also broached, in somewhat different terms, during the 1960s and '70s, in a public debate about the aims of higher education and academic research. The debate was dominated by two vogue words: on the one side, "excellence", on the other side, "relevance". Spokesmen for *excellence* saw institutions of higher learning as conserving the traditional wisdom and techniques of our forefathers, while adding whatever novelties people could contribute to this corpus of knowledge. The focus was on the value of established disciplines, which embody and transmit various parts of our inheritance: these subjects should keep their intellectual instruments polished and sharpened, adding them perhaps, but at all cost preserving their existing merits. The spokesmen for *relevance* saw matters differently. In their view, it was not valuable to keep our knowledge oiled, clean, and sharpened, but stored away: it was more important to find ways of putting it to work for human good. From this standpoint, the universities should attack the practical problems of humanity: if the established disciplines served as obstacles in this enterprise, new interdisciplinary styles of work were needed, that would be better adapted to this task. The inherited corpus of knowledge was no doubt excellent in its way, but academics in the 1970s could no longer afford to behave like Mandarins. "Learning [it was said] is too important to be left to the Learned."

Notice in what terms this debate between excellence and relevance— between conservers and appliers of knowledge—was engaged. Pitting relevance against excellence redirected attention to the practical, local, transitory, and *context bound* issues that were close to the heart of

16th-century humanists, but were set aside by 17th-century rationalists for abstract, timeless, universal and *context free* issues. In our day, formal calculative rationality can no longer be the only measure of intellectual adequacy: one must also evaluate all practical matters by their human "reasonableness". A proposal was even put forward to reorganize the Massachusetts Institute of Technology, and replace existing departments responsible for technical disciplines like electronics and civil engineering by administrative units responsible for addressing particular types of human needs; for example, transportation, communication, or urban problems. The traditional academic preoccupation with refining techniques could thus be balanced against the different ways of applying those techniques to the good of humanity.

Artistic issues ran parallel to academic ones. Twelve-tone music, non-representational painting, and architecture stripped of local color or function, were exaggerated products of a new rationalism, magnified by the early 20th-century crisis; but this time the formalism had been too extreme, and the renunciation too drastic. Anton Webern, for instance, reportedly argued that twelve-tone themes would, in time, come to sound just as "natural" as diatonic ones; but this, like the hope of grounding everyday mathematics teaching in "group theory", was at best a dream. (For Arnold Schoenberg, more realistically, the appeal of twelve-tone music was intellectual rather than sensuous: "How the music *sounds* is not the point.") By the 1980s, composers were returning to music whose harmonies and rhythms were clearly audible, and painters were again producing images that were representational, or even hyper-realistic. Mathematical prodigies, likewise, were less concerned to carry their analyses to ever more abstract heights, and more concerned to master the computers that matched formal techniques to human applications.

Like questions of "nationhood" in the political realm, questions of "formal rationality" in the intellectual realm started off fruitfully in the 17th century, because the historical conditions favored the autonomous operation of sciences and states, all of them developed around "systems" of logical structure or political organization. In the late 20th century, by contrast, these systems are *un*fruitful and *dys*functional because, as things stand, the reciprocal *inter*dependence between sciences and states is as central as their mutual *in*dependence was 300 years ago. The key problem is no longer to ensure that our social and national systems are *stable:* rather, it is to ensure that intellectual and social procedures are more *adaptive.*

The choice of that last new word is no accident. The humanizing of Modernity goes hand in hand, and is of a piece, with other changes in our way of viewing our situation: from a focus on the problem of preserving stability and preventing instability, to a focus on creating institutions and procedures that are adaptive (at least, not *mal*adaptive) or adaptable (at least, not *un*adaptable). In an age of interdependence and historical change, mere stability and permanence are not enough. Like social and political institutions, formal techniques of thought too easily lapse into stereotyped and self-protective rigidity. Like buildings on a human scale, our intellectual and social procedures will do what we need in the years ahead, only if we take care to avoid irrelevant or excessive stability, and keep them operating in ways that are adaptable to unforeseen—or even unforeseeable—situations and functions.

The Recovery of Practical Philosophy

If the humanizing of Modernity in natural science undoes the effects of the 17th-century rejection of humanism, the same option is now open in philosophy. After 1630, philosophers ignored the concrete, timely, particular issues of practical philosophy, and pursued abstract, timeless, and universal (i.e., theoretical) issues. Today, this theoretical agenda is wearing out its welcome, and the philosophical problems of practice are coming back into focus.

Since 1945, the problems that have challenged reflective thinkers on a deep philosophical level, with the same urgency that cosmology and cosmopolis had in the 17th century, are matters of *practice:* including matters of life and death. Three sets of problems have attracted special attention—those of nuclear war, medical technology, and the claims of the environment: none of them can be addressed without bringing to the surface questions about the value of human life, and our responsibility for protecting the world of nature, as well as that of humanity. All the "changes of mind" that were characteristic of the 17th century's turn from humanism to rationalism are, as a result, being reversed. The "modern" focus on the written, the universal, the general, and the timeless—which monopolized the work of most philosophers after 1630—is being broadened to include once again the oral, the particular, the local, and the timely.

The Return to the Oral

The renewal of concern among scholars of language and literature, over the last twenty years, with oral language, communication, rhetoric, and "discourse" is clear enough. A century ago, a Catholic traditionalist like

John Henry Newman could write a *Grammar of Assent,* which treated rhetoric as a topic of serious intellectual interest; but, in the first half of the 20th century, his example was not much followed. Instead, the scholarly focus was on the "text", which was taken to mean a text as it appears on a page, preferably a printed page: this limitation went with the desire to isolate literary works, as products, from facts about the historical situations and personal lives of their authors, as producers—i.e., to decontextualize the text. Since the mid-1960s, rhetoric has begun to regain its respectability as a topic of literary and linguistic analysis, and it now shares with "narrative" an attention for which they both waited a long time.

The same is happening in other fields. Many American colleges and universities have departments devoted to "communication studies", or "speech". These departments are responsible for college debating teams, but their faculty members also do serious research on different aspects of oral communication and argumentation. Meanwhile, current work in developmental psychology is influenced by the ideas of L. S. Vygotsky and A. R. Luria on, for example, the role of spoken language in the shaping of a child's capacities to think and act. Instead of the child's mental equipment being part of a permanent "human nature" with which all humans alike confront sense experience—or, at most, a passive product of that sensory experience—speech, or more specifically the internalization of speech, is now seen as a tool, which the child uses in acquiring its native culture. Rhetoric even plays a part today in the social sciences: Donald McCloskey has raised powerful questions about how economists judge the relevance of their theories to concrete situations, under the title of "the rhetoric of economics."

More centrally, at the heart of academic philosophy, questions about oral *utterances* have, since the 1950s, displaced questions about written *propositions.* In retrospect, the preoccupation with propositions, which was common in the first half of the 20th century, seems to be one more aspect of the return to rationalism during the years between the Wars. Even before the Second World War, Wittgenstein was moving away from the expression of beliefs in written propositions to their transient, contextual expression in language games, speech acts, and utterances generally. Only in the last 25 years, however, have academic philosophers in Britain and the United States generally shared his underlying perception that "meaning" cannot be analyzed as a timeless relationship between propositions and states of affairs alone, but must be understood always in relation to one or another larger behavioral context.

Recently, then, analytical philosophers in Britain and America have turned away from formal logic to the study of "forms of life" and speech contexts, although these authors rarely acknowledge that the "contexts" of utterances were traditionally a preoccupation of *rhetoric*. Meanwhile, parallel moves are being made in other countries: in Germany, Gadamer's interest in conversation, and Habermas' analysis of communication, are further examples of a philosophical shift back toward a concern with the rhetorical contexts of speech and thought.

The Return to the Particular

Along with rhetoric, another discipline that came into disrepute in the mid-17th century was "case ethics" or "casuistry": after the 1650s, discussions of moral philosophy focussed almost entirely on general abstract theories, rather than on specific concrete problems. In the last 20 or 30 years, this change too has gone into reverse. In discussing the morality of war, Michael Walzer revives criteria for distinguishing just from unjust wars that the casuists clarified in the Middle Ages and the Renaissance. The 17th-century philosophers, notably Blaise Pascal, may have scorned these medieval ideas, but in our own time it turns out that we can no longer hope to talk sense about war and nuclear weapons, or other urgent matters, if we reject the whole casuistical tradition.

This revival of "case ethics" is not the only sign of recognition by contemporary philosophers of the need to avoid concentrating exclusively on abstract and universal issues, and to reconsider particular concrete problems arising, not generally, but in specific types of situation. Where, a generation ago, philosophers interested in law discussed theoretical questions about law-in-general, we now find them writing quite as much about practical problems of jurisprudence relevant to particular current cases: for example, the limits of "affirmative action" (*Bakke*), or the conditions on which a terminally ill patient can be disconnected from life support systems (*Quinlan*). The particularity of such cases no longer makes this interest "unphilosophical": on the contrary, the way in which this very particularity challenges the temptation to generalize prematurely, and too broadly, gives such cases a special relevance to philosophy.

The Return to the Local

In the late 20th century, we are also weaned from Descartes' belief that factual realms of human study like history and ethnography lack intellectual depth, and can teach us nothing of intellectual importance about, for instance, human nature. Instead, in Western Europe and North America, people these days are deeply influenced by the insights of anthropology, to such an extent that they sometimes find it hard to evaluate their own cultures, and tend to assume—often a little sloppily—that all societies and cultures are equally good in their own ways.

Anthropological and historical insights need not, however, generate philosophical confusion in general, or a sloppy "relativism" in particular. By now, there are few branches of philosophy in which we can afford to turn a blind eye to these insights. Their importance is clearest in fields like ethics, where Alasdair MacIntyre, say, appeals to them to stimulate serious-minded attention to the varied ways in which moral problems are actually discussed and dealt with in this or that cultural and historical context: in Norse saga cultures as contrasted with medieval Christianity, or in the Lutheran and Calvinist societies of Northern Europe as contrasted with the Catholic heartland of the Mediterranean. Similar points arise across the whole of philosophy, from the theory of perception—where cultural differences in the recognition of colors, say, undermine attempts to use "sense data" as the building blocks of epistemology—to the philosophy of mathematics, in which Euclidean idealizations of spatial relations have proved to be more relevant and intelligible for people in some kinds of cultures than in others.

Once the significance of "traditions" and "forms of life" is conceded, of course, one must abandon Descartes' move in the *Discourse on Method,* in which he required us to ignore traditional ideas in favor of ones whose "clarity and distinctness" to all reflective thinkers made them cultural universals. The questions, whether people in all cultures and epochs have access to the same neutral "basic conceptual framework" equally; and, if so, to what extent and in what respects, is a question of fact that we can face with intellectual honesty only if we are ready to take anthropology and history seriously.

The Return to the Timely

Finally, in recent years, the focus of philosophy has broadened to include problems whose rational significance is not eternal but depends on the timeliness of our solutions. Once again, this is true, above all, of clinical medicine, where the ability to follow the "course" of a disease through time, and to vary clinical procedures as it changes, is an essential element. Rather than medicine being one more "natural science", whose study presumably conforms to universal rules of scientific investigation, we increasingly understand that the actual practice of clinical medicine is an art that is put to work effectively only by people with extensive and carefully digested experience of dealing with flesh-and-blood human beings, in health and in sickness.

None of this would be news to Aristotle, who knew the differences between intellectual grasp of a theory (or *episteme*), mastery of arts and techniques (*techne*), and the wisdom needed to put techniques to work in concrete cases dealing with actual problems (i.e., *phronesis*). Aristotle shared Plato's hope that we would eventually discover truths that held generally ("on the whole") of human beings as well as of natural things; but he saw that our chance of acting wisely in a practical field depends upon our readiness, not just to calculate the timeless demands of intellectual formulae, but also to take decisions *pros ton kairon*—that is, "as the occasion requires."

Nor would it be any news to Ludwig Wittgenstein. In his classes at Cambridge in the 1940s and '50s, Wittgenstein presented a skepticism that shared much with that of Montaigne, Pyrrho, and Sextus Empiricus. The universal, timeless questions that philosophical curiosity leads us to ask are *unanswerable,* he implied, because they have no determinate meanings. No experience can justify asserting one answer, and denying all alternatives. Instead, we do better to regard these questions with suspicion, and reflect on the reasons why we are tempted to ask them in the first place: after 300 years or more, the methods of theoretical argument that Descartes sold to his successors as a way of escape from classical skepticism have ended by leading "theory-centered" philosophy—after its Omega-shaped trajectory—back to the point at which Sextus and Montaigne had left it.

Wittgenstein's objections, however, apply only to philosophy that is thought of as aiming at a formal theory (or *episteme*). It does not touch the more circumscribed problems available to philosophy in the realm of practice. So if philosophers today are again taking seriously fields of study which, in the *Discourse on Method,* Descartes dismissed as having no real depth, that is no accident; nor is it an accident that more and more philosophers are now being drawn into debates about environmental policy or medical ethics, judicial practice or nuclear politics. Some of them contribute to those debates happily: others look back at 300 years of professional tradition, and ask whether oral, particular, local, and timely issues are really their concern. They fear that engaging in "applied" philosophy may prostitute their talents, and distract them from the technical questions of academic philosophy proper. Yet, one might argue, these practical debates are, by now, not "applied" philosophy but *philosophy itself.* More precisely they are now (as Wittgenstein put it) the "legitimate heirs" of the purely theoretical enterprise that used to be called philosophy; and, by pursuing them, we break down the 300-year-old barriers between "practice" and "theory" and reenter the technical core of philosophy from a fresh and more productive direction.

Historically speaking, of course, the exclusion of practical issues from philosophy is quite recent. Those who are reviving them today find that such issues were actively debated by philosophers just 400 years ago. In discussing the morality of war, for example, Michael Walzer has recovered "case-based" arguments used in this field before the 17th century; and, in rhetoric, philosophers before Descartes formulated a whole range of distinctions that can still be fruitful for us today. Other current topics in practical philosophy arise in contexts and situations that have arisen from social, cultural, or technical innovations in our present modes of life. In asking about the limits to the use of medical technology to treat dying patients, for example, we have to look at the relations between human personality and physiology in ways that breathe fresh life into the older "mind/body" problem. Far from that problem raising purely theoretical issues, about how physiological and psychological explanations connect, for instance, it now generates intense moral dilemmas about how to treat human beings in the last days or hours of their lives. Already, the problem divides the staffs of psychiatry departments into two camps—on one side, those who believe in "talking cures"; on the other, those who prefer to control mental illness by psychopharmaceutical means. Once we add a further moral component, however, the role of physiological processes in mental life gives rise to concrete clinical problems, whose details demand analysis from moral philosophers.

Equally central philosophical issues underlie practical issues about ecology and the environment. Notice, first, that ecology raises not just utilitarian but cosmological questions. We often think of cosmology as a part of theoretical physics, and so overlook its original goal, which was to describe the fundamental "order" or "pattern" in Nature. Both for the classical Greeks, and in 17th-century Europe, the *cosmos* (i.e., "order of nature") could be equated with the "order" in the heavens, which were the backcloth or stage setting for the drama of human life. Now in the late 20th century, however, our ideas about "order" in nature are very different. To our eyes, Nature can no longer be seen as stable, as it was for the Greeks or Newton: rather than being the fixed, causal backcloth for rational human action, it has an evolutionary history that is the longer-term context against which many things in human history, too, must ultimately be understood. Even on the most intimate levels, our lives today are touched by whatever seems to have happened to green monkeys in Africa some twenty or thirty years ago, or whenever the HIV (or human immunodeficiency virus) responsible for AIDS first made its appearance, and migrated to the human species.

Rather than assuming that we can still measure the political and social affairs of human beings against a fixed astronomical template—viz., a stable Solar System—so that we can expect people of different classes and genders, races and occupations to keep to separate orbits or "stations", we are learning that, in an evolving world, institutions must be adaptable to deal with evolving human problems. In a dozen respects, therefore, our cosmology today is in course of evolution, and our ideas about human affairs can no more be limited by the modern cosmopolis, with its emphasis on *stability* and *hierarchy,* than can our ideas about biology, astronomy, or the rest of the natural world. In the realm of social and political practice, as in theoretical natural science, our new and rehumanized ideals must also address issues of *adaptation.*

Throughout history, the development of philosophy has displayed a sequence of pendulum swings between two rival agendas. On one agenda, the task of philosophy is to analyze all subjects in *wholly general* terms; on the other, it is to give *as general an account* as the nature of the field allows. Theoretically minded Platonists speculate freely, framing broad generalizations about human knowledge; practical-minded Aristotelians hesitate to claim universality in advance of actual experience. So read, the move from 16th-century humanism to 17th-century exact science was a swing from the practical, Aristotelian agenda, to a Platonist agenda, aimed at theoretical answers. The dream of 17th-century philosophy and science was Plato's demand for *episteme,* or *theoretical grasp:* the facts of 20th-century science and philosophy rest on Aristotle's *phronesis,* or *practical wisdom.* When Wittgenstein and Rorty argue that philosophy today is at "the end of the road", they are overdramatizing the situation. The present state of the subject marks the return from a theory-centered conception, dominated by a concern for *stability* and *rigor,* to a renewed acceptance of practice, which requires us to *adapt* action to the special demands of particular occasions.

From Leviathan to Lilliput

In both science and philosophy, then, the intellectual agenda today obliges us to pay less attention to *stability* and *system,* more attention to *function* and *adaptability.* This shift of attention again has its counterpart in the social and political realms. For 300 years, Europe and its dependencies learned the lessons of "nationhood" all too well, and must now in some respects unlearn them. The task is not to build new, larger, and yet more powerful powers, let alone a "world state" having absolute, worldwide sovereignty. Rather, it is to fight the inequalities that were entrenched during the ascendancy of the nation-state, and to limit the absolute sovereignty of even the best-run nation-states. The social, political, and economic functions that need serving after the year 2000 call for more subnational, transnational, or multinational institutions and procedures. Like the multiplicity of jurisdictions and state authorities in the United States, when the Constitution works well, "*non*-national" institutions can check the extremes of nationhood, hamper the claims of absolutism, and obstruct the arbitrary uses of force into which sovereign power so often tempts the established rulers of all nations.

In this respect, social and political developments today run parallel to current moves away from the "modern" orientation in intellectual life, with its formal conception of "rationality". The charms of logical rigor were also learned too well, and must now in crucial ways be unlearned. The task is not to build new, more comprehensive systems of theory with universal and timeless relevance, but to limit the scope of even the best-framed theories, and fight the intellectual reductionism that became entrenched during the ascendancy of rationalism. The intellectual tasks for a science in which all the branches are accepted as equally serious call for more subdisciplinary, transdisciplinary, and multidisciplinary reasoning. Like the informal procedures of the common law when it is functioning at its best, these interlocking modes of investigation and explanation check exaggerated claims on behalf of all universal theories, and reinstate respect for the pragmatic methods appropriate in dealing with concrete human problems. In clinical medicine and jurisprudence, human ecology and social history, historical geology and developmental psychodynamics alike, the model of Euclid's axioms and theorems was from the start misleading in orientation and confused in outcome. From now on, every science will need to employ those specific methods that have proved, in concrete experience, to match the characteristic demands of its own intellectual problems.

The original pattern for the "exact sciences" of Modernity was set by physics—specifically, by the Newtonian theory of central forces. Within a humanized Modernity, ecological ideas and methods of thought will increasingly be a model in both scientific and philosophical debate. Does this mean that we can also replace the modern cosmopolis, based on the stability of the solar system, by a new "post-modern" cosmopolis based on the ideas of ecosystems and adaptability? To that, the answer is both "Yes" and "No"; but the "No" is easier to explain.

As a political instrument, the notion of cosmopolis has an unhappy track record. Historically, rhetorical analogies between nature and society have too often been used to legitimate inequality and domination. The function of cosmopolitical arguments is to show members of the lower orders that their dreams of democracy are *against nature;* or conversely to reassure the upper class that they are superior citizens *by nature.* Whatever else our inquiry has achieved, it surely was not intended to replace one system of oppressive rhetoric modeled on physics by an equally oppressive one modeled on ecology. On the other hand, we can also reply with at least a qualified "Yes". Ecological perspectives on social and political issues differ in one crucial respect from the Newtonian view of a stable system "kept in order" by universal and unchanging central forces. In the social realm, the Newtonian view called for stable institutions, unambiguous class structure, centralized power, and defense of the state's sovereign auton-omy from external interference. The resulting hierarchy of class institu-tions had a part to play in the reconstruction of Europe after the Religious Wars; but today, once we begin to think in ecological terms, we shall soon learn that every niche or habitat is one of its own kind, and that its demands call for a careful eye to its particular, local, and timely circumstances. The Newtonian view encouraged hierarchy and rigidity, standardization and uniformity: an ecological perspective emphasizes, rather, differentiation and diversity, equity and adaptability.

Writing shortly after Descartes, with a knowledge of his arguments, Thomas Hobbes presented the theory that shaped so much later political and social theory of Western Europe and North America. A modern state (specifically, a nation-state) requires, in his view, overwhelming force concentrated at the center, under the authority of a sovereign, whom he likens to an irresistible monster, or Leviathan. As willful social atoms, all of his subjects will otherwise go their own ways, and pursue their indi-vidual goods independently; so they must be made to understand that their personal activities take place under, and are constrained by, the shadow of this overwhelming central force.

Given this theory, the Newtonian image of the state as a planetary system, and the power of the sovereign as a counterpart of the central force of the sun, fleshed out and added detail to Hobbes' basic picture. The stability of society required not just centralized force, but also a system of fixed orbits (or stations) in which different parts of society follow predictable paths. So long as this image carried conviction, some other questions, which arise naturally on an ecological model of society, could not even be *asked:* for example, how we can justify, or change, the geographical boundaries of any particular state, and whether some of the powers of the national state will not be better performed on a *sub*national or *trans*national level.

An ecological cosmopolis may thus avoid the objection to which the earlier, astronomical image was subject: viz., that it is arbitrary and oppressive in its effect. Biology provides less constricting analogies for thinking about social relations than physics did. In the organic world, diversity and differentiation are the rule and not the exception, while the universality of physical theories is rare. Different ecosystems or food chains, for instance, may coexist within a single habitat, without one species establishing dominance over all others; and the measures to maintain a balance between species vary from case to case. If an image of "central forces" and "stable equilibria" made the modern cosmopolis oppressive, an ecological model opens up the possibilities for diversity and change, and so can be emancipatory.

There is no need to deny that "nation-building" helped to make 18th-century and 19th-century Europe productive and self-confident: during this time, "national" institutions and habits of mind were largely constructive and creative. But a belief in the omnicompetence of the autonomous sovereign nation often works for the benefit of the current rulers, and against the interests of those who are "subject" to those self-appointed betters. Worse, those peoples who develop a consciousness of "nationhood" late in the day are open to a pathological nationalism, which insists on anachronistic forms of unqualified sovereignty. The appeal of dogmatic nationalisms today—to extremist Sikhs in India, for example, or to Tamils in Sri Lanka—is the Djinn let out of the bottle, and awakens nightmare echoes of Europe centuries ago. Created in the aftermath of the wars of religion, the idol of the "nation" haunts a world that now needs more *adaptive* ways to meet its human needs.

What is true of politics is equally true of ethics. The idolization of "traditional values" has disadvantages, and its dogmas stand in the way of more discriminating and discerning approaches to moral issues. In the aftermath of the Religious Wars, continuing hostility between "heretics" and "papists" led to a competition in *rigor;* but there is no virtue today in letting the perfectionists monopolize the discussion of ethical issues, and ignoring the other, more humane modes of moral thinking that were just as respected in historical Christianity. On occasion, a censorious Puritanism can be in order; but dogmatic appeals to "tradition" are, in biblical terms, the teachings of the Pharisees more than those of Jesus. One can understand an Archbishop in the 1960s objecting to the tyranny of the Polish State, or to the corruption of the Communist *nomenklatura;* but *autres temps, autres moeurs.* The moral world has other dimensions beside the Cold War; charity and loving kindness stand higher on a scale of Christian values than censorious scrupulosity; and the wise firmness of an Archbishop may become inappropriate dogmatism in a Pope.

One notable feature of the system of European Powers established by the Peace of Westphalia, then, was the untrammeled sovereignty it conferred on the European Powers. Before the Reformation, the established rulers—the grand duchies, counties, kingdoms, and other sovereign territories of Europe—exercised their political power under the moral supervision of the Church. As Henry II of England found after the murder of Thomas à Becket, the Church might even oblige a King to accept a humiliating penance as the price of its continued support. Popes and Bishops did not always use their power prudently or judiciously; at times, it was unclear where the final locus of moral authority lay—in Rome or, say, Avignon; nor did the Church invariably succeed in enforcing its wishes on recalcitrant rulers. Throughout the Middle Ages, however, few secular rulers ever claimed to be wholly exempt from this external judgment.

After 1648, the new diplomatic and political order relieved rulers of the European Powers of outside moral criticism. Modern Europe had no central focus of moral and spiritual authority. The Peace of Westphalia did not just reaffirm the right of each ruler to decide the "established" denomination of the State: it gave rulers an absolute moral sovereignty. People in Anglican England, and even more in Presbyterian Scotland, were indifferent to moral criticism from French Papists. Catholic subjects of Louis XIV and XV were unmoved by the moral views of English Heretics. Nor could the Pope, in dealing with a monarch like Louis XIV, or with the Gallican Cardinals who were the King's agents, insist on his Supremacy: instead, he had to proceed diplomatically, as one among equals.

What was true in practice also took on theoretical respectability. In Thomas Hobbes' theory of the State, the Sovereign is both the wielder of supreme Power and the source and guarantor of Rights. Under the high patronage of Leviathan, effective Law and Morality meant *positive* law and morality, which had the sanction of the Sovereign—*le Roi le veult.* Throughout the centuries of Modernity, political theorists thus took the moral self-sufficiency of nation-states for granted. For them, the only question was, "How does the power of the state come to be binding on its subjects?"; and they gave little attention to the question, "Who can pass moral judgment on the exercise of State power?" True, flagrant malefactors like King Bomba of Naples became objects of ridicule throughout Europe, and William Ewart Gladstone thundered in the House of Commons against

Turkish atrocities in Bulgaria. But such isolated rhetorical episodes set no precedents, and created no authoritative non-national institutions.

We live today in a different age. After the First World War, the Allied Powers sponsored the League of Nations, and from the start this multi-national institution was meant to have a moral authority capable, on occasion, of overriding that of any single associated Power. This limitation on the moral authority of all national rulers is also, of course, a feature of the United Nations Charter; and the same limits are implicit in the oper-ations of the International Court of Justice at The Hague, and in the founding documents of the European Community. Still, even these limits are interpreted as *self*-limitations. They are not *external* constraints, which bind such states willy-nilly, but *internal* glosses on the modern nation-state's exercise of its undoubted sovereignty: each state accepts them as a condition of entering into voluntary association with other, co-equal states. As a result, the moral authority of the United Nations and similar institu-tions is less striking and less influential than the spiritual authority of the Medieval Popes.

In apparent paradox, that external authority today belongs to other, *non-governmental* institutions. No one takes wholly seriously the moral opinions voiced—whether in outrage, sorrow, or excuse—in the General Assembly or Security Council of the United Nations, as they are always presented by official spokesmen for the Member States, whose status marks them as "interested parties." The only institutions whose moral opinions command general respect and are generally heard as stating "the decent opinion of Humankind" are Amnesty International, the World Psychiatric Association, and similar organizations, which are devoid of physical power or "armed force."

At this point, the underlying confusion between *power* and *force* in Hobbes' account of the modern state is crucial. In a moment of cynical joviality Josef Stalin once asked, "How many divisions has the Pope?" The fact is that, in the eyes of decent human opinion, moral challenges are *never* answered by displays of force. The day that Amnesty International takes possession of a machine gun, let alone an atom bomb, its ability to gain a hearing and influence events will be at an end. Institutions with bigger and bigger guns have, in practice, less and less claim to speak on moral issues with the small voice that carries conviction. Here lies the effectiveness of Jonathan Swift's image of *Lilliput*. Stalin failed to see that the military triviality of the Pope's Swiss Guard increases his claim to a hearing, rather than undermining it; while Amnesty International's moral authority is that much the greater, just because it is a Lilliputian institution.

To this day, the patterns of our lives are shaped politically by the actions of State authority; yet, morally, rulers of contemporary states are open to outside moral criticism of kinds that have not been widely available since before 1650. Even the most forceful superpowers can no longer ignore the fact. Mikhail Gorbachev sees, as Josef Stalin never did, the harm that a challenge from Amnesty can do to the Soviet Government. Lilliputian organizations cannot compel immoral rulers to apologize on their knees, as Henry II had to do; but they do subject rulers who refuse to mend their ways to damaging embarrassment in the eyes of the world. If the political image of Modernity was Leviathan, the moral standing of "national" powers and superpowers will, for the future, be captured in the picture of Lemuel Gulliver, waking from an unthinking sleep, to find himself tethered by innumerable tiny bonds.

The Rational and the Reasonable

When we asked about the starting point of Modernity, we had no way of knowing how deep our inquiry would cut: in particular, it was unclear how far the standard accounts of modern science and philosophy, fine art and technology, politics and society, were bound together by common assumptions. Yet the parallels we have seen here, between developments over a wide range of practical and intellectual fields, are neither mirages nor the imagined effects of an intangible *Zeitgeist* or "spirit of the age"—let alone empty products of psychic projection and wishful thinking. On the contrary, they are held together by one shared thread: a shared conception of *rationality,* which came to the fore in the 17th century and has dominated much in Western thinking ever since.

How close the ideas of *rationality* and *reason* are to the heart of the contemporary critique of Modernity, and to the doubts about the coming millennium to which it gives rise, is evident also in other ways. Let us notice two recent books. To begin with, Paul Feyerabend has followed up his earlier attack on rationalism, *Against Method,* with a new collection of essays called *Farewell to Reason;* yet the "reason" that Feyerabend bids farewell to is not the everyday ideal of being "reasonable" or "open to reason", which Montaigne and the humanists embraced. Rather, it is what he calls "scientific rationalism": i.e., the 17th-century dream of a *logical* rationality, shared by philosophers from Descartes to Popper:

> The appeal to reason [Feyerabend argues] is empty, and must be replaced by a notion of science that subordinates it to the needs of citizens and communities.

For his part, Alasdair MacIntyre has published his critique of rationality with the title, *Whose Justice? What Rationality?* There, he explores the development of four European cultural traditions, in which the idea of "rationality" has subtly but crucially different meanings. This study confirms what we found in our own inquiry, that the history of Western culture falls into a series of periods in each of which different ideals of reason and rationality were dominant.

Our revised narrative of the stages in Modernity, indeed, embodies implicitly a history of "modern" ideas about rationality. For 16th-century humanists, the central demand was that all of our thought and conduct be *reasonable.* On the one hand, this meant developing modesty about one's capacities and self-awareness in one's self-presentation: all the things that Stephen Greenblatt calls "Renaissance self-fashioning." On the other hand, it required toleration of social, cultural, and intellectual diversity. It was unreasonable to condemn out of hand people with institutions, customs, or ideas different from ours, as heretical, superstitious, or barbarous. Instead, we should recognize that our own practices may look no less strange to others, and withhold judgment until we can ask how far those others reached their positions by honest, discriminating, and critical reflection on their experience. We can judge people's ideas or customs fairly only if we know not just where they ended up, but also (in the language of the 1960s) "where they were coming from." Sound rhetoric demands that we *speak to* the condition of an audience; honest human understanding requires us to *listen to* their condition with equal care.

After 1620, many Europeans found this intellectual and practical tolerance inconclusive, permissive, and open to abuse, and adopted other, stricter ideals of rationality instead. For Descartes, rational thought could not rely on inherited tradition: empirical procedures rooted in experience rather than theory were in his view compromised, since they perpetuated the folklore of a given culture and period, and rested finally on superstition, not reason. He felt that if everyone cleaned their slate, and started from the same sensory "impressions" or "clear and distinct ideas", there would be no need to ask what personal or cultural idiosyncrasies each of them brought to their common debate. Wherever possible, then, the "rational" thing to do was to start from scratch, and to insist on the certainty of geometrical inference and the logicality of formal proofs. Only so could a way be found, he believed, to avoid both the interminable quarrels of the dogmatic theologians, and the uncertainties and contradictions implicit in Montaigne's skepticism.

The ideals of reason and rationality typical of the second phase of Modernity were, thus, intellectually perfectionist, morally rigorous, and

humanly unrelenting. Whatever sorts of problem one faced, there was a
supposedly unique procedure for arriving at the correct solution. That
procedure could be recognized only by cutting away the inessentials, and
identifying the abstract core of "clear and distinct" concepts needed for its
solution. Unfortunately, little in human life lends itself fully to the lucid,
tidy analysis of Euclid's geometry or Descartes' physics. Aside from these
abstract fields of study, the methodology was unrealizable and practically
irrelevant, though it kept its attractions for all those who welcomed the
stability and hierarchy of the New Cosmopolis.

In the search for a "rational" method which took a central place in
17th-century science and philosophy, Descartes' agenda was only one
variant. This decontexualized ideal was a central demand of rational
thought and action among "modern" thinkers until well into the 20th
century. In due course, further variants joined it: the economist's equation
of "rationality" with efficiency, for example, and Max Weber's view of the
"rationalization" of social institutions. These further twists, however, were
still directed at issues that could be judged by rational, objective and
preferably quantitative measures, and they too left little room for cultural
or personal idiosyncrasies.

As we enter a fresh phase in the history of Modernity—seeking to
humanize science and technology and reappropriate the aims of practical
philosophy—we need to recover the idea of rationality that was current
before Descartes. There are some substantial advantages in doing this.
Rationally adequate thought or action cannot, in all cases equally, start by
cleaning the slate, and building up a formal system: in practice, the rigor
of theory is useful only up to a point, and in certain circumstances. Claims
to certainty, for instance, are at home *within* abstract theories, and so open
to consensus; but all abstraction involves *omission,* turning a blind eye to
elements in experience that do not lie within the scope of the given theory,
and so guaranteeing the rigor of its formal implications. Unqualified
agreement about these implications is possible, just because the theory
itself is formulated in abstract terms. *Supposing that* we adopt the standpoint of Newton's dynamics, for instance, it will *follow necessarily* that any
"freely moving satellite" must trace an orbit of elliptical, hyperbolic, or
parabolic shape. Once we move outside the theory's formal scope, and ask
questions about its relevance to the external demands of practice, however, we enter into a realm of legitimate uncertainty, ambiguity, and
disagreement.

Here, too, the stage in Western culture and society that we are now
entering—whether we see it as the third phase in Modernity, or as a new
and distinctive "post-modern" phase—obliges us to reappropriate values

from Renaissance humanism that were lost in the heyday of Modernity. Even at the core of 20th-century physics, idiosyncrasies of persons and cultures cannot be eliminated. The quirks and backgrounds of creative scientists are as relevant to our understanding of their ideas as they are to our understanding of the work of poets or architects. There are things about Einstein's general theory of relativity, for example, that are understood best if we learn that Einstein was a visual rather than a verbal thinker, and things about quantum mechanics that are best explained if we know that Nils Bohr grew up in a household where Kierkegaard's ideas about "complementary" modes of thought were (as Gerald Holton has reminded us) discussed at Sunday dinner.

Within a humanized Modernity, the decontextualizing of problems so typical of High Modernity is no longer a serious option. The axioms of Modernity assumed that the surface complexity of nature and humanity distracts us from an underlying Order, which is intrinsically simple and permanent. By now, however, physical scientists recognize as well as anyone that natural phenomena *in fact* embody an "intrinsically simple" order only to a limited degree: novel theories of physical, biological, or social *dis*order (or "chaos") allow us to balance the intellectual books. We may temporarily ("for the purposes of calculation") shelve the contexts of our problems, but, eventually, their complete resolution obliges us to put these calculations back into their larger human frame, with all its concrete features and complexities.

Looking back at the intellectually challenging years between 1650 and 1950, from a position of lesser confidence but greater modesty, we can appreciate why the projects of Modernity carried the conviction they did. Not the least of these charms was an oversimplification that, in retrospect, was unrealistic. With this point in mind, we may recall the comment on social and political affairs made by that humane, grumpy, but normally clearheaded commentator, Walter Lippmann, which distills much of what has come to light in our own inquiry. "To every human problem," he said, "there is a solution that is simple, neat, and *wrong*"; and that is as true of intellectual as it is of practical problems. The seduction of High Modernity lay in its abstract neatness and theoretical simplicity: both of these features blinded the successors of Descartes to the unavoidable complexities of concrete human experience.

Facing the Future Again

A pproaching the third millennium, we are at the point of transition from the second to the third phase of Modernity—or, if you prefer, from Modernity to Post-Modernity. Placed at this transition by changes beyond our control, we have a choice between two attitudes toward the future, each with its own "horizons of expectation". We may welcome a prospect that offers new possibilities, but demands novel ideas and more adaptive institutions; and we may see this transition as a reason for hope, seeking only to be clearer about the novel possibilities and demands involved in a world of practical philosophy, multidisciplinary sciences, and transnational or subnational institutions. Or we may turn our backs on the promises of the new period, in trepidation, hoping that the modes of life and thought typical of the age of stability and nationhood may survive at least for our own lifetimes.

To speak more precisely, these two attitudes to the future—one of imagination, the other of nostalgia—do not imply different horizons of expectation. The choice is one between *facing* the future, and so asking about the "futuribles" open to us, or *backing into* it with no such horizons or ideas. Conditions of life and thought today differ in a dozen ways from those in the 18th and 19th centuries, when the theory and practice of Modernity were most fruitful, and it is unrealistic as things stand to imagine a future that preserves the hallmarks of Modernity: the intellectual autonomy of distinct sciences, a confident reliance on self-justifying technologies, and separate independent nation-states with unqualified sovereignties. An attitude of nostalgia implies few expectations, aside from the hope of preserving the *status quo:* the task of defining realistic "futuribles" is open only to those who are ready to adopt imaginative attitudes, think about the directions in which we might be moving, and recognize that the future will reward those who anticipate the institutions and procedures we shall need. How, then, will the modes of life and thought of the third phase of Modernity differ from those of its second phase?

Scientifically, they will abandon the assumption that physics is the "master" science, which gives an authoritative model of rational method to all science and philosophy. Instead, they will let each field of inquiry develop its proper methods, adapted to its own special problems. Some authors may continue to write, as popularization, of high-energy physics and cosmology as seeking "the key to the universe": in practice, however, scientific inquiry will increasingly shift from abstract laws of universal application to particular decipherments of the complex structures and detailed processes embodied in concrete aspects of nature. The model of "theoretical grasp" as the formal ability to master a deductive system that describes a permanent and ubiquitous "order" in nature, is giving way to a substantive ability to discover the local, temporary relations embodied in one specific aspect of nature, here and now, in contrast to another, elsewhere, a million years ago. Ecology and molecular biology between them are, in this respect, beginning to figure out the detailed vocabulary of Galileo's Book of Nature. Among all the subdisciplines of the natural sciences, therefore, relations will become more egalitarian as fresh multidisciplinary fields open up to research, bearing complex names like "developmental neuropsychology".

In the arts, a similar egalitarian move away is already under way. One lasting effect of the critique of Modernity has been to undermine the role of "respectability" as a reason to esteem certain styles, genres, or even media, at the expense of others—for example, classical (or "serious") music at the expense of popular music. That shift implicitly began when Mozart found a middle-class audience for irreverent *opere giocose* like *The Marriage of Figaro* and *Don Giovanni,* to balance the established Court taste for *opere serie* like *Idomeneo* or *La Clemenza di Tito;* it resurfaced between the two World Wars, when Berthold Brecht and Kurt Weill used popular music as a mode of political critique; but it became explicit and irreversible only during the last twenty-five years. Alongside the attack on claims for the superior status of "high" media and genres, much of the striking innovation in the arts, at present and for the future, ignores the traditional separations between distinct media, finding ways to express ideas more effectively than the established genres sometimes permit. The critical singularity of "the" sonata, "the" landscape, or "the" drawing room comedy, is thus losing ground to the new pluralism of multimedia experiments.

In the field of technology, our ability to handle material processes and civil-engineering techniques has passed beyond the stage at which their benefits are self-evident and self-justifying. Hiroshima might have done enough to prove the point; but it has recently been underlined by the explosion at Chernobyl, the oil spill at Prince William Sound, the hole in the polar ozone layers, and the wanton burning of tropical rain forests. Preaching before Modernity got off the ground, John Donne reminded his congregation that "No man is an island", untouched by the fate of his fellows; and the same is true of technological and engineering projects. They cannot be judged in isolation from the rest of human life, or from the interests of the other species whose existence is affected—even threatened—by their execution. Initially, the Soviet authorities tried to suppress news of the Chernobyl disaster, but it was soon clear that they could only benefit from cooperating with people in other countries. In all the ecological problems of our own time, indeed, natural processes do not stop at human frontiers, but can be controlled only through the free cooperation of people and governments from many (if not all) countries and states. The limits to which technology will be subject in the new, third phase of Modernity thus lead directly on to the social, political, and institutional changes demanded by the third millennium.

———————

At last, then, we can return to the questions raised in the prologue. The countries that played most prominent parts in the second phase of Modernity are, we now see, least prepared, and worst placed, to move into the third. The superpowers that led the last confrontation of High Modernity—not between "heretics" and "papists", but between the "free" and "socialist" worlds—developed institutional sclerosis in the process; while other highly successful nation-states were affected more than most by the short-term thinking of the 1980s, and the resulting sense that the historical horizon was unusually dark and foggy.

After the turbulence of the 1960s and '70s, the decade of the '80s was a time for nostalgia rather than imagination. From the 1960s on, in many countries, too much social stress developed too quickly: notably, the unresolved conflicts left over from the Vietnam War, and the rapid economic changes arising from automation of industry, the growing service economy, and international competition. The modern dream of an order of sovereign "nations" again became attractive, and nostalgia led people to revive their pride in nationhood, and to do as little as possible to upset the nation-state system. In Britain, the War over the Falklands stirred an old pride in national glory; in Japan, the long decline of the Emperor Hirohito postponed a restructuring of the country's institutions; in the Soviet Union, failures in agriculture, the quicksand of Afghanistan, and the revival of divisive nationalisms, delayed the adoption of more moderate policies; in the United States, years of rearmament and self-congratulation merely bandaged over the wounds of Vietnam, while tax reform extinguished all hopes for serious social reform. In all four countries, most people preferred to look backward at past achievements, rather than forward to future uncertainties; so no wonder, in those countries, the future looked unusually cloudy and dark, and the "horizon of expectation" was obscured.

In other countries, the 1960s and '70s generated less of a reaction, nationhood was less of an issue, and structural change was not so hard to contemplate. If we are to understand the possibilities opening up in the third stage of Modernity, then, we may look less at the superpowers and other naturally conservative societies, and more at those regions where the institutional structures are less fixed. In Europe, where the theory and practice of the nation-state first emerged, its weaknesses are now being challenged. The history of the European community shows us how states that had been committed to pre-existing modes of stability, domestically and diplomatically, proved to be unexpectedly adaptable, and ready to set up the institutions needed to create a functional union. In two spasms of War—from 1914 to 1918 and 1939 to 1945—Europeans had proved that "nationhood" is as limited a basis for claiming state loyalty as religion had been 300 years before, at the time of the Thirty Years' War: so began an institutional flux that has turned a collection of suspicious neighbors, with rival economies and hostile memories, into an economic union and, foreseeably, a political unit with a power to command common loyalties. Few doubt that, a century hence, the State of Rhode Island will have the same boundaries and the same two Senators as it has now; but, by then, the sovereign state of Luxembourg will probably be as much of a memory as an independent Anjou and a sovereign Burgundy.

From now on, the overriding concern of administrators and politicians can no longer be to enhance the scope, power, and glory of those centralized national institutions that took shape and worked unfettered in the heyday of the nation-state, when sovereignty was its own reward. Rather, we need to disperse authority and adapt it more discerningly and precisely: on the one hand, to the needs of local areas and communities, and on the other, to wider transnational functions. Nor is this proposition merely abstract and hypothetical. On a *sub*national level, many people in America like to believe that the 1960s left no trace on its institutions, but that is an exaggeration. The events of those years still resonate in a dozen ways in the minds and hearts of those who were actively involved: "Bliss was it in that Dawn . . ."; but they also saw the creation of many "nonnational" institutions, from local consumer groups to transnational networks for monitoring national governments, which remain as thorns in the flesh of established powers, whether the utility company, the city and state authorities, or the institutions of the nation-state. Indeed, the vigor of "non-national organizations" is a good index of the health of a country's democracy. After a military coup, such groups are (from a junta's point of view) uncontrolled and the first to feel the pinch. Until the other day, in the socialist states of Eastern Europe, too, the state authorities saw these groups as alarming and suspect: even now, the Soviet government finds it painful to acknowledge the right of "Lilliputian" institutions to sit in moral judgment on the Soviet State.

Valuable examples can be found, equally, on a *multi*national level. So long as the model of Leviathan dominated Western political thinking, the vertebrate cohesion of Mao's China made it appear the very model of "nation building": by contrast, the politics of India looked disorganized. Now, twenty years later, we can ask whether, in a country with so large an area and so diverse a population, it is not more adaptive to be disarticulated, and so ready to react to limited problems by local changes. Independent India took over from the British Raj the techniques of indirect rule that allowed a tiny *émigré* Indian Civil Service to govern a subcontinent; and these constitutional devices still serve today in balancing the powers of "the Centre" with those of the States. Reflective Indians, thus, concede that India is not a "nation" in the European sense, but a confederation of nations that gain more than they lose from staying in the Union. Perhaps the country also pays a price for its disarticulation; but this at least is clear. When we are interested in comparing the merits of governmental forms, the sprawling, heterogeneous commonwealth of India is as good an object of study as the centralized Leviathan to its North.

All in all, then, life and thought in the third phase of Modernity will be shaped as much by activities and institutions on *non-national* levels—whether subnational or transnational, international or multinational—as by our inheritance from the centralized nation-state. Rather than deploring this change by blanket condemnation of, say, multinational corporations or the International Monetary Fund, it is more useful to ask how the ideal of "representative government" can be extended to these institutions, so as to bring their activities under scrutiny from the people whose lives they most affect. In asking this, one last institution that needs to be reconsidered is the United Nations itself. In some ways, the name of the U.N. organization is a misnomer: the structure and *modus operandi* make it, rather, a Cooperative of States. The vulnerable communities, today, are those that lack recognized channels of expression within any single state. In the industrially developed economies, for example, those who are "structurally unemployed" have no unions to speak in their interest; while, in the

United Nations, the unrepresented "non-state" communities are the first to go to the wall. The Kurds, for example, have lived for centuries in an area that is today divided arbitrarily among four States, none of which acknowledges their claims to autonomy or to protection, as Kurds. This fact serves to remind us that we lack an organization of nations, as distinct from nation-states—and need, at least, a better-funded collective of *non-state nations.*

Finally, on the transnational level, let us not forget Lilliput. Local communities and unrepresented groups need the means of self-expression and protection; and nonviolent ways of drawing attention to their needs are more persuasive than those of murderers by night. When antinuclear demonstrators march with candles through the streets of Leipzig, when prisoners of conscience bring General Pinochet's torturers into public scorn, when women's organizations speak for their fellow-women in fundamentalist states, they question the nightmare side of the Modern inheritance, and challenge the moral authority of absolute, centralized nation-states. In this resistance, the candles, voices, and other tools of the powerless may seem of little help. Even the intellectual model of ecology, with its decentralized concern for each distinct habitat, gives us little foundation for building institutions that are more just. But, in the long run, we have seen power and force run up against their limits. In the third phase of Modernity, the name of the game will be *influence,* not *force;* and, in playing on that field, the Lilliputians hold certain advantages.

The impression from which our inquiry began, that the countries of the West were preoccupied in the '80s with their pasts, and turned their back on the future, thus has some warrant. As Peter Drucker saw thirty years ago, in working on the essays in *Landmarks for Tomorrow,* the age of absolute sovereign states is past. The only serious questions are, "How can we best respond to this fact? Are we ready to take advantage of the novel opportunities it provides? Or shall we go on acting as though nothing had happened?" Like corporations and institutions that learn the lesson of internal diversification, and give practical responsibility to work-groups within the organization, the countries that can look forward with most confidence and eagerness to the third millennium are those that welcome the chance to divide their "national" powers and responsibilities among internal, domestic groups, and to enter into multinational and transnational networks that are able to serve human needs more effectively and adaptably than a fragmented collection of sovereign nation-states can still do.

From Hobbes to Marx and beyond, political theory has largely been written in national and international terms. Our reflections on the order of society, as well as nature, are still dominated by the Newtonian image of massive power, exerted by sovereign agency through the operation of central force, and we have lost our feeling for all the respects in which social and political achievements depend on *influence,* more than on *force.* For the moment, the varied political relations and interactions between transnational, subnational and multinational entities, and the functions they can effectively serve, still remain to be analyzed, by an "ecology of institutions" that has, as yet, scarcely come into existence.

Bibliographical Notes

This book is a product of reading and experience across a spectrum from physics and ethics to theology and history. The argument outruns any stock of reference cards, and at times I can do no more than say what authors I am most indebted to, and which scholarly debates I knowingly draw on. Only over crucial points (e.g., Chapter 2, on the significance of Henry of Navarre's assassination, and the evidence of René Descartes' knowledge of the event) is the text based on fresh research, which calls for exact documentation.

General Background

In developing my narrative, I am guided by 35 years in the history of "early modern" Europe, beginning from Roland Mousnier's pioneer work, *Les XVIe et XVIIe Siècles* (1954) and Eric Hobsbawm's essay, "The crisis of the seventeenth century" (*Past and Present,* nos. 5 & 6), and continued by British, American and French historians, at Princeton and elsewhere. The anthology, *The General Crisis of the Seventeenth Century,* ed. by Geoffrey Parker and Lesley M. Smith, is a useful survey of this research. Theodore Rabb's book, *The Struggle for Stability in Early Modern Europe,* helped to confirm my confidence in the central thesis of this book.

In all matters to do with Michel de Montaigne, I have relied on the work of Donald Frame, notably his fine edition of the *Essays,* and also on conversations with Philip Hallie. I did not find it possible to accept the position of Jean Starobinski's well-known book, *Montaigne in Motion;* but Léon Brunschvicg's older *Descartes et Pascal, Lecteurs de Montaigne,* was helpful, especially in throwing light on the relations of Montaigne to his 17th-century successors.

For the English Civil War and the Commonwealth, Christopher Hill's books were an invaluable guide, especially in regard to the interplay of psychology, theology, and politics typical of the time. For 18th-century France, above all the Enlightenment and the Revolution, I rely on Robert Darnton; while on Isaac Newton's life and ideas (notably, his Arian theology) I am in debt to R. S. Westfall's splendid biography, *Never at Rest.* Richard Ashcraft's *Revolutionary Politics & Locke's 'Two Treatises of Government'* came to my attention late, but enriched my picture of politics in the late 17th- and early 18th-century England. For the same period, I learned much from the perceptive writings of Steven Shapin, and also from Margaret Jacob's books, particularly *The Newtonians and the English Revolution.* Finally, Richard Popkin's writings on skepticism in the 16th and 17th centuries are the indispensable warp on which all later writers on the subject weave their own texts.

Descartes and Henry of Navarre

My work on the Jesuit College at La Flèche began from the copy of Baron Sébastien de la Bouillerie's *Histoire de l'Imprimerie à La Flèche* (Mamers, 1896) in the research library at the University of California, Los Angeles. Item 20 in that bibliography of the La Flèche press was the *In anniversarium,* the set of student compositions prepared for the first *Henriade* in 1611. La Bouillerie refers also to the history of the College by Fr. Camille de Rochemonteix, S. J. (Le Mans 1889), of which copies are available in several major libraries, including UC at Berkeley; that history was invaluable.

The copy of the *In anniversarium* which I found in the Bibliothèque Nationale at Paris, in the circumstances described earlier, was listed in the *catalogue des anonymes* with the call number $Lb^{35}1208$; but, when requested, the volume bearing this number proved to be a reprint of a lecture by C. Höfler to the Royal Bohemian Society of Sciences, on March 14, 1859: *Heinrich's IV.,/König von Frankreich/Plan/dem Hause Habsburg/Italien zu entreissen* (Prague, 1859). Where, then, was the B.N.'s copy of the book? The head of the catalogue room, M. Peyraud, directed me to the catalogue printed in 1855, when the B. N. was reclassified: the supplementary list of "anonymous works" provided an alternative call number—$Lb^{35}1177$. This time the book that reached my desk was the *In anniversarium,* and the Sonnet discussed here turned up on p. 163 of the original text. Inside the front cover of this volume, the handwritten annotation can be found, *Ex libris ff^{m} Praedicatorum Parisiensum ad S. Honoratum,* which places it in the pre-Revolutionary Priory in the rue St. Honoré. The title page bears the B. N. acquisition stamp of "type 17", as described in "Estampilles du Département des Imprimés de la Bibliothèque Nationale", by P. Josserand and J. Bruno, in *Mélanges d'histoire du livre et des bibliothèques offerts à Monsieur Frantz Calot* (B. N. Bureau, no. 2532, pp. 261–98, and Pl. XXIII): the design of that stamp dates the acquisition of the book to 1792–1803. The volume also carries an older call number (Y. 2892. A′) struck through: before the B. N. collection was reclassified, this suggests that it was listed under 'Y' for "Latin Verse". Another copy of the *In anniversarium* is in the Houghton Library at Harvard University.

Notes and References

Prologue

The notion of "horizons" is familiar to readers of H.-G. Gadamer and other contemporary German philosophers. For the more specific concept of "horizons of expectation", see Reinhart Koselleck, *Vergangene Zukunft* ("Former Futures") and *Kritik und Krise*. The term *futuribles* ("achievable futures") was coined by Bertrand de Jouvenel for his writings about the methodology of *prévision sociale* ("social forecasting"): for example, in his book, *Ars Conjectandi*. On the case for readmitting the Jews to England under the Commonwealth, see David Katz, *Philo-Semitism and the Readmission of the Jews to England, 1603–1655*.

Chapter One

Dating the Start of Modernity. The controversy over Modernity and post-modernity has two chief battlegrounds: architecture and critical theory. As to architecture, Heinrich Klotz's book, *The History of Post-Modern Architecture* (1988), gives a full account of Robert Venturi's reaction against the influence of Mies van der Rohe, and what followed. Just recently, I saw a reference to J. Hudnut's *Architecture and the Spirit of Man,* as having used the term "post-modern architecture" before Venturi, but I was not able to verify this. For Mies van der Rohe, see the notes to Chapter 4, below.

In philosophy and criticism, the controversy has generated a large literature. Here, I take Jean François Lyotard's *The Post-Modern Condition,* and Jürgen Habermas' *Philosophical Discourse of Modernity* as representing the opposing camps. We must also take note of John Dewey's Gifford Lectures, *The Quest for Certainty,* and Richard Rorty's *Philosophy and the Mirror of Nature* and *Consequences of Pragmatism.* For "post-modernity" in natural science, the pioneer is Frederick Ferré; but see also the final essays in Stephen Toulmin, *The Return to Cosmology.* Note that Marshall Clagett's standard work, *The Science of Mechanics in the Middle Ages,* takes Galileo as its *end* point.

On the retrospective invention of allegedly "immemorial" customs, see the anthology on *The Invention of Tradition,* edited by Eric Hobsbawm and Terence Ranger.

The Standard Account. The current convention among English historians, of dating the start of Modernity to the years around 1600, is exemplified in Lawrence Stone's *The Crisis of the Aristocracy:* "it is between 1560 and 1640, and more precisely between 1580 and 1620, that the real watershed between medieval and modern England must be placed." For the curious separation of the history of science and the history of philosophy from early modern history generally, the essay cited in the text is "The Scientific Movement and its Influence, 1610–50", by A. C. Crombie and M. A. Hoskin: it appears in *The New Cambridge Modern History,* Vol. IV ("The Decline of Spain and the Thirty Years' War: 1609–49/59"), pp. 132–68.

The Flight from Humanism. I discuss the transition from Renaissance humanism to 17th-century exact science in my inaugural lecture at Northwestern University, "The Recovery of Practical Philosophy": cf: *The American Scholar,* Vol. 57, no. 3 (Summer 1988), pp. 337–52. For the dismissal of case ethics in the mid-17th century, under the lead of Blaise Pascal, see Albert R. Jonsen and Stephen Toulmin, *The Abuse of Casuistry* (1988), pp. 231–49.

In presenting Montaigne's position, I quote from four of his essays, as translated in *The Complete Essays of Montaigne,* by Donald M. Frame. For his ridiculing of attempts to divide the mental and bodily aspects of human life, I draw chiefly on the final essay, *Of Experience,* Book III, no. 13 (Frame tr., pp. 815–57); for his defense of sex and his attack on prudery, on the essay, *On Some Verses of Virgil,* Book III, no. 5 (Frame, pp. 638–85); for his remark on farting, on the essay, *Of the Power of the Imagination,* Book I, no. 21 (Frame, pp. 68–76); for his insistence on finitude and the uncertainty inevitably resulting from it, on the essay, *Apology of Raymond Sebond,* Book II, no. 12 (Frame, pp. 318–457).

On Descartes' private confession, *larvatus prodeo,* see the essay by Alexandre Koyré included as a preface to Descartes' *Selected Writings,* edited by P. T. Geach and G. E M. Anscombe.

Chapter Two

Henry of Navarre. The general literature on Henri IV is too vast to summarize here. A good recent general biography in English, *Henry IV,* is by David Buisseret of the Newberry Library, Chicago. The "novels" by Heinrich Mann, *Young Henry of Navarre* and *Henry, King of France,* give a good sense of the court intrigues among which Henry grew up. As to Henry's famous remark that he wished his subjects "a chicken in every pot", Alma Lach has a refined reading of this: viz., that "every Sunday, my peasants of France may have *la poule au pot.*" The phrase, *la poule au pot,* refers to the richest and most filling dish in the cuisine of Henry's native Béarn: the recipe calls for one to stuff the chicken with pork, bacon, veal, cognac, madeira, and vegetables, simmer it for two or three hours, and serve it with a heavy cream sauce. (*Hows and Whys of French Cooking,* p. 473.)

On the reaction to Henry's assassination, both at home and abroad, see Charles Mercier de Lacombe, *Henri IV et sa politique,* pp. 461–66. The description of the dismay at Rheims Cathedral is taken from the contemporary *Histoire de l'Église de Reims,* by P. Cocquault. This reads in the original,

> Les Chanoines, dans le Chapitre, ne pouvoient parler, estant les uns pleins de pleurs et sanglots, les autres saisis de douleur. L'on voit les habitants de Reims pâles, defais, tous changez de leur contenance, car ilz estimoient, ayant perdu le Roy, que la France estoit perdue.

The public reaction in France, as evidenced in contemporary pamphlets, is analyzed in Robert Lindsay and John Neu's *French political pamphlets: 1547–1648:* the event prompted much more spontaneous publication of handbills, sermons, denunciations, and other pamphlets than any other in the entire century covered in that book. On the customary manner of dismembering the King's body, the standard work is E. H. Kantorowicz's discussion of medieval political theology, *The King's Two Bodies* (1981). Em. L. Chambois describes the burning of Henry IV's heart in the marketplace at La Flèche after the Revolution—and the retrieval of its ashes by a local surgeon—in the *Revue Henri IV*, Vol. I (1912), pp. 33–36.

On the deteriorating relations between Protestants and Catholics in France after Henry's death, see the papers of his Protestant lieutenant, Philippe Duplessis de Mornay, *Testament, codicille et dernières heures de Messire Philippes de Mornay, Seigneur du Plessis Marly* (La Forest: Iean Bureau, 1624), which is in the B. N., under call number Ln^{27}21789, *La lettre de M. de Plessis Mornay, envoyé à M. le Duc d'Espernon le 1 de May 1621* (Lb^{36}1631), and *Advis sur ce qui s'est passé en la ville de Saumur entres les Catholiques et ceux de la R.P.R. le mars 1621* (Lb^{36} 1573): see also the manuscript letters of Du Plessis Mornay held in the Bibliothèque Protestante in the Rue des Saints Pères, Paris, and catalogued under MSS nos. 370, 753, and 789.

René Descartes. The opening of Descartes' biography in *La Grande Encyclopédie* cited in the text reads in the original:

> Il suffirait presque de deux dates et de deux indications de lieux à la biographie de Descartes, sa naissance, le 31 mars 1596, à La Haye, en Touraine, et sa mort à Stockholm, le 11 février 1650. Sa vie est avant tout celle d'un ésprit; sa vraie biographie est l'histoire de ses pensées; les événements extérieurs de son existence n'ont d'interêt que par le jour qu'ils peuvent jeter sur les événements intérieurs de son génie.

On Descartes' experience at La Flèche, I have profited from a chance to correspond and talk with Mme. Geneviève Rodis-Lewis: since she is the leading expert on René Descartes' schooling and early career, I found it gratifying to have her agree that my attribution of the *In anniversarium* sonnet to the young Descartes was *très probable.*

As to Descartes' knowledge of and involvement in the Thirty Years' War: aside from the time he spent as a gentleman-observer studying the military doctrines and techniques of Maurits of Nassau, he volunteered to serve with the armies of the Catholic League, and joined in the army of 30,000 League troops under Count Tilly which occupied Upper Austria in 1620. In Geoffrey Parker's recent book on *The Thirty Years' War* (1984), the general index includes an entry reading: "Descartes, René, b. 1596; Jesuit-educated philosopher and scientist; served in Dutch army; lived in Holland (1628–49) and Sweden (1649–50); d. 1650: *invades Upper Austria (1620), 61.*"

John Donne. The critical and biographical material on John Donne is almost as vast as that on René Descartes, and cannot be digested here. The sketch of his life quoted here is in *The Oxford Companion to English Literature,* edited by

Margaret Drabble, (5th ed., 1985), p. 283. The poem *Ignatius his Conclave,* often omitted from collected editions of Donne's verse, is available in the Early English Text Society series.

For the part played by Donne in the narrowing of intellectual and spiritual preoccupations in the early 17th century, see Hiram Haydn's book on "the Counter-Renaissance". On the character of Baroque culture as it developed in and after the Counter-Reformation, mainly but not only in Spain, and its relationship to the social stresses associated with the theological conflicts of the time, the view presented here owes much to José Antonio Maravall's *Cultura del Barocco.* For the Baroque emphasis on theatrical illusion, and the changes in stagecraft resulting from a switch from an apron to a proscenium stage, I have learned from Tobin Nellhaus: on the importance of this change for our understanding of Shakespeare's last plays—notably *The Tempest,* in which Prospero plays the part of a Counter-Reformation impresario and magician—Julian Hilton has many good things to say.

The Politics of Certainty. The manuscript in the Bibliothèque Ste. Geneviève cited in the text as *Traité l'autôrité et de la réception du Concile de Trent en France*—65 pp. in 4° early 18th Century—is MS 1347 in that library, Cat no. 1, pp. 618–19. It opens, *Le concile de Trent avoit été convoqué pour extirper les erreurs de Luther,* and concludes with the claim to *prouver invinciblement nôtre dernière proposition.*

For the comparative adventurousness of intellectual discussions in Christian Europe before the Reformation, as showing the chilling effect of the post–Reformation confrontation, see H. J. Berman, *Law and Revolution.* For religious freedom in Poland during the liberal years from 1555 on, the establishment of Unitarian congregations at Rakow and elsewhere, and the renewal of persecution after 1600, consult Earle Morse Wilbur's *History of Unitarianism: Socianianism and its Antecedents,* notably pp. 356–66 and 442–65.

Two points help remind us how long the "cold war" between Papists and Heretics continued to shape European culture and politics after 1650. As late as 1987, the lawyers advising the Synod of the Irish Presbyterian Church gave their opinion that Ministers of the Church were still bound by the terms of the Westminster Covenant of 1649, which declared that the Pope is "the Man of Sin and the Anti-Christ": Only by a fresh Act of the British Parliament could they be freed of the obligation to accept this doctrine. Visiting Jerusalem in the 1930s, again, Evelyn Waugh wrote to a friend in England, "For me, of course, Christianity *begins with* the Counter-Reformation."

Chapter Three

The Rise of the Nation-State. After 1690, the balance between the new sentiment of "nationhood", and a continued reliance on old feudal loyalties, was evidently struck in France and England in different ways; though (in the sense explained) both countries equally made "absolute" claims to national sovereignty. On this topic, see the essay, "The exponents and critics of absolutism", by R. Mousnier, *The New Cambridge Modern History,* Vol. IV, pp. 104–31. How the English conception of "popular" sovereignty carried over to the North American Colonies, and helped shape the debates around the United States Constitution, is shown in Edmund S. Morgan's book, *Inventing the People.*

On the connection between the revocation of the Edict of Nantes and James II's flight from England, see Emmanuel Le Roy-Ladurie's preface to Bernard Cotteret, *Terre d'exil,* reprinted in the French Protestant weekly, *Réforme,* no. 2084, March 23, 1985, "Révocation et 'Glorious Revolution' ": also Janine Garrisson, *L'Édit de Nantes et sa Révocation: Histoire d'une Intolérance,* written for the tercentennial of the revocation in 1985.

For Pope Innocent X's objections to the Peace of Westphalia, see *The New Cambridge Modern History,* Vol. IV, chapter 5, "Changes in Religious Thought", by G. L. Mosse, p. 186.

Leibniz Versus Newton. Leibniz's wish to develop a universal language, to "express all our thoughts" without ambiguity, took shape early on. He was born in 1646: the passages quoted here are either in his *Préface à la Science Générale* or in the essay, *Zur allgemeinen Characteristik,* both of them from 1677. (See, for example, Leibniz, *Selections,* ed. Philip P. Wiener, § 4 and 5.) Leibniz's ecumenical dreams are discussed in the collection, *Leibniz, 1646–1716: Aspects de l'Homme et de l'Œuvre,* published by the Centre International de Synthèse (1968), especially in the three essays, "L'Irénisme au temps de Leibniz et ses implications politiques" by Jean B. Neveux, "Bossuet devant Leibniz" by Jacques Le Brun, and "L'Idée de religion naturelle selon Leibniz" by Emilienne Naert.

Leibniz's rivalry with Newton over the invention of the infinitesimal calculus and other matters was a long-lasting affair, and is analyzed in Robert Westfall's biography of Newton. It culminated in the exchange of letters with Samuel Clarke, which began with a letter from Leibniz to Caroline, Princess of Wales, in November 1715. (The Princess had been Leibniz's pupil in Hanover, before moving to London with the Royal Court.) This exchange between Leibniz and Clarke became longer and more detailed: each party had completed five letters before Leibniz died in 1716. The correspondence was reedited in 1956 by H. G. Alexander, and published by Manchester University Press as *The Leibniz-Clarke Correspondence,* along with extracts from Newton's *Principia* and *Opticks.* The suggestion that this argument should not be taken wholly at face value, but that it shows signs of a "hidden agenda", was put forward in Steven Shapin's essay, "Of Gods and Kings" (*Isis,* 1981).

On the interdependence of Newtonian physics and the epistemology of both the rationalists and the empiricists, from the 1630s on, see my Ryerson Lecture, "The Inwardness of Mental Life", given before the University of Chicago, reprinted in *Critical Inquiry* (Autumn 1979), vol. 6, no. 1, pp. 1–16.

The Scaffolding of Modernity. This account of the presuppositions of the Newtonian world view draws on a broad range of material. The argument repeats, in a shorter form, the interpretations presented earlier; for example, in the three "Ancestry of Science" books by Stephen Toulmin and June Goodfield, *The Fabric of the Heavens, The Architecture of Matter,* and *The Discovery of Time.*

For the reasons why philosophers from Descartes to Kant dismissed the notion that psychology could ever aim at the status of a Science, see the introduction by Theodore Mischel to the book, *Human Action.* For the assumed passivity of Matter, and its incompatibility with Thinking, see Toulmin, "Neuroscience and Human Understanding", in *The Neurosciences,* ed. G. Quarton, Melnechuk, and Schmitt, pp. 822–32: this essay shows that the criteria invoked in this debate changed with the general standpoint of 17th, mid-18th and late 20th-century thinkers. For a scholarly account of the 18th-century debate, see John Yolton, *Thinking Matter.*

On the History of Nature, the first key document is Immanuel Kant's *Allgemeine Naturgeschichte und Theorie des Himmels* (1755), Eng. tr. by W. Hastie. On the rise of historical geology, and the groundwork it laid for the debate about the origin of species, Charles C. Gillispie's *Genesis and Geology* remains a first resource for general and scholarly readers. Since the centennial of *The Origin of Species* in 1959, a vast literature has grown up: Howard E. Gruber and Paul H. Barrett, *Darwin on Man,* opens up the world of Darwin's "M" and "N" notebooks, in which he kept a record of his thoughts about the material basis of Life and Mind.

The "Subtext" of Modernity. The problem of recovering beliefs that "go without saying" for the educated oligarchy of 18th-century Europe is like that which faces the history of popular culture: for example, Carlo Ginzburg has pointed out that illiterate Italian peasants for many generations transmitted oral world views that were at variance with those of educated people in the same period. The things that are left unwritten include not only the beliefs of unlettered people who have neither the means nor the reasons to commit them to writing: they include also all beliefs that "go without saying" and *a fortiori* without writing. The Newtonian presuppositions were regarded as self-evident—"allowed by all men"—and so were rarely stated, let alone argued.

The illustrative quotation about the Sedgwick burial ground in the Stockbridge churchyard forms the opening words of Jean Stein and George Plimpton's memoir, *Edie,* p. 3.

Chapters Four and Five

The narrative and analysis in the last two chapters cover familiar territory from a standpoint as much personal as scholarly, and require less documentation. My central claim, that post-1918 Modernism replays the themes of 17th-century Rationalism, is confirmed by new material published for Mies van der Rohe's centennial in 1986. On the Platonist side of Mies' style, and his debts to Augustine, see Fritz Neumeyer, *Das Kunstlose Wort: Manifeste, Texte, Schriften zur Baukunst;* and the essay on Mies by Martin Filler in *The New York Review of Books,* June 12, 1986. For the contrast between the attitudes of Mies and those of the pre-1914 Viennese Modernists, see Eduard F. Sekler, *Josef Hoffmann.*

As to the myth of the "clean slate" in politics and intellectual life: the quotation about the French Revolution at the beginning of Chapter 5 comes from Robert Darton's essay in the *New York Review of Books,* Feb. 1989. The evidence that undermines Descartes' and Locke's supposed "neutral starting point" for epistemology is discussed in well-respected papers and books on cognition and classification by authors like L. S. Vygotsky and A. R. Luria in the U.S.S.R., and Eleanor Rosch and Donald Campbell in the U.S.A. See, for example, *The Influence of Culture on Visual Perception* (1966), by M. H. Segall, D. T. Campbell, and M. J. Herskovitz.

The current revival of rhetoric is exemplified in several fields—in English in the writings of Wayne Booth; in Speech, in current discussions of communication and argumentation; in philosophy, in the work of John Austin and John Searle; in economics, in the work of Donald McCloskey. The new cultural anthropology, which uses Clifford Geertz's method of "thick description" (cf: Geertz, *The Interpretation of Cultures* and *Local Knowledge*) deploys the same feeling for the importance of the local that Aristotle taught, but Descartes dismissed; and current work on clinical medical ethics and jurisprudence does the same for the significance of the timely and the practical.

The incompletely answered issues with which Chapter 5 ends—i.e., the relations between *rationality* and *reasonableness*—call for a fuller reconstruction of the history of the ideas of Human Reason. For the time being, the field is divided between rationalist philosophers (e.g., Alan Gewirth) who ask, "Is 'reasonableness' *rational?*"—i.e., "Can we formally demonstrate that 'reasonable' modes of thought and conduct conform to systematic rational principles?"—and those who stand the question on its head, asking in a more pragmatic spirit, "Is 'rationality' *reasonable?*"—i.e., "In what types of cases and situations can we reasonably appeal to 'systematic' rules and 'rational' demonstrations?"

Epilogue

In conclusion, let me acknowledge the generous help of Susanne and Lloyd Rudolph, not only for sharing their insights into "state formation" in India, and the significance of current developments in that fascinating and complex country, but also for inviting my wife and myself to spend Christmas 1987 with them at Jaipur, in Rajasthan. As we then learned, present-day India has customs that would surely have pleased Montaigne and Henri IV. On the holy days of any religion, professional-class Indian families of that community receive courtesy calls from their neighbors and friends of other religions, congratulating them on their sacred day. If only some prophet could have persuaded the Catholic League and their Huguenot rivals to practice this custom in France around 1600: Europe might then have been spared much blood and many tears, and intellectual history could have followed a more tolerant course. See Susanne Hoeber Rudolph and Lloyd I. Rudolph, *Essays on Rajputana*. Our Indian visit was enriched, as well, by the hospitable company of the Herwitz family, who shared with us a dozen of their friends in Bombay and New Delhi, most notably that remarkable artist, M. F. Husain.

Finally, I may add that the comments on China in the Epilogue were written long before the student occupation of Tiananmen Square, Beijing, in May 1989, and its violent suppression by the "People's Liberation Army." This sad episode only underlines the maladapted inflexibility of sovereign central force, when exercised over so large, varied, and cultivated a population. So we saw China joining the other "superpowers" in placing shackles on itself, as it approaches the new millennium.

Index